W9-BDM-143

"This book is a fascinating and scholarly exploration of ancient cosmologies, which focuses on the relationships between the spiritual destiny of mankind and the solstitial position of the sun and the centre of our galaxy. The great changes we are witnessing today are shown to be mysteriously coordinated with cosmic movements that we wrongly thought the Ancients knew little or nothing about."

Robert Bolton, coauthor of The Order of the Ages

"Archeoastronomy, art, and ancient gnosis from world traditions break through the limits of the zodiac to embrace the Galactic Center in a rediscovered vision of evolutionary cosmology. Extensive and intriguing research."

Christine Rhone, coauthor of Twelve-Tribe Nations and translator of Sacred Geography of the Ancient Greeks

"Jenkins provides the 'alignment generation' with a galactic portal to pass through, giving all humankind an opportunity for spiritual renewal by recognizing the astounding significance of the galactic alignment of 2012. Galactic Alignment is the definitive source book for understanding the historical significance of important astronomical events, and how many cultures of the past—and right up to modern times—wove this astronomical information into their sacred architecture and spiritual belief systems."

Willard Van De Bogart, CEO of The Portal Market

"John Major Jenkins is the most global and erudite voice of a swelling chorus of Galactic Center theorists. By framing the subject in the context of the Primordial Tradition, he raises it to a new level of seriousness, and of reassurance."

Joscelyn Godwin, author of The Theosophical Enlightenment and Arktos: The Polar Myth

GALACTIC ALIGNMENT

The Transformation of Consciousness
According to Mayan, Egyptian,
and Vedic Traditions

JOHN MAJOR JENKINS

Bear & Company
Rochester, Vermont

Bear & Company
One Park Street
Rochester, Vermont 05767
www.InnerTraditions.com

Bear & Company is a division of Inner Traditions International

Copyright © 2002 by John Major Jenkins

All rights reserved. No part of this book may be reproduced or utilized in any form or by
any means, electronic or mechanical, including photocopying, recording, or by any information storage and retrieval system, without permission in writing from the publisher.

Library of Congress Cataloging-in-Publication Data

Jenkins, John Major.
  Galactic alignment : the transformation of consciousness according to
Mayan, Egyptian, and Vedic traditions / John Major Jenkins.
      p. cm.
Includes bibliographical references and index.
  ISBN 1-879181-84-3
  1. Maya cosmology. 2. Maya astronomy. 3. Maya calendar. 4.
Cosmology, Egyptian. 5. Hindu cosmology. I. Title.
  F1435.3.R3 J45 2002
  529'.329784152—dc21

                                                            2002006139

Printed and bound in the United States at Lake Book Mfg., Inc.

10 9 8 7 6 5 4 3 2

Text design by Priscilla Baker
This book was typeset in Caslon, with Caslon Antique and Agenda as display typefaces

Permissions and Acknowledgments

The author gratefully acknowledges the following authors for the use of their images from the following sources:

Frontispiece: Athanasius Kircher's *Turris Babel*, Amsterdam, 1679.

Figures 1.1, 1.3, 18.1, and 19.1: photographs by John Major Jenkins.

Figures 3.1 and 3.2 : adapted from *A Forest of Kings* by David Freidel and Linda Schele.

Figure 3.4: Miguel Angel Vergara's *Chichen Itza: Astronomical Light and Shadow Phenomena of the Great Pyramid*, Centro de Investigacion Maya, Haltun-Ha, Nolo, Yucatan.

Figure 3.5 (left side): adapted from *Code of Kings* by Linda Schele and Peter Mathews.

Figures 4.2 and 7.1: drawn by Christine Rhone.

Figure 4.2: photograph courtesy of Archive Press Communications, Boulder, Colorado (www.ArchivePress.com).

Figures 5.1, 5.7, and the left portion of Fig. 23.2: courtesy of Darlene, from *A Monument to the End of Time* by Jay Weidner and Vincent Bridges.

Figure 5.8: photograph of the cross in Urcos, Peru, was taken by Jay Weidner.

Figure 7.2: adapted from Jean Richer's *Sacred Geography of the Ancient Greeks*.

Figures 8.1 and 8.2: Maarten Vermaseran's *Corpus Inscriptionum et monumentorum religionis mithriacae*. The Hague: Martinus Nijhoff, Volume 1, 1956, where they are designated Figure 810 (London) and Figure 650 (Nersae). Used with kind permission from Kluwer Academic Publishers, and they cannot be reprinted or used without express written permission of the publisher.

Figure 9.3: R. A. Schwaller de Lubicz's *Sacred Science* (Rochester, Vt.: Inner Traditions), page 97.

Figure 10.1: photograph of Jnanavatar Swami Sri Yukteswar Giri that appears on the cover of his book *The Holy Science* is used with the kind permission of Self-Realization Fellowship, Los Angeles, California.

Figure 10.3: used by permission of Patrizia Norelli-Bachelet, with the important clarification that the model of the Matrimandir in this photograph, explained in detail in Norelli-Bachelet's book *The New Way*, was done according to the Mother's original plan and differs entirely from what has been made the centerpiece in the Auroville rendition.

Figure 14.1: adapted from a Flammarion diagram used in *Hamlet's Mill* by Giorgio de Santillana and Hertha von Dechend.

Figure 18.7: adapted from a photograph by C. Prahl on the Michigan Technological University Volcanoes website (www.geo.mtu.edu/volcanoes/tacana/).

Figures 19.2, 19.3 (adapted), 19.4, and 19.7: Sydney David Markman's *Colonial Architecture of Antigua, Guatemala*, used by permission of The American Philosophical Library.

Part 5: artwork by Virgil Finlay.

Thanks to Jim Reed for encouraging (and participating in) the first Izapa expedition, to Geovany Mendoza in Antigua for telling us of the *portada* of La Concepcion, and to Moira Timms for feedback on the Egypt chapter. Special thanks to Jeanie Levitan, Cannon Labrie, Jon Graham, and everyone at Inner Traditions who have contributed to the manifestation of this book.

To the memory of my father,
William Barnum Jenkins, Sr.
(1936–2002)

This book is dedicated to all those who know that to desire
more of everything is to have less than nothing.

Contents

INTRODUCTION

Galaxia Nuncius
(A Message from the Galaxy)

T he phrase "Galaxia Nuncius" (Message from the Galaxy) follows the lead of two great pioneers: Galileo and Oliver Reiser. Galileo's seminal work, *Sidereus Nuncius* (*Message from the Stars*), is now recognized as a paradigm-shattering breakthrough, even though it was condemned when it was written. Oliver Reiser's work, including his unpublished book *Messages to and from the Galaxy*, has yet to be recognized as such. Perhaps someday it will. At times I feel a deep kinship with these thinkers because the discoveries and concepts I write about are also unpopular with the establishment paradigm. However, let us pursue the analogy. Galileo's revolutionary discovery was that all things do not revolve around the earth and a higher center, the Sun, must be recognized. Likewise, my work has sought to break the bubble again so that we might recognize an even higher center, the Galactic Center, and integrate it into conventional thought as a fundamental player in the affairs of Earth. And like Galileo, my work is really just a reintroduction, a rediscovery, of perspectives that were espoused thousands of years ago by ancient metaphysicians and cosmologists whom we are just beginning to understand.

Galactic Alignment: The Transformation of Consciousness According to Mayan, Egyptian, and Vedic Traditions is more ambitious than I intended it to be. I simply wanted to assemble and present all the evidence from the ancient traditions for a particular knowledge about the galaxy and our changing orientation to it over vast periods of time. In the process of tracking down the underlying meaning of often fragmented systems of belief, new ideas and connections emerged that were worth exploring. But there is one concern retained throughout, a singular pursuit that follows directly upon the discoveries in my book *Maya Cosmogenesis 2012*. In that book, I identified the rare alignment of the December solstice sun with the Galactic Center as the reason why the Maya chose to end their 13-*baktun* calendar on December 21, 2012. This topic must serve as a foundation for everything in this new book, so I thought it necessary to summarize those findings. Part 1 is dedicated to that purpose, as well as to presenting some recent discoveries in my reconstruction of the galactic parameters of Mayan cosmology. Then, in part 2, we are ready to pose the questions: Did other ancient civilizations know, as the Maya did, about the Galactic Center? Did they know about our impending alignment to it, as encoded into the 2012 end-date? If so, what did these other traditions have to say about it?

And so we embark on a round-the-world journey, an adventure of ideas that will explore sacred topography in Greece and England, esoteric astronomy in Homer's *Iliad*, the symbolism of obelisks in France, alchemy, Gothic architecture, Islamic astrology, Egypt's wonders, and finally arrive in ancient Vedic India to examine the doctrine of the *yugas* (World Ages) as found in the Laws of Manu. In all of these traditions, I identify important concepts, some buried but others overt, relating to a widespread recognition that alignments to the galaxy periodically occur and that these alignments offer spiritual renewal for humanity.

In part 3, I explore the ideas of the Traditionalist school, in particular the writings of esteemed scholar Ananda Coomaraswamy and symbolist philosopher René Guénon. These writers pioneered the resurrection of the Primordial Tradition, or Perennial Philosophy, and a major idea in this school is that the current cycle of history is ending amid a proliferation of inverted spiritual values and rampant materialism—we are approaching the end of Kali Yuga. In the Vedic doctrine of World Ages, Kali Yuga is the final age, the age of greatest spiritual darkness, and its end signals the shift to a new World Age. Clarifying some undeveloped areas within Traditionalist thought, and drawing from the insights of various Vedic commentators, I identify the galactic alignment of era 2012 as the key to the timing of this transition, anchoring the Vedic *yuga* doctrine to a real astronomical event.

A model of how the cycles of time map onto the globe and manifest as a westward flow of civilization is discussed in part 4, leading us into esoteric mysteries in the Americas, including the Masonic origins of

Washington, D.C., and the ley-line grid over the early Mayan site of Izapa—the place where the Long Count calendar that gives us the famous 2012 end-date was invented. And in all of this, the uniting thread that reemerges at various points, like the full moon from behind clouds, is the archetype of the Great Mother: Isis. We find her, of course, in the Mayan material, as the womb of the Milky Way from which the solstice sun god is reborn at the end of the age. She is also in the Vedic soma rite, the Finnish *Kalevala*, Egyptian cosmology, Masonic symbolism, Peruvian mythology, and even Spanish colonial architecture. How far back into history she goes is one of the great unsolved mysteries. As the ultimate source and center of all life, her true domain is, of course, beyond time and space, but I think we can now say with confidence exactly where her throne is in the sky.

To say that the Mayans, Hindus, and Egyptians were aware of the Milky Way galaxy should surprise no one—after all, the Milky Way is dramatic and prominent in the night sky. But to demonstrate, as I will, that they also knew about the Milky Way's center and believed that our periodic alignments to it have something to do with the transformation of consciousness should stand the history of science and religion on its head. And what if the commonsense conclusion to be drawn from all the evidence I've gathered together here is true? What if ancient civilizations were aware of the Galactic Center and the precession of the equinoxes and believed that eras of galactic alignment—like the one we are struggling through right now—somehow contribute to the unfolding of consciousness on Earth? Furthermore, could global weather changes as well as the intensification of synchronicities and anomalous experiences that many people are increasingly reporting be an effect of our alignment with the Galactic Center? Part 5 explores these questions, as well as the unforgettable refrain: "Will the world end in 2012?"

New vistas have opened up while researching and writing this book, ones that elevate "metaphysics" to its traditional place as a superior framework for understanding the nature of time, reality, and consciousness. This brings me full circle back to my earliest philosophical preoccupations. Metaphysics is the answer to the limitations and dead ends of the physical sciences, for as a "meta" physics it takes a "higher" view than conventional physics. And this is not semantic sleight of hand; the sacred sciences of antiquity, closely allied with metaphysical ideas that are now largely misunderstood, were the multidimensional and holistic precursors to our modern profane sciences that today amount to nothing more than a kind of shortsighted thingism.

As we narrow down our search and venture into metaphysical territory, we dig into the unpublished work of Coomaraswamy and emerge with a Vedic teaching that addresses our end-of-cycle concerns and connects us right into the Galactic Center. That teaching is encoded into the Vedic theft of soma myth, and in pursuing its underlying wisdom regarding the transformation of consciousness, all of the book's themes will be integrated into the metaphysical importance of the solstice-galaxy alignment.

PART ONE

Mayan Cosmology and Calendrics

ONE

Search and Research

The brilliant and complicated legacies of our ancient ancestors come down to us today fragmented, eroded, misinterpreted, and degraded. These legacies were drawn from a profound realm of higher consciousness, a realm from which modern humanity is largely alienated. This is why the wisdom of these ancient cultures appears so mysterious—we are confounded by their profound grasp of very large questions. It has been easy, and disingenuous, for the modern media to assemble the riddles of the past, set them out for all to see, and be entertained by the mysterious ways of those clever Ancients. Nevertheless, we are currently being overwhelmed by an astonishing array of evidence and clearheaded interpretations that reveal a definite fact about these archaic cultures—that is, they recognized our impending alignment with the center of our galaxy and considered this alignment to be the moment of greatest spiritual opportunity for human beings on Earth. Put more simply: the Ancients understood that our supreme source and center is the Galactic Center, and they oriented their belief systems and cosmologies around it.

My research has focused on elucidating the galactic mysteries in Mayan and Mesoamerican calendar cosmology, but recently I have learned to see these same ideas in the Egyptian and Vedic esoteric traditions. This new panorama of interrelated ancient belief systems reveals to me nothing less than an archaic mono-myth, a galactic paradigm of immense genius and depth, a true *primordial tradition* formulated by brilliant human beings—our ancestors—next to whom we are but neophytes groping in the darkness.

Gaining an appreciation for the accomplishments of other civilizations requires that we briefly step outside of our culturally conditioned mindsets. This is perhaps no more true than with regard to our appreciation of the Mayan and Aztec civilizations, for we have been so inundated with information about how brutal and barbaric they were that we are predisposed to see nothing but that. But all large civilizations will engage in the entire range of human experiences—brutalities, artistic expressions, wars, and spiritual accomplishments—and when exploring the intellectual achievements of Mesoamerican cultures, we first need to suspend our deeply engrained cultural stereotype—still present in the twenty-first century—of the "primitive savage" incapable of advanced or sustained intellectual effort. To overcome this bias doesn't require that we deny barbaric episodes or practices in Mesoamerican culture—we can find such things in any culture. Instead, our focus can be to reconstruct the aspects of the ancient Mesoamerican worldviews that embrace the higher concerns of astronomy, religion, mathematics, calendar making, writing, and architecture. Central to these concerns is cosmology—the curiosity about human origins and the nature of the ever-changing cosmos. With this orientation, we can transcend stereotypes and approach Mayan science and religion honestly and accurately.

Mayan studies have progressed tremendously since the early 1980s. Advances in hieroglyphic decipherment and major archaeological discoveries have resulted in a huge quantity of artifacts, data of all kinds, and new theories pouring forth from the universities. Indeed, academic interpretation has not been able to keep up with this inundation of raw

Figure 1.1. The astronomical observatory at Chichen Itza

data. We are now in need of a synthesis of this data, a challenge made all the more difficult because aspiring Mayan scholars are encouraged to specialize, which makes interdisciplinary synthesis less viable as a career track.

In many fields of study, an outsider comes along to assemble the pieces and present a "big picture" breakthrough. In *The Structure of Scientific Revolutions*, Thomas Kuhn noted that major scientific breakthroughs have often come from outsiders or newcomers, precisely because they didn't carry with them any of the biases or prejudices that prevented the veterans from seeing the obvious. Commenting on the discoveries of R. A. Schwaller de Lubicz, Deborah and Robert Lawlor wrote in their introduction to his *Temple of Man*, "Historically, in many specialized branches of knowledge, it has been the non-specialized, integrative minds that have made the ground-breaking innovations."[1]

The history of Mayan studies is filled with these nonspecialists who, with self-funded research and self-motivation, have entered the ongoing discussion and provided missing keys. In the 1920s John E. Teeple, a New York–based chemical engineer, contributed major breakthroughs to deciphering the Mayan script. Joseph T. Goodman, a journalist and editor by profession, "made some truly lasting contributions" according to Mayan scholar Michael Coe.[2] Goodman contributed early insights into the correlation problem and was ignored for decades, but his work resulted in the Goodman-Martínez-Thompson correlation (hereafter, the GMT: 584283) that is now widely accepted. Yuri Knorosov, a Russian linguist, broke new ground in identifying both phonetic and ideogramic components in Mayan hieroglyphs. He was discouraged by his advisors from pursuing such a hopeless and foreign topic as Mayan glyph decipherment. And of course Linda Schele, the great doyenne of recent breakthroughs in hieroglyphic decipherment and champion of the close relationship between Mayan astronomy and mythology, was trained as an art historian.[3]

My solution to the problem of 2012 unavoidably falls into the category of maverick scholarship, as I am not affiliated with any university. My research into Mayan cosmology began in the 1980s when I lived and worked among the highland Maya. A brief description of my early research will provide some background for the discoveries set forth in my *Maya Cosmogenesis 2012*, and—it is hoped—assure the reader that I've done my homework.

I was first drawn into the mysteries of the Maya in 1986, after reading

The *tzolkin*: 260 days, consisting of 20 day signs combined with a number from 1 to 13. According to the Quiché language, the day signs are: Imox, *Iq*, Aq'ab'al, K'at, Kan, Kame, *Kej*, Q'anil, Toj, Tz'i, B'atz, *E*, Aj, Ix, Tz'ikin, Ajmak, *N'oj*, Tijax, Kawuq, Junajpu.

Dennis Tedlock gives their Yucatec Mayan counterparts and translates their meanings as: Lefthanded, *Wind*, Foredawn, Net, Snake, Death, *Deer*, Yellow, Thunder, Dog, Monkey, *Tooth*, Cane, Jaguar, Bird, Sinner, *Thought*, Blade, Rain, Marksman.[4] Four of these day signs (italicized) are called "year-bearers" and only they can initiate a New Year.

The *haab*: The 365-day "vague" year. Combined, the *tzolkin* and *haab* create a 52-*haab* period called the Calendar Round. It is 13 days less than 52 years, because the 365-day *haab* is slightly less than the 365.2422-day solar year. This causes New Year's Day to shift slowly backward through the year at the rate of 1 day every four years. The complete backward transit takes 1,507 years and this year-drift formula has its own astrological implications.

Venus cycle: Venus reappears as morning star every 583.92 days (approximate to 584 days). Five of these Venus cycles equal eight *haab*. Thus, Venus traces a five-pointed star around the ecliptic every 8 years.

Venus Round: 104 *haab* (2 Calendar Rounds). This is when the cycles of *tzolkin*, *haab*, and Venus resynchronize on the *tzolkin* day 1 Ahau, the sacred day of Venus. The math: 260 x 146 = 365 x 104 = 584 x 65 = 37,960 days.

Long Count: A system of at least five place values, consisting of: *baktun* (144,000 days), *katun* (7,200 days), *tun* (360 days), *uinal* (20 days), and *kin* (1 day). Thus, 9.16.4.1.1 indicates a Long Count date of 9 *baktuns*, 16 *katuns*, 4 *tuns*, 1 *uinal*, and 1 *kin*, meaning that a total of 1,412,661 days have elapsed since the first day of the Long Count: August 12, 3114 B.C.

A period of 13 *baktuns* (5,125.36 years) is indicated on creation monuments as one World Age. Five of these equal a precession cycle (25,627 years).

The correlation of the Mayan calendar with the Gregorian calendar has been determined by the Goodman-Martínez-Thompson correlation such that the last day of the 13-*baktun* cycle will be December 21, 2012.

Figure 1.2. Mesoamerican calendar systems

Frank Waters's *Mexico Mystique*. At that time, I was living and working in Boulder, Colorado. I left for my first trip to Mexico and Central America in December 1986, and my first book, *Journey to the Mayan Underworld* (1989), described my trip and my many misadventures. I returned to Central America in 1988, 1989, 1990, 1994, and 1998. During these years I tackled the core questions of Mayan cosmology:

* ★ The correlation of the Mayan calendar with the Western Gregorian calendar
* ★ Reconstructing the Mayan Venus calendar
* ★ Identifying the core principles of Mayan time philosophy
* ★ The meaning of the 2012 end-date

The first question involved determining "what day is it, today, in the 260-day Mayan calendar?" Scholars have spent decades examining this calendar correlation problem, and in the 1990s the problem was very simply answered by taking a look at the academic literature. The important result of solving the correlation problem is that we now know that the end-date of the 13-*baktun* cycle in the Long Count calendar (a Great Cycle or World Age) is December 21, 2012. Furthermore, Mayan creation texts and modern ethnographic data state that the associated sacred day in the 260-day *tzolkin* calendar is 4 Ahau. As we approach the 2012 end-date, written 13.0.0.0.0 in Long Count notation, we also approach the Creation Day, 4 Ahau—a fact supported by the Quiché Maya day-count in Guatemala.

I explored this issue thoroughly in my *Tzolkin: Visionary Perspectives and Calendar Studies* (1994), and though my answer agreed with the surviving day-count among the highland Quiché Maya (revealing an unbroken calendar tradition going back almost 3,000 years), my support for this placement put me at odds with the sector of Mayan calendar enthusiasts who were following the work of José Argüelles. Argüelles had promoted a day-count placement that was not consistent with the surviving, unbroken Mayan day-count, which I called the "true count." In response to this debate, I wrote an article in 1995 called "A Manifesto for Clarity" specifically for the Institute of Maya Studies in Miami, Florida, and generally for anyone seeking the facts of the matter. That's where I let the matter rest, because the facts were in, and the correlation question was only one facet of my work.

A related issue here is the two-day discrepancy reported by scholars such as Linda Schele and Michael Coe, making the end-date appear to be December 23, 2012, rather than December 21. I had already researched the origin of this discrepancy, and found it to be based on a misconception in the work of Schele's mentor, Floyd Lounsbury. The misconception was also noted by Dennis Tedlock and Victoria Bricker. I discussed this issue at length in an appendix in *Maya Cosmogenesis 2012*, and it was a primary focus of my book *Tzolkin*. Suffice it to say that December 21, 2012, remains the best candidate for the end-date.

My second challenge involved tracking the evolution of the Mayan Venus calendar. In doing this reconstruction work, I made dozens of charts and tables and approached the problem from two angles. The first acknowledged that the ancient placement of the Venus table in the Dresden Codex (one of the four surviving Mayan books) had grown, over many centuries, hopelessly out of synchronization with actual morning-star appearances of Venus. So I proposed simply to locate the next time that Venus rose as morning star on the sacred day of Venus, 1 Ahau, and restart the prediction table there. This date turned out to be April 3, 2001—a strangely significant date because it was exactly eight *haab* (one *haab* is 365 days) after the commencement of the final *katun* of the Long Count calendar on April 6, 1993. Incredibly, this *katun* commencement date in 1993 was also a morning-star Venus rising (as well as a full moon). Furthermore, my tables indicated that twenty Venus Rounds equal 2,080 years—which is thirteen conjunctions of Uranus and Neptune, as well as one zodiacal "age" in a thirteen-sign zodiac. The sacred numbers 13 and 20 had conspired on a higher level to structure outer-planet conjunctions and the duration of zodiacal ages. But this worked only when following the thirteen-sign zodiac of the Maya, an apparently superior system.

My second approach was more academic. I attempted to reconstruct how the Dresden Venus table evolved into a prediction sequence used by the Ixil and Quiché people who migrated into the Guatemalan highlands beginning in the twelfth century A.D. By making the chief year-bearer equivalent to the sacred day of Venus, this newer Venus table would bring the Venus Round into alignment with the Calendar Round. All of these explorations, and a great deal more, were published in *Tzolkin*, which has recently been updated and reissued.

The third challenge was to identify the core principles of Mayan time philosophy. The constant refrain in my research was the question, "What is at the heart of the Mayan calendar?" This led me deeper into sacred geometry, mathematics, and Mayan time philosophy. In research published through 1994, I identified three root-principles that are identical to the three root-principles of Egyptian sacred science. By *root* principle I mean the universal principles associated with the square roots of 2, 3, and 5. In Egyptian sacred science these principles are responsible for the creation, maintenance, decline, and regeneration of the spiritual and material worlds. Following the essays of Mayan ceremonialist Martín Prechtel and Mayan ethnographer Robert Carlsen, I was able to show how two of these root-principles corresponded to the contemporary Tzutujil Maya paradigm of change called *jaloj kexoj* (pronounced hah-*low* kay-*show*). The parallel was significant because it showed how the mathematical framework I had arrived at in my own research was confirmed by ethnographic information. This phase of study culminated in *Jaloj Kexoj and PHI-64* (1994), which has been reissued with four new appendixes as *Mayan Sacred Science* (2000).

Now we get to the central concern of my work: the true meaning of the 2012 end-date of the Mayan calendar, a key insight into the Mayan perception of time. My research shifted to the end-date question in early 1994. My basic insight, which I wrote about in *The Center of Mayan Time* and *Maya Cosmogenesis 2012*, was that the Maya intended their 2012 end-date to mark the alignment of the solstice sun with the Milky Way galaxy, and that the mytho-astronomical players in the scenario were One Hunahpu (First Father), the dark-rift Road to the Underworld, and the Milky Way Great Mother. Early on in my research, I recognized that the solstice-galaxy alignment would occur around 1998 or 1999. This was based on precise astronomical concepts (e.g., galactic equator and solstice colure) and a rough estimate I made with EZCosmos astronomy software, confirmed by the calculations of European astronomer Jean Meeus and the U.S. Naval Observatory.[5] I'll have more to say about this precise timing in chapter 21, but suffice it to say two things here. First, the fourteen-year error between 1998 and 2012 amounts to less than one-fifth of a degree— a tiny sliver of the width of the full moon and thus negligible, considering it was a forward calculation in precession of at least 2,000 years. Second, the Sun itself is one-half a degree wide, so an alignment zone between 1980 and 2016 must be allowed, thus embracing the 2012 end-date.

A few general principles of Mesoamerican cosmology need to be summarized before proceeding further. This is a broad-brush summary, and interested readers can find the details in *Maya Cosmogenesis 2012*. From the earliest beginnings, shamanism played a central role in Mesoamerican culture. As with Siberian shamans, the primary duty of the Mesoamerican shaman was to journey into the "cosmic center" to retrieve sacred knowledge and healing abilities. When the office of sacred kingship was instituted, the journeying king-shaman also had to obtain the power and wisdom of rulership. The important concept here is "cosmic center." Ancient Mesoamerican skywatchers perceived that location to be the source and center of the world. The king's throne—and, by extension, city centers—were intended to represent this cosmic center, which had a very real astronomical location.

Following the "as above, so below" principle, cities, towns, regions, and even trading routes to distant provinces were structured according to a cosmological prototype perceived in the sky. That prototype was organized around the cosmic center and consisted of four quadrants united by the sacred center. As a result, Mesoamerican cities obeyed a quadripartite design, with the ruler's temple and throne at the center.

For the Olmecs, who created the first Mesoamerican civilization, the cosmic center was located in the Pole Star, for a very simple reason: All the stars and constellations appear to revolve around it. There were other candidates for the cosmic center, however. The Olmecs noticed that the Pole Star does not remain fixed. Because of the astronomical shifting known as the precession of the equinoxes, the Pole Star changes over long periods of time. We know the Olmecs became aware of precession around 1000 B.C. because the axis of the temple complex at La Venta was oriented to polar north, but was relocated over the centuries to account for precession. The discovery of precession led to a cosmological crisis, a disenchantment with the erratic polar center. It now appears self-evident that the history of Mesoamerican cosmology—the battles between various ruling deities, competing mythologies, and cosmo-conceptions—is actually defined by evolving ideas about which cosmic center is the best. And there were three possibilities.

First was the polar center, as mentioned, ruled over by Seven Macaw, a deity who in the Mayan Creation myth is associated with the Big Dipper. Second there was the zenith, the precise geometrical center of the sky overhead. Within the tropical latitudes of Mesoamerica, the Sun's passage through the zenith at high noon takes place twice each year, but on different dates depending on one's exact latitude. The great central Mexican city of Teotihuacan was oriented to the horizon position of sunset on the solar zenith-passage date, and Monte Alban used a zenith-tube sighting device as early as 250 B.C. Quetzalcoatl is the deity associated with the zenith center, though his true reference is to the Pleiades. Finally, between 200 B.C. and A.D. 50 the early Mayan site of Izapa acknowledged these two cosmic centers, but made an overall preferential statement about a third—the Galactic Center. Izapa did this with its orientation to horizon astronomy and with the pictographic imagery carved on over sixty monuments found at the site in the mid-1900s. In the Creation myth recorded at Izapa, which

Figure 1.3. The Pyramid of Kukulcan at Chichen Itza

is equivalent to the *Popol Vuh*, One Hunahpu is the deity associated with the December solstice, and is reborn when the December solstice sun aligns with the Galactic Center in era 2012.

We have thus sketched several general principles:

★ A cosmology based in visionary shamanism
★ City designs that mirror the cosmos above

★ A concern for correct orientation to a cosmic center
★ An awareness of precession, with a likely resulting effort to calibrate it
★ Three possible cosmic centers of interest to Mesoamerican skywatchers

With this orientation we can confidently approach the unresolved mysteries of the ancient Mayan calendar, revealing a lost cosmology of galactic proportions.

TWO

Reconstructing Ancient Mayan Cosmology

I n attempting to figure out why the early Maya picked A.D. 2012 to end a large period of time in their Long Count calendar, I took the seemingly self-evident approach of looking carefully at the early Mayan site that created the Long Count calendar: Izapa. Since nobody had taken this approach before to answer this question, my findings are unique and somewhat surprising. As I discussed in *Maya Cosmogenesis 2012*, studies on Izapa have been limited to archaeology and iconography (symbol studies). Only a few researchers have had anything to say about astronomy, and those who did arrived at incomplete conclusions.[1] Using astronomy software, I first studied the celestial movements observable at Izapa during its heyday (ca. 100 B.C.). Then I was ready to interpret the dozens of carved monuments at the site. I noticed that the site has two important orientations, one northward to the peak of Tacana volcano, and the other southeastward to the December solstice-sunrise horizon. This layout embodies a basic "north-south" framework for Izapan cosmography. I noticed that the Big Dipper would rise straight over Tacana volcano, but (as the Olmecs had realized) precession causes it to rise farther and farther east along the horizon as the centuries go by. This precessional shifting gained speed precisely during the era of Izapa's rise to dominance as the region's premiere ceremonial and astronomical center—800 B.C. to A.D. 100.

In the Izapan-Mayan Creation myth, Seven Macaw (the Big Dipper) had to be defeated before the Hero Twins' father (One Hunahpu, the December solstice sun) could take his place as the next World Age ruler. The earlier circumpolar deity of the Olmec (the Big Dipper) had to be dethroned, and I have suggested that precessional movement was the basis of this myth. In other words, the story of Seven Macaw's fall

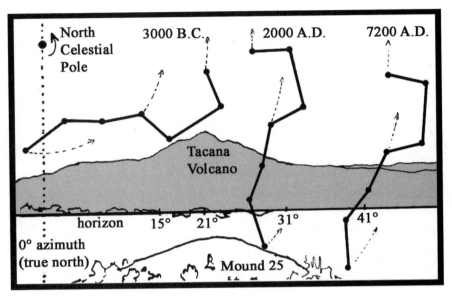

Figure 2.1. The Big Dipper precessing away from the North Celestial Pole

encoded the astronomical process by which the Big Dipper "fell away" from the North Celestial Pole (fig. 2.1). Furthermore, the transition from the older Olmec paradigm to the newer Izapan-Mayan worldview heralded an abandonment of the old polar paradigm, an evolution in cosmological doctrine. But what cosmology would take its place?

To the southeast, the December solstice horizon provided an alternative cosmic center. Many of Izapa's monuments face the December solstice horizon, and the ballcourt in Group F is aligned to it. While the Big Dipper in the north was falling away from its polar perch, to the south the December solstice sun was slowly converging—again, as a result of precession—with the bright and wide "nuclear bulge" of the Milky Way's center. The Maya mythologized this location as the womb of the Cosmic Mother as well as the mouth of a snake or frog. Being adept astronomers and mathematicians, the Izapans calculated forward to when the alignment between the solstice sun and the galactic heart would culminate, and they arrived at the year that we call A.D. 2012, which is 13.0.0.0.0 in their Long Count calendar—the end of the thirteenth *baktun*.

If this seems far-fetched, we need only look at the imagery on Izapa's monuments for confirmation. Stela 11 at Izapa (fig. 2.2) is one of those monuments that face the December solstice sunrise. It shows the First

Figure 2.2. Izapa Stela 11, the solstice
sun in the Milky Way's dark rift

Father solar deity (One Hunahpu) being reborn from the mouth of the cosmic frog deity. His arms are outstretched, which is a measuring gesture that indicates a period-ending event (like the end of a World Age). We can understand the meaning of the frog's mouth by looking at the astronomical features along the Milky Way. A major feature near the Galactic Center is a dark rift in the Milky Way, caused by the thick accumulation of interstellar dust in the dense region near the center. From our viewpoint on Earth, it appears to be a dark ridge or road running northward away from the center. This feature was poetically labeled by the Maya in several ways, depending on which metaphor was being used for the Milky Way. If the Milky Way was thought of as the Great Mother, then the dark rift was her birth canal; if the Milky Way was the cosmic ballcourt, then the dark rift was the goal ring; if the Milky Way was the great temple, then the dark rift was the king's throne; if the Milky Way was the cosmic serpent of death and regeneration, then the dark rift was its mouth. The frog regurgitates First Father after his death, thus facilitating his rebirth. Without a doubt, Stela 11 depicts the alignment of the December solstice sun with the dark rift that lies along the Milky Way near the Galactic Center, an event determined by precession that culminates in the years around 2012. This type of alignment occurs once every 26,000 years.

If we are still unsure, we can look at the monuments in Izapa's ballcourt for final confirmation. As mentioned, the lengthwise axis of Izapa's

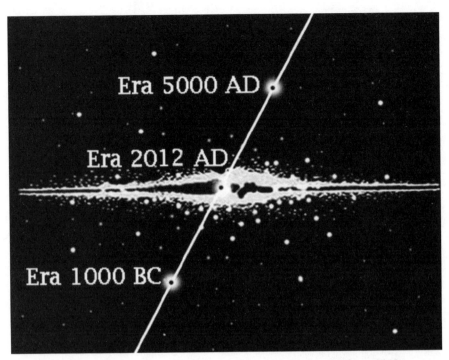

Figure 2.3. The galactic alignment, culminating in the era of A.D. 2012

ballcourt is aligned to the December solstice horizon. A monument on the eastern end of the ballcourt shows one of the Hero Twins standing victorious over a completely fallen Seven Macaw (who must be deposed before One Hunahpu can be reborn). On the western end of the ballcourt we find a throne and several small monuments that each encode the different metaphors by which the alignment was understood. The throne itself has carved legs between which a solar god's head, or solar Ahau face, is emerging. This birth scene faces eastward down the axis of the ballcourt toward the December solstice sunrise, where the convergence of solstice sun and dark rift was tracked. Clearly, the throne depicts the future alignment as a birth.

Next to the throne we find a circular stone ring in which a stone ball was placed. In the symbolism of the ball game the December solstice sun is the game ball and the dark rift (or the Galactic Center) is the goal-ring. Finally, next to the ring and ball we find a serpent's head, which, like most ballcourt markers, originally had a solar Ahau face in its mouth. This is the devouring end-of-age image of the sun in the snake's mouth—implying that death must precede rebirth. All of these images clearly portray the future alignment toward which they face, the December solstice sun's alignment with the Galactic Center (see chapter 18 for more details on the Izapan ballcourt).

In Mesoamerican cosmology, a set of interlocking myths and symbols constellates around the galactic-alignment event. My work has been to show how the alignment was encoded into important Mayan institutions such as the ball game, the Creation myth, and rites of royal accession. These findings gather significance because they are supported by a wide spectrum of disciplines, including archaeology, iconography, etymology, ethnography, mythology, and archaeoastronomy. The overall continuity of my interpretation, as well as the involvement of the most important institutions in Mesoamerican culture, favors the likelihood of one conclusion: *The early Maya intended the 2012 end-date to target the rare alignment of the December solstice sun with the bright band of the Milky Way near the Galactic Center.* The Maya wove an entire cosmology around this alignment, which I have called the "galactic cosmology."

Zenith and Quetzalcoatl-Kukulcan

By the time Izapa was fading and the Maya were on the rise, circa A.D. 200, Mesoamerican civilization had split into two major streams with two cosmological orientations. In central Mexico, Teotihuacan was founded around A.D. 150 and was oriented to sunset on the zenith-passage date at Teotihuacan, May 17. In addition, on this passage date (circa A.D. 150) the Pleiades rose just before the Sun in the predawn skies (its heliacal rising). This "keying" of the Pleiades to the zenith-passage date of May 17 defines a very specific and datable era in the precession cycle. For within a hundred or so years from the founding of Teotihuacan this celestial coincidence fell out of synchronization. The shifting of precession caused the heliacal rise of the Pleiades to move forward through the year, such that by A.D. 1800 the Pleiades were rising heliacally in June. The hidden effect of this shifting was that around 1800 the Pleiades were in conjunction with the Sun *on the zenith-passage date*, which meant that the sun and the Pleiades rose together, in conjunction, and passed through the zenith together! Of course the conjunction would be hidden in the glare of the Sun, but I discovered evidence that the Teotihuacanos used a well-known tradition to calibrate this Sun-Pleiades-zenith conjunction—the New Fire ceremony.

What this discovery reveals is another cosmological tradition in Mesoamerica that was not concerned with either the polar or galactic centers, but with the zenith center and the Pleiades. This implies a bifurcation in Mesoamerican consciousness, a split in the original Olmec polar tradition that had provided a unified cosmovision. With the advent of more complicated considerations—namely, precession—different cosmic centers were explored, and thus there arose two separate Mesoamerican streams. This schism manifested in the early Mesoamerican psyche between the Nahuatl civilization in central Mexico and the Mayan civilization to the east, in Peten, Chiapas, Yucatan, and Guatemala.

The defining characteristic of these two worldviews involved their calendars, which were intended to calibrate the timing of World Ages. For the Maya, the supreme World Age calendar was the Long Count. As we have seen, this calendar was designed to target a future alignment between the solstice sun and the plane of the galaxy (visible as the Milky Way), defining the end of a World Age. The early central Mexican civilization, centered on the great city of Teotihuacan that flourished between A.D. 150 and A.D. 750, focused its eschatological doctrine of a future World Age shift on the movements of the Pleiades in relation to the Sun and the zenith. This system tracked a completely different precessional alignment, timed with the fifty-two-year Calendar Round. The New Fire ceremony is critical to how the Calendar Round was used to track the movements of the Pleiades, so let us take a look at what it involved.

The astronomical purpose of the New Fire ceremony is revealed in Bernardino de Sahugún's report from Aztec informants, recorded shortly after the invasion.[2] The New Fire ceremony occurred at the end of every fifty-two-year Calendar Round. Just prior to the invasion, the ceremony always occurred in November. The Pleiades were observed carefully, and on the expected night they were supposed to pass through the zenith precisely at midnight. If we accept this account as accurate, and there is no reason not to, we have a very precise measurement. The Pleiades, being on the ecliptic, actually pass through the zenith quite often during the year, but only once every year do they arrive at the zenith precisely at midnight. If they didn't, so goes the popular myth, the world would end. This tells us that the New Fire ceremony is a doctrine that was designed by the

Teotihuacanos to predict the end of the current World Age. However, the encoded implications are not quite so simple. If the Pleiades failed to pass through the zenith at midnight on the expected day, they would pass through the zenith on the very next day. Why? Because precession slowly moves the timing of the phenomenon forward, one day every seventy-two years, and by 1507 the central Mexicans had already made at least two dozen such adjustments without the world coming to an end. There would have to be an ultimate future target, or culmination, for the process—but what could it be?

The key to understanding this problem is the fact that *the midnight zenith passage of the Pleiades defines the day exactly six months later when the Pleiades and the Sun are in conjunction.* Earlier I described how Teotihuacan (where, by the way, the New Fire ceremony was first performed at least 1,700 years ago) was oriented to the sunset horizon on the solar zenith-passage day, and in that era the Pleiades rose heliacally on that day. The Pleiades emerge in the predawn skies (heliacally) after six weeks of being lost in the rays of the Sun. This six-week period is generally referred to as the "Sun-Pleiades" conjunction, but to calculate the precise day of the Sun-Pleiades conjunction one needs to use another measurement. The event most readily available upon which to base such a measurement would be the Sun-Pleiades opposition, which is precisely what the midnight zenith passage of the Pleiades is.

The forgotten meaning of the New Fire tradition now comes into focus: The periodic recalibration of the New Fire date was a way to recalibrate the conjunction date of the Sun and the Pleiades in May. Most significantly, however, like the date of the midnight zenith passage of the Pleiades (the diametrically opposed event), this conjunction date had been slowly moving forward through the year ever since the founding of the New Fire ceremony at Teotihuacan. Furthermore, the Sun-Pleiades conjunction had been slowly moving forward through the month of May toward the unchanging date of the Sun's zenith passage on May 17 (at the latitude of Teotihuacan). The alignment of the Sun and the Pleiades *in the zenith* must have been the ultimate target of the New Fire ceremony! This convergence of celestial phenomena is caused by precession and, like the Maya's galactic cosmology of 2012, it defines a specific era for the world's ending.

The complication with this New Fire system is that the timing of the world's end is a function of one's latitude of observation, because that variable affects the date of the solar zenith passage—the target of the alignment doctrine. Because Teotihuacan is situated at 18° north latitude, the convergence of Sun, Pleiades, and zenith actually occurred in the early 1800s. South of Teotihuacan, the era of the world's end would have arrived sooner; north of Teotihuacan it would arrive later. The fact that the world did not end in the 1800s does not matter—ancient eschatologies do not have to be prophetically true in order for them to have once existed. On the other hand, we might say a world did end, for the Aztecs at least, long before the 1800s. Of greater interest here is what happened to this New Fire–World Age doctrine when Teotihuacan disintegrated in the eighth century A.D., and its inhabitants (and ideas) fled to the Yucatan.

By that time it had been almost a millennium since the split in the Mesoamerican psyche occurred. The Teotihuacanos—the people of the Pleiades—worshiped deities of death and rebirth located in one part of the sky, while the Maya calibrated death and rebirth according to events in the opposite direction. For all intents and purposes, both the Mayan and Teotihuacano realms were disintegrating by the eighth century A.D., suffering perhaps under the conflict of their unintegrated worldviews. And the conflict apparently involved disagreement over when the world was to end and be reborn. Something needed to happen. Teotihuacanos began arriving at Chichen Itza around A.D. 780, and they revived a straggling and weary kingdom. New life was kindled, and as the end of Baktun 10 approached (in A.D. 830), the Great Ballcourt and the famous Pyramid of Kukulcan were built. It is this pyramid-temple that preserves the New Fire doctrine of the Sun-Pleiades reaching the zenith throne— the famous legend of the return of Quetzalcoatl.

The Pyramid of Kukulcan

It has never before been shown how the Pyramid of Kukulcan at Chichen Itza encodes precession. Every equinox, thousands of visitors swarm around the pyramid to observe a shadow serpent appear and slither down the northern stairway. The shadow is caused by the ingenious orientation of the pyramid to the rays of the late-afternoon sun. It is said that this hierophany heralds the return of life-giving solar energy on the spring equinox, but the shadow serpent also appears on the fall equinox. At any rate, this famous event is the exoteric pointer to the alignment of the Sun and the Pleiades in the zenith that literally makes Kukulcan's pyramid a precessional star clock in stone. In other words, the equinoctial shadow serpent is not the ultimate purpose of the Pyramid of Kukulcan. This may sound surprising, as the shadow serpent manifestation on the equinox is impressive, and indeed it required amazing architectural design and engineering abilities. But the shadow serpent also points symbolically to an astronomical event that is invisible, or, we might say, esoteric. The visible manifestation of the shadow serpent on the equinox is merely the exoteric pointer, and should not be considered the deepest intention of the pyramid's message.

We must first visualize the shadow serpent and include an element that is rarely considered—the serpent's tail. The tail (or rattle) has no counterpart in the shadow that appears, but must be deduced or extrapolated to complete the picture of the snake (fig. 2.4). The snake descends the stairway headfirst, and to make sure the viewer's perception is correct, a serpent's head is carved in stone at the base of the stairway. Since the serpent descends from the apex of the four-sided pyramid, we can envision the erect tail of the Yucatec Mayan rattlesnake, *Crotalus durissus*, rising through the small temple on the top platform, pointing up into the center of the sky. Four-sided Mayan pyramids represent the four directions, with the top or center representing the fifth direction, the zenith.[3] Thus, the tail points to the zenith, indicating a location where something hidden might occur.

Mexican researcher José Diaz Bolio spent many years showing that Yucatec rattlesnakes were solar deities because, in part, they often display a little circular design near their rattles.[4] Oddly, the three dots in the design resemble the solar Ahau face used by the Maya to represent the sun. The rattle next to this solar symbol provides the key to the pyramid's hidden cosmology. In the Yucatec Mayan language, the word for the snake's rattle is *tzab*, which is also the word for the Pleiades—the rattle constellation. Here we find a perfectly integrated symbolism that points us to an astronomical event that will not be visible to the naked eye: *the Sun conjunct the Pleiades in the zenith*. This is none other than the World Age alignment doctrine encoded into the New Fire ceremony of the Teotihuacanos, brought to Chichen in the eighth century A.D. Confirma-

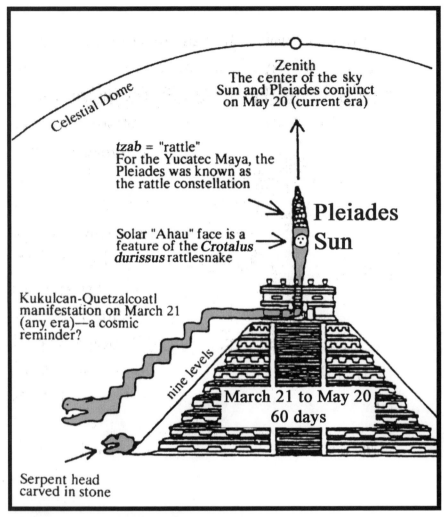

Figure 2.4. The alignment of the Sun and the Pleiades in
the zenith over Chichen Itza

tion comes from the *chac mool* statue discovered in the inner chamber of
the Pyramid of Kukulcan, just below the floor level of the upper platform,
in whose stomach the New Fire was drilled.

At the latitude of Chichen Itza, the solar zenith passage occurs
between May 20 and May 25. A range of zenith-passage dates must be
allowed, especially at more northerly latitudes.[5] Remember how the New
Fire ceremony was designed to track the changing date of the Sun-
Pleiades conjunction, and how at Teotihuacan they reached the zenith

together in the early 1800s? Well, at Chichen they don't reach the zenith together until the early twenty-first century A.D., which is extremely significant because it brings the world-ending doctrine of central Mexico into alignment with the end-date of the Mayan Long Count calendar. The relocation of core elements of Teotihuacano science to Chichen thus allowed a prolongation of their world and a unification, or healing, of the ancient split in the Mesoamerican psyche.

Quetzalcoatl first emerged as a deity image at Teotihuacan, and it has been shown that his earliest astronomical association was with the Pleiades. But, I would add, he also had solar attributes, and we might think of him as the Sun and the Pleiades in conjunction. His flight from south to north over the Mesoamerican landscape could be envisioned as his returning to his throne in the zenith center, bathing different regions with his presence as he slowly moved northward. His return was annual (as the Pleiades rose heliacally), but occurred in the zenith throne only in a specific region during a specific era. Perhaps this explains the general northward movement of Mayan culture, from beginnings in the far south at Izapa and Copan, through the latitudes of Peten and Palenque, farther north to Yucatan.

Unification at Chichen Itza in the Ninth Century

Central Mexican and Mayan culture fused at Chichen Itza in the ninth century A.D. to declare a unification of two World Age cosmologies. They were united by virtue of the way that Chichen's latitude afforded a slightly later era for the Sun-Pleiades-zenith alignment—an adjustment that brought central Mexican eschatology into alignment with the Mayan 2012 end-date. Now both the zenith cosmology and the galactic cosmology would occur over Chichen Itza in the same era, that is, in the twenty-first century of the Christian calendar.

Figure 2.5. Captain Sun Disk and Captain Serpent

My reading of Chichen as a place of unification is supported by the prevalence of two pseudohistorical leaders depicted in various states of battle and alliance all over Chichen Itza. Scholars refer to them as Captain Sun Disk and Captain Serpent, because one sits in a sun disk and the other is encircled by a serpent companion (fig. 2.5). In the overly literal interpretations of academicians, these characters have been forced to become historical personages—a perspective that occludes their deeper symbolism. Captain Sun Disk represents the paradigm of solar rebirth in the Mayan doctrine of 2012. Captain Serpent clearly represents the central Mexican obsession with the Pleiades (serpent rattle) as the focus of future world renewal. That they appear together at Chichen is significant, for it conforms to the historical meeting of Teotihuacanos and Mayans at Chichen, and validates my reading of a unification that healed an ages-long schism in the Mesoamerican psyche. It also supports the idea that this unification was essentially a union of two esoteric cosmologies, and thus requires a metaphysical dimension. The captains were latter-day versions of One Hunahpu and Quetzalcoatl, the deities who are reborn in their respective World Age mythologies. In chapter 3 we will review how the mural depicting the union of captains in the Upper Temple of the Jaguar is bathed by the light of the setting sun on certain days of the year—notably, the zenith-passage days.

As if this weren't astounding enough, we can recognize something else in the esoteric astronomy encoded at Chichen. The Pleiades are roughly opposed to the Galactic Center; a Scorpio-Pleiades polarity is recognized in Mayan as well as Incan cosmography. The Pleiades are thus an approximate indicator of the Galactic Anticenter. We can envision an axis extending up from the Galactic Center, passing through Earth, and stretching outward past the Pleiades into the vast empty spaces beyond our galaxy. It is on this axis that the two precessional alignments occur, both in the twenty-first century. Metaphysically speaking, Mesoamerican cosmologists must have recognized this as some kind of supreme convergence of intragalactic and extragalactic forces, which would converge on Chichen Itza in the distant future. All of these considerations provide material for further explorations, some of which will be taken up in chapter 3.

Aftermath

Something that sets *Maya Cosmogenesis 2012* apart from other books on the Maya—both popular and academic—is that it offers an interdisciplinary synthesis of the academic scholarship, which results in a new picture of Mayan calendrics and cosmology. Careful source documentation, a comprehensive grasp of the issues, and rigorous adherence to reason guided by intuition contribute to what amounts to the first in-depth, serious, and comprehensive exploration of the galactic alignment as it manifests in a cosmological system. I would like to summarize the salient points of this new reconstruction.

1. The Maya intended the 2012 end-date of the 13-*baktun* cycle of their Long Count calendar to target the rare alignment of the solstice sun with the Galactic Center of our Milky Way galaxy.
2. They encoded this alignment into their basic institutions, including the Hero Twin Creation myth, king accession rites, and the sacred ball game. I call this complex of ideas the galactic cosmology.
3. Izapa is the origin place of both the Long Count and the Mayan Creation myth, which serve as the astronomical, calendric, ritual, and mythological foundation of the galactic cosmology.
4. An unrecognized astronomical message in the Pyramid of Kukulcan at Chichen Itza (where the famous shadow-serpent event occurs every equinox) involves the alignment of the Sun and the Pleiades in the zenith. My reconstruction here is supported by evidence in Mayan iconography, calendrics, and archaeoastronomy. I call this the zenith cosmology.
5. In addition, I identified the New Fire ceremony and the Calendar Round as the systems used to track the alignment of the Sun and the Pleiades in the zenith.
6. Thus, Chichen Itza was identified as a place that recognized not only the future 2012 alignment of the Sun with the Galactic Center, but a future convergence (in the twenty-first century) of solar and Pleiadian energy. In the sociopolitical realm, the avatars Captain Sun Disk and Captain Serpent symbolize the union of these essentially cosmological doctrines.

7. Given that the Pleiades and the Galactic Center are roughly opposed in the sky, I proposed that the Maya understood the two alignments that will occur in the twenty-first century (over Chichen Itza, at least) to be an opening of the evolutionary axis that extends from the Galactic Center, through Earth, and out toward the Galactic Anticenter region of the Pleiades. The implications of this are profound, and point to ideas in Vedic and Egyptian cosmology.

In the largest context of what is demonstrated here, the Maya were interested in two parts of the sky and two precession-caused alignments that occur in those regions. Both alignments are extremely rare and involve the entire frame of the sky rather than merely local conjunctions of planets. The Maya created an entire set of myths and deities to encode these celestial convergences. The first alignment concerns the resurrection of One Hunahpu; the second describes the return of Quetzalcoatl. Astronomically speaking, Earth is aligning, via the solstitial axis, with the Galactic Center and the Galactic Anticenter. Metaphysically speaking, a galactic chakra system can be envisioned in this convergence, with the evolutionary energy (or *shakti*) being funneled through Earth as a result of the alignments identified in ancient Mayan cosmology. In parts 3 and 5 we shall explore in greater detail the metaphysical implications of the solstice-galaxy alignment as a temporal key to the Perennial Philosophy.

These ideas suggest a very compelling (and ancient) model of human spiritual evolution. One thing I learned from writing *Maya Cosmogenesis 2012* is that *it is important to distinguish between the reconstructed cosmology of the ancient Maya and having to believe in it ourselves.* The idea that periodic alignments to the galactic plane and to the Galactic Center stimulate consciousness on this planet is an intriguing and profound concept. What I have demonstrated is that the ancient Mayan astronomer-priests understood the astronomy involved in this statement, that they accurately calculated the next big alignment, and that *they believed* it would herald something significant for planet Earth. I did not make these claims without assembling a huge amount of evidence from diverse academic sources, and I demonstrated quite clearly how the Maya encoded this end-date alignment concept into their core institutions. I also briefly explored the argument for whether such alignments have any effect on life on Earth.[6] In the foreword to *Maya Cosmogenesis 2012,* Terence McKenna suggested that a resonant relationship between DNA molecules and the Galactic Center might be elaborated through the growing paradigm of chaos dynamics. This is without doubt the right track—resonant relationships rather than cause-and-effect "astrology"—a perspective I discussed in *Tzolkin* in the chapter "Causality vs. Synchronicity." My feeling is that any argument for a causal, scientifically rigorous explanation, or even a metaphysically elegant quantum model, is not as important as *the potential for spiritual and social transformation that the knowledge of our impending alignment with the Galactic Center might have for people.*

I must emphasize that even if the ancient "alignment" model were proved to be empirically invalid in terms of demonstrable effects on human beings, that does not mitigate against my reconstruction of the ancient Mayan cosmology, nor would it disprove the presence of these galactic concepts in other ancient traditions. Must we believe in the details of ancient Greek political science or Vedic philosophy to study and appreciate those perspectives? The lingering unresolved suspicion here, of course, is that this ancient galactic cosmology does offer a valid insight superior to any developed by our own cosmologists. We might state this insight in a surprisingly simple way: Our changing relationship to the larger galaxy changes *us.* A child of ten might understand this as self-evident, yet many scientists reject this as naively based in some idea magical correspondence, which we can call either "silly superstition" or "Bohm's nonlocality theorem," depending on our attitude.

After publication of *Maya Cosmogenesis 2012,* I discovered that other researchers were active on the galactic alignment question, although usually from a purely astrological viewpoint, as was the case with an article in the May 1998 issue of *Mountain Astrologer* by Daniel Giamario reporting on "a shamanic look at the turning of ages" suggested by the alignment. I found his research to be clear and his perspective interesting. Right after publication of *Maya Cosmogenesis 2012,* Jay Weidner called to tell of his collaboration with Vincent Bridges on a book called *A Monument to the End of Time,* which was published in August 1999. Their book is superbly argued and thoroughly examines the enigmatic French alchemist Fulcanelli's commentary on a monument in southern France that clearly encodes the galactic alignment as an "end of time" signal. Their work made it clear to me that the Maya's galactic cosmology might have a wider base; in other words, that the same compelling insight was noticed by other civilizations around the globe. Weidner and Bridges's work showed that this knowledge came from ancient Egypt. Subsequent research indicates to me that this knowledge derives from the Vedic World Age doctrine and its metaphysical conception of spiritual transformation in general.

THREE

Recent Discoveries

Since publication of *Maya Cosmogenesis 2012* I have made several new discoveries that further support my reconstruction of the galactic parameters of ancient Mayan cosmology. Two of them are worth taking up here. The first involves a careful reappraisal of Chichen Itza's astronomical alignments, which reveal an attempt to integrate the three cosmic centers of Mesoamerican cosmology—polar, galactic, and zenith. The second concerns the iconography of Copan's Stela C, which reveals an awareness of the Galactic Center–Galactic Anticenter axis. Chichen Itza, as discussed in chapter 2, integrated two cosmological traditions in the ninth century A.D., and Copan is especially significant because it is at the same latitude as Izapa.

Alignments at Chichen Itza

We can make some general assessments about the overall program of architecture and alignments at Chichen Itza. The entire effort—what it endeavored to encode—is complicated by the insistence on integrating all three of the cosmic centers that were recognized at various times in Mesoamerican history. As we have seen, the primordial polar tradition gave way to two newer traditions adopted by the central Mexicans on the one hand, and the Maya on the other. Centuries later, Chichen Itza, as a place of unification, integrated the two cosmological traditions in Mesoamerica—cosmologies centered on precessional alignments involving both the Pleiades and the Galactic Center. These two celestial locations are equivalent to the Scorpio-Pleiades polarity recognized in South American and Mesoamerican ideas and, more important, they represent the Galactic Center–Galactic Anticenter axis.

The westerly and easterly sides of the Pyramid of Kukulcan align with sunset on the May solar zenith passage and sunrise on the day of the New Fire ceremony in November, respectively, and this alignment matches the axis of the Upper and Lower Jaguar Temples, whose murals and symbology implicate the zenith center. The Pyramid of Kukulcan is a key to understanding the overall astronomical program of Chichen's other structures and alignments, whose purpose is to integrate the three cosmic centers—and their axes—into a unified vision of cosmic alignment set to occur in the twenty-first century of the Judeo-Christian calendar.

Because it can be occupied by the Sun, the Moon, planets, or stars, it should be noted that the zenith is a "center" in a provisional or transparent sense. The most important periodic occupants of the zenith are the Pleiades and the Sun. And since the Sun is always moving in its annual course around the zodiac, it is the Pleiades that target a specific sidereal location; thus, the zenith cosmology might more appropriately be called a Pleiades cosmology. An early Arabic word for the Pleiades means "center," and, as we shall see in the Old World's cosmological shift from a polar to a solar orientation, the seven stars of the Big Dipper were mapped (or conceptually relocated) to the seven stars of the Pleiades. The underlying meaning here is that the Pleiades, like the Big Dipper, are the head point of a world-centering axis, with the astronomical reference for the Pleiades, though approximate, being to the Galactic Anticenter. Obviously, the other end of this axis is rooted in the Galactic Center. By way of the ballcourt's solstitial alignment with the Milky Way, which is nevertheless a north-south alignment, the north-south axis of Chichen is conflated with polar north and Galactic Center south. While the Pole Star hovers some 20° above the northern horizon, the nuclear bulge of the Galactic Center can be seen to pass through the southern meridian at twice that height—thus again the north-south dialogue between polar and galactic centers. Although on one level an opposition between the Galactic Center and the northern polar region can be viewed (as just described), a primary axial opposition between the Galactic Center and the Pleiades also exists. Chichen integrates and measures the ever-changing relationship between the seasonal quarters and this galactic axis, with due reference to the original polar axis. Luckily, at Chichen, we have more than just structural alignments to go on—we also have the murals and symbolism that back up this reconstructed model of Chichen's cosmological preoccupations. The integration of the Galactic Center and the

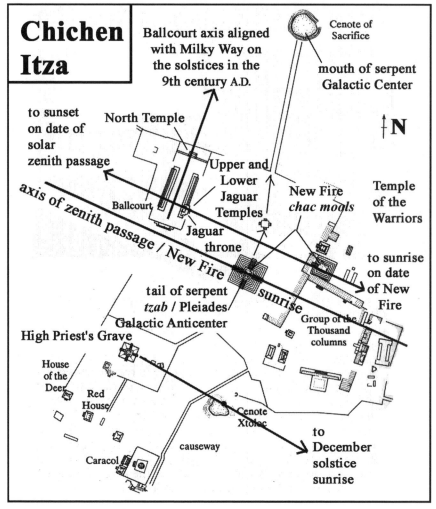

Figure 3.1. Alignments at Chichen Itza

Galactic Anticenter is consecrated in the pact between Captain Sun Disk and Captain Serpent.

The Upper Temple of the Jaguars

The westward face of the Upper Temple of the Jaguars (the UTJ), like the westward face of the Pyramid of Kukulcan, is oriented toward sunset during the solar zenith-passage date-range, May 20–25. A row of cross-shaped shields lines the upper register. The cross form, of course, may have a deep—though possibly obscure—correspondence with the Milky Way–ecliptic cross. The register just below contains two horizontal rattlesnakes emanating from the center of the facade. Basically, this "center" is an origin place, and the snakes springing from the center symbolize the cycles of time and the manifest structure of space (conceived by the Maya as having four directions). The snake is all over Chichen, and has a deep resonance with the Pleiades, the Sun, and the zenith. Because it is on the westward-facing wall of the UTJ, the center-place from which the two rattlesnakes spring faces the horizon along which the sun sets on the solar zenith-passage date at Chichen. In the era of the zenith cosmology's culmination (the twenty-first century A.D.), this date will be exactly six months removed from the date of the New Fire ceremony, which is when the Pleiades are observed passing through the zenith at midnight. Also, as encoded into the nearby Pyramid of Kukulcan, the first solar zenith-passage date is when the Sun and Pleiades will be conjunct during the alignment era.

This interpretation is based on the astronomical fact that the date of the midnight zenith passage of the Pleiades is exactly one-half year removed from the Sun-Pleiades conjunction. The center-place "portal" is above the door of the UTJ, which, of course, also faces sunset on the zenith-passage day. The door is flanked by inverted serpent columns. Four *pawatuns—bacabs*, or year-bearer symbols of the four directions—give the visual impression of surrounding the door. This means that the doorway represents the fifth, central direction. As with the apex of the Pyramid of Kukulcan (or any pyramid for that matter), this portal is an entrance into the "fifth direction," a cosmic center that Linda Schele identified in the inscriptions as the Na Ho Kan (the Five Sky Place).[1] Inside the doorway, many murals and an altar-block supported by numerous raised-arm "Atlantean" figures repeat scenes of the two avatars joined in sealing a pact of cosmic union. As one might expect, the mural on the back wall gets illuminated at sundown in late May, during the zenith passage at Chichen. The mural depicts the two avatars, Captain Sun Disk and Captain Serpent, who represent the two precessional cosmologies that both culminate with alignments in the twenty-first century. These two alignments, as mentioned, are in the directions of the Galactic Center and the Galactic Anticenter. Although these observations are full of profound implications, they are only one aspect of the full cosmological statement made at Chichen Itza.

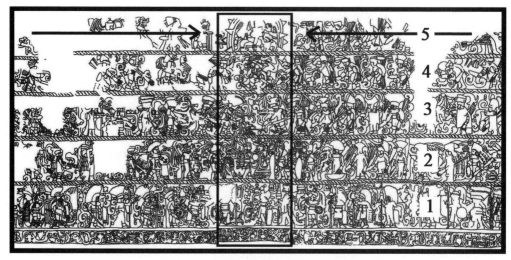

Figure 3.2. Inner mural from the Lower Temple of the Jaguars

The west-facing UTJ is counterposed by the east-facing Lower Temple of Jaguars (hereafter LTJ), situated directly below. Its open doorway faces sunrise on the date of the New Fire ceremony (in the twenty-first century) and contains a jaguar throne. This throne is much like the *chac mool* statue in the upper room inside the Pyramid of Kukulcan. In the LTJ the jaguar throne is flanked by two columns, each containing four carvings on each of the four sides. These depict four aspects of the creator couple, one column being male and the other female. Inside the chamber, we find complex murals operating on five levels (not including a narrow base panel).

In the center of the fourth and fifth levels, directly behind the jaguar throne, we find Captain Serpent and Captain Sun Disk. Notice that Captain Sun Disk sits on a jaguar throne on the fifth level. Captain Serpent sits on (or rides) the serpent, which may serve as his throne. Each level has something going on in the middle of the relief, and human figures approach the center from both sides, as if in propitiation or worship. It is difficult to determine what is occurring in the corresponding central areas of the other levels. On the third level, directly below Captain Serpent, bird feathers are visible exactly in the center, suggesting that this might be Seven Macaw, the regent of the polar center. This would be consistent with the integration of three cosmic centers. On the second level we see a ballplayer holding a game ball and on the first level there is an eroded fish of some kind. The vertical organization seems to be primarily a temporal one, from the older

Figure 3.3. Close-up of central thrones on the fourth and fifth tiers

cosmological systems up through the more recent—and advanced—models, reminiscent of the doctrine of five World Ages. The highest or most advanced model is indicated by Captain Sun Disk, the ancient One Hunahpu/First Father of the Izapan Creation myth, the solstice deity conjoined with the Galactic Center.

It goes without saying that this five-level vertical statement faces sunrise on the morning of the New Fire ceremony. From the vantage point of the jaguar throne, the eastern sunrise horizon is viewed directly over the Temple of the Warriors, where a *chac mool* and inverted serpent columns are located (see fig. 3.1). On the Pyramid of Kukulcan, only the eastward face is illuminated at sunrise on this date, the other three faces being in shadow. The opposite is true at sunset on the May zenith-passage date—that is, only the westward face is illuminated. At midnight on the New Fire date, the Pleiades can be observed directly over the apex of the Pyramid of Kukulcan, and no doubt new fire was at this moment drilled on the *chac mool*'s belly in the upper chamber of the pyramid, situated directly underneath the little temple on the top.

The sunrise-sunset axis discussed here conforms to the orientation of the UTJ and LTJ as well as the Pyramid of Kukulcan. As Miguel Angel Vergara illustrates in his book *Chichen Itza: Astronomical Light and Shadow Phenomena of the Great Pyramid*, the corner-to-corner orientation of the Pyramid of Kukulcan is aligned with June solstice sunrise and December solstice sunset.[2] As a result, on those two dates the sun illumines exactly two faces of the pyramid at sunrise and sunset (fig. 3.4).

The solstices are also implicated in the north-south orientation of the ballcourt, which, in fact, is situated perpendicular to the UTJ-LTJ axis. This is because the ballcourt was aligned with the Milky Way on the solstices when it was built in the ninth century A.D. And on the northern end of the ballcourt we find yet another temple filled with murals that conform to the "three cosmology" integration achieved at Chichen Itza.

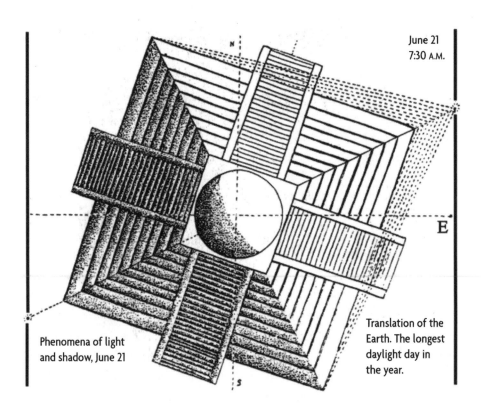

Figure 3.4. Shadows and seasons on the Pyramid of Kukulcan (from Vergara)

The North Temple

On the North Temple, pillars representing the world tree flank the southward-facing doorway. From the ballcourt's playing field, the significant horizon is viewed directly over the North Temple, in the direction of the northern polar skies, rather then the horizon toward which the doorway faces. (Something else can be viewed *from* the doorway, however, as we shall see.) The mural inside, like the one in the Lower Temple of the Jaguars, is arranged in five levels with significant action in the middle of each tier. The most interesting image is seen on the lowest level, where a huge deity lies prostrate with vines growing from its belly. Directly above the navel manifestation, on the second level, we see an unoccupied throne. It is difficult *not* to think of the Hindu deity Vishnu, who manifested the universe from his navel. (In chapter 12, we shall see that Vishnu's navel represents the Galactic Center in Vedic astrology.) Here, because of the North Temple's orientation as viewed from the ballcourt, it seems to represent the North Celestial Pole, around which all the stars are observed to revolve.

Recall that the polar center counterposes the Galactic Center as it passes through the southern meridian. Thus, the southern orientation of the North Temple's doorway may indeed be doubly significant: The navel manifestation honors the polar center as viewed over the temple (from the ballcourt) while at the same time it honors the Galactic Center direction viewed *from* the temple doorway. Those privileged to occupy the North Temple, and having seen the mural inside, might understand a deeper, dual symbology in the ball game. The implication is that a dialectic exists between the polar center and the Galactic Center—a dialectic that we first encountered in the alignments, iconography, and orientations at Izapa, where the older polar cosmology was superseded by the galactic cosmology. These two cosmologies are combined in Chichen's ballcourt alignment with the Milky Way and the perpendicular axis to the New Fire dates that integrates the zenith and the Pleiades.

Thus, we have a triangulation between the North Pole, as vertex, the east-west axis that frames the Galactic Center–Galactic Anticenter relationship, and the Sun-zenith-Pleiades phenomenon. This replicates the cosmological framework described by Michael Coe in which a primary Mesoamerican framework of orientation was identified that united four astronomical directions targeted by the Big Dipper (N), Cygnus (S), the

Pleiades (E), and Scorpio (W).[3] This model generally conforms to the well-known sacred-tree image formed by the Milky Way (north-south axis) and the ecliptic (east-west axis).

This interpretation of Chichen Itza requires more study to flesh out the background to these ideas in Mayan and central Mexican religion, ethnography, calendar ritual, iconography, and archaeoastronomy. My hope is that this brief presentation provides a better picture than I was able to draw in *Maya Cosmogenesis 2012*. Further evidence for an ancient knowledge of the axis formed by the Galactic Center and the Galactic Anticenter is found at Copan.

Copan Stela C: Sun King in the Creation Place

Perhaps the most striking new evidence for a Mayan understanding of the galactic dimensions in which the earth moves comes from Copan, the southernmost Mayan city. Copan Stela C (fig. 3.5) is the well-known 18 Rabbit statue that Schele and Mathews note is dated 9.14.0.0.0 (December 5, A.D. 711, according to the 584285 correlation).[4] This would have been the first *katun* ending after 18 Rabbit's succession to rulership. But, as Schele points out, this political anniversary was also attended by astronomical events occurring in the eastern sky that faces the side of Stela C containing the young 18 Rabbit. The iconography of the statue helps us understand what it may portray astronomically.

The east-facing image is of the young solar king standing in the maw of a crocodile form, holding a double-headed serpent bar that represents the ecliptic. He is wearing a draped loincloth that is ornamented with the jaws and teeth of a crocodile, which means he is in the crocodile's mouth. What is the significance of this? As David Kelley points out, the upturned frog-mouth glyph means "to be born," and the upturned crocodile's mouth probably has a similar meaning.[5] For a king, accession to rulership was a kind of rebirth into a new identity, thus the motif of "being born" is appropriate for Stela C. We see this imagery on many Mayan monuments. For example, even the early Mayan Stela 11 from Izapa, replicates this basic idea (see chapter 18).

As noted above, Copan Stela C is dated December 5, 711 (Gregorian calendar). Schele notes in *Code of Kings* that on December 5, 711, Venus was on the Milky Way (as evening star right after sundown), and this confirms the Venus iconography identified on the statue. However, another important conjunction occurred on that date: *the Sun was aligning with the dark rift in the Milky Way.* This dark-rift feature appears like a great cleft near Sagittarius, and is called the *Xibalba be* (Road to the Underworld) by the modern Quiché Maya. As a portal, this astronomical feature was symbolized by a door, a road, a cave, or a mouth (as in a crocodile's or snake's mouth). Clearly, the crocodile mouth in which 18 Rabbit stands could very well be the dark rift in the Milky Way.

It is worth mentioning that the west-facing side of Stela C depicts an aged 18 Rabbit. The turtle altar that is in front of him symbolizes Orion, whose belt stars outline the Ak turtle's back. In early December, when the monument was dedicated, an east-west hierophany occurred: the Sun, aligned with the dark rift, rose in the east, while Orion set in the west. This is the Galactic Center–Galactic Anticenter axis, and the Janus-faced Stela C seems intended to encode this information.

But what, essentially, can we conclude the eastern side of Stela C

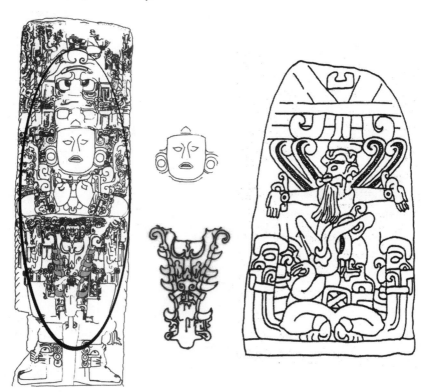

Figure 3.5. Copan Stela C, the sun king in alligator-mouth regalia

depicts? We see a solar king (sun) holding a serpent bar (the ecliptic), "inside" a crocodile mouth (the dark rift). Stela C depicts the sun inside the dark rift. This interpretation is confirmed by the celestial event toward which Stela C faces—*on December 5, 711, the Sun was indeed aligning with the dark rift in the Milky Way*. Is this simply a coincidence? In Mayan ceremony and symbolism, the meaning of this image involves the rebirth of the sun and the authority of kingship. If the ancient Maya of Copan consciously intended Stela C to encode this alignment, then we need to look seriously at the concept of "sun in dark rift" and how it may have been included in other facets of Mayan cosmology—most notably, in the end-date astronomy.

☾

It is an astronomical fact that alignments of the solstices and equinoxes with the plane of our Milky Way galaxy occur periodically over the 26,000-year precession cycle. Such alignments, in fact, occur every 6,450 years. Joseph Campbell pointed out that knowledge of the precessional cycle is implied by the importance given the number 25,920 in Hindu, Nordic, and Babylonian doctrines. Frank Waters showed how the Native American Circle of the Law Belt adds up to precessional numbers, and Gordon Brotherston's *Book of the Fourth World* examines South American and Central American cosmological number systems with the same result.[6] The 26,000-year precession cycle, in all these traditions, is understood as a vast cycle of collective spiritual gestation for humanity.

But where is the anchor of this cycle, how can we identify its beginning and end? Clearly, an alignment of the solstice axis with the Milky Way can provide an unambiguous "anchor" for the precession cycle. Could this anchor have been known to those same cultures that seemed to have been aware of precession? The case is strong for the Maya, for the ancient calendric cosmology of the Maya considers the impending solstice-galaxy alignment to be a critical metaphysical event for collective human transformation, and the centerpiece of their eschatological doctrine.

If we accept that the ancient Mayan cosmologists intended their 2012 end-date to target the rare alignment of the solstice sun with the galaxy, the inevitable question arises: What about other astronomically sophisticated civilizations, such as ancient Egypt, Persia, and Vedic India? If we find evidence for knowledge of this alignment among these civilizations,

Figure 3.6. Scorpio as center of the celestial sphere
(from Jacob Boehme, *Theosophische Werke*, 1682)

the Maya then appear to be merely the latest promoters of a very ancient cosmological science.

Our course is set to seek the existence of the Galactic Cosmology in other civilizations. Did they have a knowledge of the galaxy? Certainly. Were they aware of precession? Yes, I would wager. Did they recognize, as did the Maya, the location of the Galactic Center as an important player in human origins and future transformation? And do our periodic alignments to the Galactic Center trigger world-shattering events? If it is true that the most ancient civilizations possessed this knowledge, then relatively recent survivals might still be found. For example, what about the Renaissance woodcut that places Scorpio (whose stinger points to the Galactic Center) in the center of a celestial sphere (fig. 3.6)?

This illustration from the works of Jacob Boehme is tantalizing and suggestive, to be sure. Is it an isolated case, or might it be just one fragment in an ocean of related pieces of evidence? Luckily, other independent researchers have tuned in to this profound question, and a reappraisal of long-neglected and underappreciated academic research in the light of this new perspective provides extensive ready-made support. Beginning with the cultures and esoteric traditions of Europe, we might be able to trace this knowledge, from fragmented recent practices such as geomancy and sacred topography, back in time to the profound and sophisticated perceptions of the ancient Egyptians and Vedic astronomers. Along the way, surprising ideas will be uncovered, bringing us full circle back to the Maya and our own tumultuous times.

FOUR

Sacred Cartography in the British Isles

The megalithic monuments of Avebury and Stonehenge—to name but a few—reveal that England was once home to a people who mapped the terrain, filling it with mythic meaning and magical lore. Stonehenge is arguably the best-known megalithic site in England, and recent decades have shed more light on its mysteries. It is now known, for example, that the huge stone blocks used to construct Stonehenge came from a quarry some sixty miles away, across the Severn River, in Wales. Why would the ancient builders of Stonehenge go to such great trouble to find stones when there were plenty of quarries much closer to the site? It is believed that a high concentration of minerals in certain stones was desired so as to channel the earth energy that runs along a crisscross network of alignments known as the ley-line grid.[1]

Over seventy-five years ago a man named Alfred Watkins stood on a low hill and gazed over the Hereford countryside in west England. He suddenly became aware of a system of lines hidden in the landscape that connected old churches, road intersections, ancient standing stones, and hilltops. His integrative vision lasted just a moment, but it made sense of all the local lore about sacred spots and old place-names that he had been collecting over many years of traveling around the back-country districts as a delivery man for his father's brewing company. He had discovered the ancient ley-line grid—subtle energy pathways that were known to the ancient inhabitants of England and marked by the placement of stone circles and processional paths.

The subsequent mapping of sacred sites and ley lines in England—in fact, in the entirety of the British Isles—reveals that megalithic sites such as Stonehenge were intentionally located at the intersection of major ley lines. This, of course, brings up the question of what ley lines actually are. Sur-

Figure 4.1. Stonehenge reconstructed

prisingly, the ley lines were found to align not only with underground waterways but also with astronomy, most notably equinox and solstice horizon points. For example, a major ley line runs from the tip of Cornwall in southwest England through the entire width of England to the northeast coast. Known as the Michael-Mary line, it runs through many major stone circles and sanctuaries dedicated to Saint Michael, including Avebury and the tower on Glastonbury Tor. The entire line, hundreds of miles long, is oriented to sunrise on May 1, the cross-quarter day upon which the maypole dance occurred to celebrate fertility and the arrival of spring.

The four seasons and the four directions provided a larger generalized framework for the subdivisions of the ancient ley lines discovered and mapped by Alfred Watkins in his book *The Old Straight Track*. The lay of the landscape was very important to the ancient bards and shamans of the British Isles. Each river, boulder, hill, glade, and forest pathway was imbued with sacred meaning, and the human impulse to map the terrain manifested in a curious practice: the quartering of the landscape. In order to learn more about the intentions and methods of this ancient science as practiced in the British Isles, we need to understand the principles of sacred cartography.

Divine order was established on Earth by centering a given region, which might be delimited by geographical features such as mountains, rivers, or ocean. In the British Isles, an entire island—for example, Ireland—could be identified as a complete and separate entity. It would then be "centered" by dividing it into four parts. This was accomplished by first determining its longest lengthwise axis (usually north-south), and then its widest east-west axis. Where these two axes crossed defined the sacred central precinct from which the high druid or, later, the Celtic king, would rule. Evidence of the existence of the ancient sacred precincts survives today in boundary roadways and the old county names. In Ireland, County Meath—which means "middle" in Old Irish—stands in the middle of the island, uniting four ancient quadrants that were later subdivided into smaller districts. Thus a central fifth element is introduced that unites the surrounding four districts.

John Michell has decoded the principles of sacred cartography, showing how (and where) the sacred centers of many of the British Isles and other places were located. His combined reading of old maps, travelers' accounts, historical archives, folklore, and local traditions resulted in important books, including *At The Centre of the World* and *Twelve-Tribe Nations*, the latter of which was cowritten with Christine Rhone. Michell identified the sacred centers of England, Ireland, France, Wales, the Isle of Man, the Orkneys, Iceland, and other islands. He was frequently able to locate the axes of the quadripartite divisions, which today often correspond with modern roads or paths. But we may wonder, what impulse was behind this tradition of quartering the terrain?

An important function of sacred cartography is to map the celestial realm of the night sky onto the local landscape. This follows from the ancient belief that processes in the sky reflect processes on Earth—the ancient doctrine of "as above, so below." In keeping with this concept, natural landmarks in local topography were perceived to reflect prominent celestial features such as planets, bright stars, constellations, or the Milky

Way. In fact, the Milky Way was recognized as a major cosmic axis whose terrestrial counterpart was the long north-south axis of a given island or region. Since this north-south axis also points to the North Celestial Pole, the Pole Star or polar axis could also have the same meaning. The east-west axis was seen to indicate the rising and setting points of the sun on the equinox dates in March and September, and thus it reflected the ecliptic path of the Sun, Moon and planets. So, the Milky Way and the ecliptic form the two axes that, together, divide the cosmos into four parts. The point where they cross is the sacred center on a celestial level. We already know that one of the crossing points formed by the Milky Way and the ecliptic is in the Sagittarius-Scorpio region, and it pinpoints the Galactic Center. And, of course, when this cosmic grid is mapped onto the local topography, the sacred center then marks the place of ruler-ship and spiritual authority. In the example of Ireland, this was County Meath, where the ancient Irish kings lived.

According to Michell, the likeliest candidate for the sacred center of England is the crossroads formed by two old roadways that mirror the two celestial roads—Fosse Way and Watling Way. A little town called Venonae is located right where these two ancient roads intersect. Watling Way runs from Dover in the southeast to north Wales in the northwest. The folklore associated with this ancient road identifies it with the Milky Way. Fosse Way runs southwest to northeast, and the two roads intersect precisely at the sacred center of England. In addition, Michell notes that England is roughly triangular, and the central district, the location of Venonae, is close to the geometrical middle of the triangle (see fig. 4.2).

To be consistent with other "sacred center" traditions, we should expect there to be a pillar, a cross, or a monument of some kind at this location, and sure enough, at one time there was. A high cross survived at the site into the nineteenth century. History records that it reproduced an older Roman monument placed at this sacred crossroads, which in turn overlaid an even older druid sanctuary. An eighteenth-century engraving (fig. 4.3) survives of the high cross that marked the sacred center of England.

Notice in the illustration that there is a cross on top of a globe on top of the pillar. This is an ancient esoteric symbol with many levels of mean-ing. Simply put, it says "this is where the center of the world is," or, "this is the cosmic navel." Since Watling Way represented the Milky Way and the cross it forms with Fosse Way indicates a "center," then the high cross

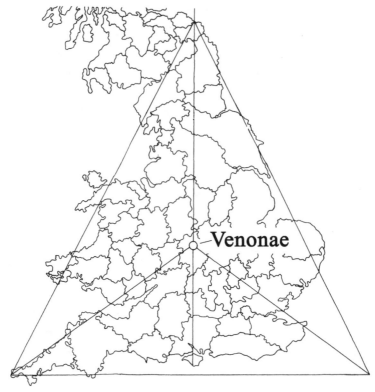

Figure 4.2. Venonae, the sacred center of England

at Venonae would apparently indicate a "cosmic center" that resides along both the Milky Way and the ecliptic. Despite the preoccupation with the polar center that we find in northern cultures, this information quite clearly indicates a different celestial center—the Galactic Center. (Today, the region of the Galactic Center cannot be viewed from the latitude of England, as it is always below the horizon. Before roughly 2,000 years ago, however, it was quite high over the southern horizon; more on this in chapter 14.)

At the very least, the Venonae high cross probably replicated or paid homage to the ancient esoteric knowledge of how, according to the time-honored principles of sacred cartography, that spot represented the Galactic Center. We should remember here that the Galactic Center occupies a region of the Milky Way that is quite bright and wide, visible to the naked eye, and subject to being seen as a cosmic womb or birthplace of stars.

The folklore and symbolism associated with the crossroads of Venonae paint a simple picture, and it would be difficult to avoid the inevitable conclusion that the high cross was intended to mark the Galactic Center rather than (or perhaps in addition to) the polar center. My interpretation is in keeping with the principles of sacred cartography identified by Michell and others. My identification of the Venonae cross with the Galactic Center may, however, conflict with the other cosmic center that many writers exclusively emphasize: the North Celestial Pole, or Pole Star. The Pole Star is clearly an important celestial symbol, especially for northern people, because in the far north it is almost straight overhead

Figure 4.3. The high cross at the Venonae crossroads

and all the stars appear to revolve around it. Here we begin to encounter two different astronomical locations that nevertheless map onto the same symbolic structure—but as we shall see, this enriches rather than prevents understanding.

The north-south axis of many lands is a polar indicator because it points northward. In England, however, the north-south axis of Watling Road has a specific and very ancient association with the Milky Way. According to Richard Hinckley Allen's *Star Names: Their Lore and Meaning*, a variant of Watling Way, Walsyngham Way, was considered in Norfolk tradition to be the road leading to the Virgin Mary, seen in the sky as the Milky Way. And yet many other traditions honor the polar center and the nearby Big Dipper as primary "center" places. How can we explain the apparently conflicting presence of galactic symbology? A single example of this, such as we find in England, might be easily dismissed, but let us take a look at the traditions of the Isle of Man, which lies between Wales and Ireland, for there we find some other compelling artifacts that point right to the Galactic Center.

The Isle of Man

The sacred center of England's association with the Galactic Center is compelling and simple, but it is not an isolated instance of this kind of relationship in the British Isles. We can identify the sacred center of the entire group of islands and find even better evidence. John Michell determined that the center of the entirety of the British Isles can be identified by running a north-south line from Land's End in Cornwall to Duncansby Head in northern Scotland. This is the terrestrial counterpart to the Milky Way overhead as the World Axis. The east-west line (corresponding to the ecliptic) consists of the east-west diameter running through the middle of the north-south axis. The resulting crosshairs precisely target the Isle of Man as the sacred center of the British Isles (see fig. 4.4).

This in itself is a pretty astounding "coincidence," and immediately makes the Isle of Man into a geographical omphalos. Tradition tells that druids and bards traveled to this island from distant lands to study the arts of astronomy, poetry, song crafting, medicine, and shamanism. Named after the Manx people, its remote location has preserved intact many

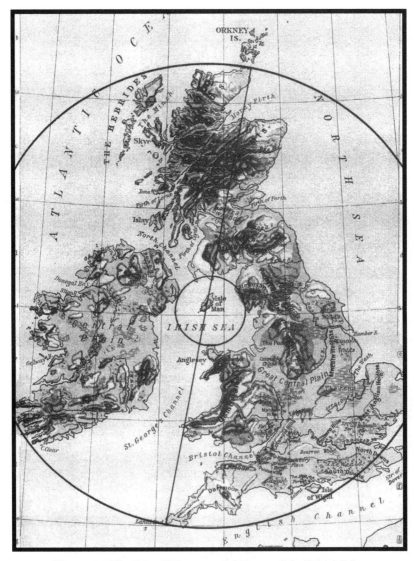

Figure 4.4. The Isle of Man as sacred center of the British Isles

ancient pathways and monuments. When we zero in on the Isle of Man, we find that its four districts conform to the larger quadripartite pattern that was just described. Most intriguingly, the north-south axis of the Isle of Man corresponds to an ancient pilgrimage path into the center of the island, today called the Millennium Way. In local lore it is known as the Manx Royal Road or the Great Road of King Orrey, who is associated in the following legend with the Milky Way.

As told in the island's *Historical Account* of 1858, when Orrey landed on the northern beach he was met by a group of the island's inhabitants, asking where he had come from. "That is the way to my country," he said, pointing up at the shimmering Milky Way. He then proceeded to march southward, along a route that was given his name, into the center of the island, where he installed himself as sacred ruler at Keeill Abban. This mytho-historical account is important in terms of highlighting the practice of pilgrimage to the central shrine, a type of pilgrimage similarly undertaken along the Way of Saint James to Santiago de Compostela in Spain, which culminated, in pre-Christian times, with the pilgrim's arrival at the Atlantic coast, World's End, where the dying sun was imagined to drown in the western ocean. These traditions represent the Milky Way as the Great Roadway into the center or end of the world—the "end" is the prelude to a new beginning and is thus equivalent to the source or center. Here we encounter an intriguing idea, essential for understanding the impact of precessional ages on humanity: Time does not move "up and down" (as in forward progress vs. backward regress); rather, it moves us *in and out* of intimacy with our source and center.

The Millennium Way provides clear evidence that the Isle of Man represents the center of the British Isles and also a celestial center along the Milky Way. This is a terrestrial map that points to a specific celestial location: The cross formed by the Milky Way where it crosses the ecliptic in Sagittarius is where the Galactic Center is located! How incredible it would be to walk the ancient pilgrimage route from the northern edge of the island deep into the central precinct, and to sit on the steps of Saint Luke's Church, which was built over the ancient Galactic Center shrine of Keeill Abban!

The ancient stone oratory chapel of Keeill Abban was already in ruins when Saint Luke's Church replaced it in 1836. Michell reports that some of the original stones were used, including a sandstone block with a cross carved into it, which was given a place of honor in the new church of Saint Luke, outside, facing east, below the belfry. It is tempting to imagine this stone as the surviving marker of the cosmic cross that Keeill Abban was intended to represent. In fact, Celtic and Manx tradition utilized just such cross-carved stones as thrones. As with Mayan kings, Celtic kings symbolically occupied the "cosmic center" and a cross carved on a stone throne spoke this truth perfectly (see fig. 4.5). Michell tells us,

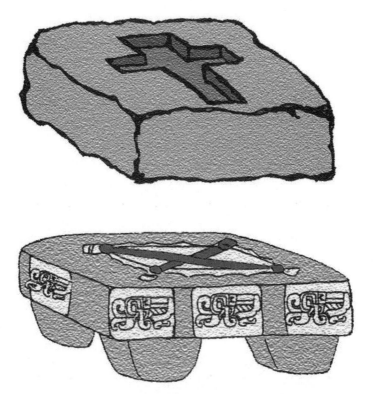

Figure 4.5. *Above,* a Celtic coronation stone; *below,* Izapan throne

"A Stone of Destiny is a Celtic coronation stone, and there is no harm in supposing that the block in the wall at St Luke's was the stone on which the old Manx kings were installed."[2]

There are similar traditions in Iceland, Wales, Ireland, the Hebrides, and the Orkney Islands, all of which indicate that the sacred central areas were meeting places, royal sanctuaries, and zones of lawgiving, oratory, proclamation, healing—even divine inspiration. It is quite impressive that the Milky Way and the Galactic Center are so clearly embedded in these ancient maps of the World Axis. But what of the polar center, clearly an important celestial symbol, especially for northern peoples? Here we have two different locations that share the same symbolic structure. As in Mayan cosmology, there may have been an age-old competition going on between these two cosmic centers, the polar and the galactic. Or, as cosmological thinking evolved, human beings mapped the older polar-centered framework onto a newer, more intriguing system involving the Milky

Way and the Galactic Center. This evolution of thought would explain the shift from polar to solar symbolism in the history of astrology, as identified by René Guénon and others. I would add that the sun could occasionally occupy the "cosmic center" in the newer, solar-oriented philosophy. In other words, the sun itself is not the center, but could periodically occupy—or be enthroned in—the cosmic center, which in the new system would be the Galactic Center. I'll have a lot more to say on this topic in a later discussion, but we already glimpse that sacred traditions in the north must belong to a very ancient and profound worldview.

A French Obelisk

England's high-cross monument and the throne-stone of the Isle of Man, symbolically situated at the "peak" of the Milky Way, belong to a larger tradition found all over England and Europe, where we find many monuments like these in old market squares and at important crossroads. But where did this practice come from? Without laboriously tracing the evolution and variant forms of this tradition over many centuries—even millennia—of development, we can observe that this tradition is very similar to, and probably derived from, the Egyptian practice of raising obelisks as symbols of the *djed* pillar, the body of Osiris. Moira Timms, in her "Raising the Djed" essay, pioneered new insights into the symbolism of the *djed* pillar. She explained that the *djed* pillar is spatially associated with the Pole Star, but in a precessional context it also relates to the Milky Way in its north-south orientation. The *djed* is also well known as the backbone of Osiris and is an important element in Egyptian cosmology.

As the *axis mundi*, obelisks were symbols of power and connection between the earth and the sky. Peter Tompkins, in his wonderful book *The Magic of Obelisks*, surveyed the uses and meanings of obelisks, from the 3,600-year-old Cleopatra's Needle to the Washington Monument. Tompkins explains that the *djed* pillar draws down power from the sky. In the human body, the spinal column is like a miniature *djed* pillar through which flows a subtle energy, known in Hinduism as the *kundalini shakti*. Rome, around the time of Christ, appropriated an Egyptian obelisk to affirm its status as new temporal power and spiritual center. Similar plundering of the spiritual heritage and political symbols of Egypt has continued into modern times; the obelisk of the Egyptian ruler Thutmose III

Figure 4.6. Egyptian obelisk at Luxor

ended up in New York's Central Park. Egypt looms in the background of a great deal of what survives in various European traditions.

An apocalypse obelisk in France was described by the enigmatic twentieth-century alchemist Fulcanelli in his book *Dwellings of the Philosophers.* Fulcanelli offers a compelling interpretation of the obelisk from Dommartin-sur-Tigeaux (Siene et Marne), which is reminiscent of his analysis of the cyclic cross at Hendaye in his *Mystery of the Cathedrals.*

According to Fulcanelli, this monument (which, unfortunately, was obliterated during World War II) encodes a double catastrophe to occur at the end of the Great Solar Period, which is divided into four ages. We can deduce that this reference is to the 26,000-year precessional cycle, divided into four periods of 6,500 years each. (Some Hinduism-influenced writers such as Fulcanelli report 24,000 precessional years, yielding four eras of 6,000 years each.) Like the high cross at Venonae, the Dommartin monument also has a ball at the top, surmounted by rods rather than a cross, and may very well symbolize the center of the Milky Way. But why should a monument that may point to the Galactic Center be involved with apocalyptic symbolism and the precession cycle? Well, having already discussed the Mayan cosmology of the galactic alignment, we know the answer, but the presence in France of a similar cosmology is

Figure 4.7 Apocalypse obelisk from Dommartin-sur-Tigeaux, France
(from *Dwellings of the Philosophers* [Boulder, Colo.: Archive Press, 1999])

astounding. This engages the main themes of this book: our periodic alignments to the Galactic Center, the ancient beliefs that developed around these events, and the encoded survival of these ancient beliefs in esoteric cosmologies worldwide.

To find out more about who Fulcanelli was and how he knew such esoteric secrets, we need go no further than the work of Jay Weidner and Vincent Bridges and their book *A Monument to the End of Time*. For although the Dommartin monument was destroyed, the cyclic cross in Hendaye, France, still stands.

FIVE

The Apocalypse Cross
at Hendaye

Before examining the evidence presented in *A Monument to the End of Time*, we need to understand the difference between *cross* and *alignment*. The esoteric symbolism examined by Weidner and Bridges envisions the galactic alignment as a cross—the cross of the equinox axis and the galactic plane that measures precisely 90° during the alignment. Thus, "equinox cross" is just another way of saying "solstice alignment"—both name precisely the same event. The concept of the cross is possibly more appropriate from the vantage point of Western astrological symbolism, which chooses the vernal equinox point as a precession marker.[1]

Weidner and Bridges's *A Monument to the End of Time: Alchemy, Fulcanelli, and the Great Cross* is a remarkable book that describes how the galactic alignment is deeply embedded within European esotericism, including Gothic architecture, astrology, and alchemy.[2] The alignment itself may be somewhat difficult to distinguish in some of these traditions, but the Galactic Center is clearly present; for example, it is found as a high initiatory location within Renaissance alchemy and in the mythos of the Holy Grail. The entire cycle of Arthurian stories about the quest for the Holy Grail involves the soul's journey to paradise, the center of the world, where the cup of immortality could quench the seeker's thirst for spiritual vision and truth. Within the Kabbalah the Galactic Center corresponds to the axis running between Kether and Malkuth, the highest and lowest *sephiroth* in the Tree of Life. Kabbalistic diagrams were encoded into Gothic architecture in the twelfth century, embodied by Saint Denis cathedral and Notre Dame. The authors of *A Monument to the End of Time* (hereafter *AMET*) closely examined the premiere authority on Gothic cathedral architecture, the enigmatic Fulcanelli, whose classic work *The Mystery of the Cathedrals* contains a revealing chapter called "The Cyclic Cross at Hendaye." This encoded information, as we shall see, pertains to both the Galactic Center and the galactic alignment.

The cross monument itself contains typical medieval symbols drawn from astrology, tarot, and alchemy, and was apparently erected in the late 1600s, but nobody knows by whom. The Hendaye cross encodes information about the Apocalyptic Day of Judgment, a barely surviving high secret of ancient Egyptian eschatology that was overlaid by more superficial interests as Greco-Roman and European priorities came to the fore of history.

Who was Fulcanelli? It is safe to say that Fulcanelli was a mysterious, enigmatic French esotericist who wrote several influential and controversial books. It is still not clear exactly who he was. Perhaps he was R. A. Schwaller de Lubicz, brilliant Egyptian symbolist who wrote the monumental book *The Temple of Man*.[3] Some believe he was René Guénon, others that he was a literary fiction who represented a consortium of alchemical writers active in France in the 1920s. None of the theories are conclusive. Fulcanelli's impact and message are perhaps more relevant than his exact identity, for, as we discover in his writings, his erudition and knowledge indicate he was no dabbler in the occult arts.

Figure 5.1. Notre Dame cathedral, Paris

As an initiate into the deep esoteric stream of European occultism, Fulcanelli was careful to walk the razor's edge between saying too much and saying too little in his 1926 book, *Mystery of the Cathedrals*. Today, we know that Fulcanelli's aim was to elevate our understanding of the secret information encoded into the sacred architecture of Gothic cathedrals, most prominently, Notre Dame in Paris. Yet a careful reading of *Mystery* hints at so much more.

Fulcanelli's work involved alchemy, and alchemy is usually misunderstood as a primitive medieval precursor to the "real" science of chemistry. Or, somewhat closer to the mark, alchemical operations and procedures were interpreted by the Jungian school as symbols of the personality's individuation toward wholeness; thus, the Philosopher's Stone of the alchemical quest was not intended to turn lead into gold but to forge a fully realized, immortal, and enlightened human being.

Beyond these interpretations, recent scholars of alchemy like Weidner and Bridges have realized that alchemy involves the secret of time such that the unfolding of history leads us into the cauldron of ultimate transformation at the end of time, which arrives at an astronomically defined moment. The term *astro-alchemy* thus designates an astronomically stimulated transmutation of consciousness. The efficacy of alchemy is time-dependent, and only the end of time allows the Philosopher's Stone to manifest. This is just to say that alchemy's high secret is connected to the doctrine of chiliasm, a belief in an eventual apocalyptic ending to the world.

AMET helps us to understand that Western eschatology, as it evolved out of primordial Egyptian gnosis, was filtered through the heavy apocalypse metaphor-making of early Christianity to become a most literal expectation of future obliteration. Chiliasm itself is not an esoteric knowledge that needs to be hidden within initiatory mystery schools—the biblical Revelation is blatantly ascribed to chiliasm—but the anchoring of Judgment Day to an astronomical alignment was potentially dangerous because it might upstage the wrath of the Judeo-Christian God. As a result, the full import of this esoteric astronomy that had descended from Isis cults would have been baffling to early church fathers, or worse, actively disdained. The mother deity associated with this lost layer of religious history was derided, even though the Isis cult did find its own underground stream into Medieval Europe, tenaciously thriving at Black

Madonna shrines and in the Mary Magdalene folklore throughout southern France.

The role of Islamic science is also significant. Although we shall explore Islamic astronomy in more detail in chapter 6, suffice it to say that Weidner and Bridges find suggestive references to the Galactic Center in the ancient illuminated manuscripts of Persian and medieval European astronomers. The material is sometimes fragmented and anecdotal, or survives only in a mute mural, as in this example:

> The Villa Farnese, in Caparola, Italy, contains an astronomical ceiling painted by an unknown master in the late 16th century, which depicts our illuminated mythology of the heavens. . . . The celestial sphere is unwrapped into an oval, with the center at the cusp of Scorpio/Sagittarius and the edges at Taurus, to the right, and Gemini, to the left. The oval is tilted toward the celestial pole, above the north pole of the earth, so that the two "snakes" of the ecliptic zodiac and the milky way, as they cross at the center and the edge, are symmetrically tilted above and below the planetary equator. Draco coils around the ecliptic polar line, which unites the composition by connecting the ecliptic poles with the center of the galaxy.[4]

How else can we interpret this but as evidence that the Galactic Center was recognized and placed in the center of a celestial map of the 1570s? And if the Galactic Center was acknowledged then, why not much earlier? For naked-eye observation alone can perceive the "nuclear bulge" along the Milky Way, and any human mind from any era couldn't help but consider this area unusual.

This example is not isolated. Figure 3.6 also depicts the Galactic Center in the middle of a celestial map, and in many of the illustrations from Jacob Boehme's books, such as in figure 5.2, celestial spheres often portray either Scorpio or Taurus (which is opposite Scorpio) in the center. Other of Boehme's hermetic engravings depict a human being standing in a circular zodiac, with Scorpio or Sagittarius at the bottom and Taurus or Gemini at the top. This should not be regarded as coincidence, as every feature within alchemical diagrams was intended to convey secret meaning.

These diagrams highlight the Galactic Center–Galactic Anticenter axis; we will see more of this later, especially in the Mithras material in chapter 8.

Figure 5.2. From Jacob Boehme's *Dreyfaches Leben*, 1682

Such iconographical evidence suggests that the cross at Hendaye belongs to a larger context of hidden information, understood only at high levels of an esoteric delegation, operating behind the scenes of history. If this is the case, then it is not surprising that our descent into deeper materialism and technological fantasies has slowly removed the monuments to the Galactic Center from our sights forever.

The unassuming stone cross at Hendaye can still be seen today, on a busy street corner near the church of Saint Vincent. Erosion and pollution have dimmed its features, but its message has grown all the more clear.

Located in southwestern France near the Pyrenees and the Atlantic Ocean, Hendaye neighbors Basque regions to the south, where pilgrimages to Santiago de Compostela along the symbolic Milky Way of Spain still take place. Because of its unique location, Hendaye occupies the center of a quadripartite landscape that is three parts earth and one part water.

The Basque people are unrelated to the Celts and to other European groups, and they speak a language vaguely Finno-Ugric, but likewise anomalous.[5] They could very well be the last remnant of the original Neolithic inhabitants of Europe, the Mother Goddess–worshiping Magdalenian culture that left beautiful paintings in France's Lascaux cave. However, the closest genetic relatives of the Basque people are, strangely enough, the Incan people of Peru. As we shall see, Peru is tied up in this Hendaye cross mystery too.

As mentioned, nobody knows who carved the Hendaye cross, but it is

Figure 5.3. Locaton of Hendaye, France

dated to the late seventeenth or early eighteenth century. In *Mystery of the Cathedrals,* Fulcanelli wrote, "The Hendaye cross shows by the decoration of its pedestal that it is the strangest monument of primitive millenarism, the rarest symbolic translation of chiliasm, that I have ever met. . . . The unknown workman, who made these images, possessed real and profound knowledge of the universe."[6]

Roughly twelve feet high, the pillar is topped with a cross containing two inscriptions: OCRUXAVES PESUNICA on one side and INRI on the other (see fig. 5.4). There is a dearth of good commentary on the Hendaye cross. Weidner and Bridges identify only three sources: a 1936 article by Jules Boucher, a strange appendix to Johnson's *The Fulcanelli Phenomenon* (1980) by Paul Mevryl, and the 1957 Hendaye chapter by Fulcanelli. The first two, according to Weidner and Bridges, are dismissed as either misleading or purposefully deceptive ruses, so we are left with Fulcanelli's chapter, reproduced in full in *AMET.* The chapter reads like a huge anagram of some kind, obliquely providing hints embedded in misinformation to lead the insincere off track.

Weidner and Bridges are guided in their own interpretation by Fulcanelli's

Figure 5.4. The cyclic cross at Hendaye

clues, and we learn that "Ocruxaves Pesunica" translates, literally, as "Hail, oh cross, our only hope." Later on we discover an anagrammatic transformation:

OCRU S AVEC

PECU NICA

Notice that the *X* was changed to *S* and one *S* was changed to hard *C,* based on Fulcanelli's clues on how to accurately represent the phonetic pronunciation of the original letters *X* and *S.* If the *R* on the top line changes place with the first *C* on the bottom line, a simple transposition of a few letters results in the anagram:

CUSCO CAVE, PERU INCA
or: INCA CAVE, CUSCO, PERU

An alternate transformation of OCRU X AVES results in AVE X URCOS, or "Hail to the cross (X) at Urcos." The authors were then able to identify a town in Peru called Urcos, a short distance from Cuzco. This pursuit of deciphering the Hendaye inscription was in response to their trying to locate the "place of refuge" from the Day of Judgment that Fulcanelli insisted was encoded into the Hendaye cross. Weidner and Bridges found it, and located a conquest-era document from Peru containing an intriguing image (see fig. 5.5).

The image is entitled "The Symbols of the Incas: The Sun, the Moon, Lightning, the Hill of Guanacaure, and the caves of Pacarictambo." It is arranged like a typical coat of arms, but the symbolism goes much

Figure 5.5. *Left,* page from the Peruvian *Chronicle* of Felipe Guaman Poma de Alaya; *right,* the four symbols on the pedestal of the Hendaye cross

deeper—in fact, these Incan symbols are astonishingly similar to the main symbols on the four sides of the Hendaye cross (the triangular mountain being analogous to the four A-shaped symbols).

Weidner and Bridges provide an in-depth analysis of the multiple meanings of the Hendaye glyphs. Briefly, though, the sun face is angry, announcing the Day of Judgment is at hand. It is in the middle of four corner stars, suggesting it occupies a fifth, "cosmic center" location. The "man in the moon" symbol is akin to the moon boats found in medieval art, suggesting an eclipse as well as an ark in which to escape the catastrophe. The starburst indicates an explosive event or perhaps Sirius, which is related to Isis and the Sothic cycle measured by the early Egyptian calendar.

Now, the four A-shaped symbols in the quartered oval refer to the cyclic nature of time. According to Fulcanelli, each of the *A*s symbolize an age of the Great Year of precession. We can interpret this either as quarter parts of the full precessional cycle, or the four ages of the traditional Vedic Yuga doctrine, which total 12,000 years (one-half of a precessional cycle according to Hindu sources). In either case, precession is indicated, and the cross that separates the four time quadrants might symbolize the cross formed by the equinox and solstice axes, which precesses around the zodiac.

Precession is also indicated in the numerology of the INRI inscription on the top of the cross. As Weidner and Bridges decipher it, the following gematria correspondences yield the precessional number 270:

I	Yod	Yam	Water	Isis	Life	10
N	Nun	Nour	Fire	Apophis	Death	50
R	Resh	Ruach	Air	Osiris	Rebirth	200
I	Yod	Yebeshas	Earth	Isis	New Life	10

The numbers in the right column add up to 270, and 270 x 8 = 2160, the number of years in one zodiacal "month" of precession. Notice the meanings, based on the Hebrew letters: four elements, Egyptian deities, and a time cycle going from life through death to new life. The pillar of the Hendaye cross, much like an obelisk, is conceptually equivalent to the Egyptian *djed* pillar, the backbone of Osiris, the World Axis. The top of the *djed* pillar is particularly compelling, as it often portrays the sun in a birth cleft (fig. 5.6).

This may be a reference to the "sun in dark rift" motif used so

Figure 5.6. Head of an Egyptian *djed* **pillar**

frequently in Mayan cosmology—a way of stating the galactic alignment of era 2012. In other Egyptian depictions the body of Nut (the sky goddess) arches overhead, and the solar disk is often placed near her birth cleft. As in Mayan iconography, "sun in cleft" can be portrayed in several ways.

Returning to the INRI inscription, the letters traditionally stand for *Iesus Nazarenus Rex Iudeorum* (Jesus of Nazareth, King of the Jews). But INRI has other possible meanings, among them *Igne Natura Renovatur Integra* (by fire nature is renewed whole) and *Isis Naturae Regina Ineffibilis* (Isis, the ineffable Queen of Nature). The latter invokes the Egyptian mother goddess, Isis, who has been shown to symbolize the Galactic Center.[7] The first obviously refers to a trial by fire and by extension to the Last Judgment that Fulcanelli says will come in the form of a double catastrophe to scorch the Northern Hemisphere.

Near the inscriptions we find two little carved crosses, *XX*, Roman numerals equaling 20. In the Tarot deck, card 20 is the Last Judgment, reinforcing on yet another level the end-times message. Interestingly, the word *hendaye* has an "egg/apocalypse/mountain" connotation: henday/end-day/Ande. According to *AMET*, the *XX* symbol could also represent the ongoing seasonal waveform defined by the solstices and equinoxes—the equinox being defined by the vernal crossover "node" of the ecliptic and celestial equator.

Fulcanelli writes that Hendaye is a marker stone of a future "double catastrophe." Based upon the assemblage of clues, Weidner and Bridges conclude that this double catastrophe must involve (1) the precessional era of the equinox-galaxy cross (around 1999); (2) an eclipse on an equinox; (3) something else that would have catastrophic results, specifically to the Northern Hemisphere.

The first point provides the general timing mechanism of the Day of

Judgment—the equinox-galaxy cross being equivalent to the solstice-galaxy alignment. The second criterion resulted in the choice of a theoretical eclipse of September 22, 2002 as the best candidate. My own work has placed importance on eclipses and the nodal axis, but I interpret solstice eclipses as significant, because then the nodal axis will be aligned with the Galactic Center–Galactic Anticenter axis. This doesn't mean that equinox eclipses aren't equally important, as a 90° aspect has greater disruptive energy than an alignment.[8]

Figure 5.7 shows the relationship between the Galactic Center–Galactic Anticenter axis and the equinox axis, forming a perfect cross. Although the constellation glyphs are reversed in this figure, in the sky the stinger of Scorpio and the arrow of the Sagittarian archer point right at the Galactic Center.

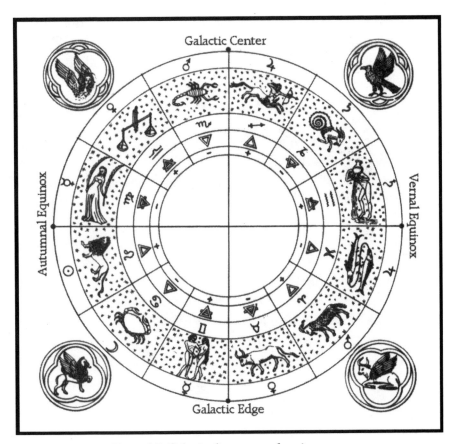

Figure 5.7. Galactic alignment and equinox cross
(from *A Monument to the End of Time*)

The third requirement led our researchers to the scientific theories of Paul LaViolette, whose work provided strange confirmation of an impending "double catastrophe." Over many years of study, LaViolette examined ice-core samples that contained increased iridium deposits dating to 14,000 years ago. He explained his theory with the idea that bursts of energy periodically emanate from our galaxy's center. Astrophysicists observe a significant percentage of galaxies in a state of great illumination, and these are called Seyfert galaxies. Due to some little-understood periodicity analogous to solar sunspot extremes, but on the galactic level, the cores of these Seyfert galaxies occasionally erupt in heightened activity. Additional data and research led LaViolette to conclude that our own galaxy periodically erupts like this, and we are approaching an active phase that will begin with the dramatic arrival of a "superwave" of energy. The timing of the superwave interval, however, is for some reason closely related to the precession cycle. LaViolette proposed a mechanism for this, involving the earth's axial tilt being "yanked" by the superwave. But the explanation seems incomplete, as the superwave timing mechanism is related not only to the precession cycle but also to *the era of alignment.* Nevertheless, the theory describes a "double catastrophe" that would result from the galactic superwave burst scorching the earth (especially the Northern Hemisphere).[9]

Bridges recently suggested an alternate theory that would not require a superwave burst. His scalar theory suggests that the angle of inclination between the solar system and the galactic plane would produce, at precise synchronization, a "scalar wave" effect, triggering all kinds of phenomena that might explain LaViolette's data and also provide a "double catastrophe."[10] We'll return to LaViolette's theory and the discussion of the mechanism of precession in relation to galactic alignments in chapter 20.

I am touching upon only a few of the many associations encoded into the Hendaye cross that were uncovered by Weidner and Bridges. Their reading of the Great Porch of the Last Judgment at Notre Dame in Paris also shows that a knowledge of the end-day cross—the perpendicular alignment of the equinox axis with the galactic plane—is not limited to Hendaye and is part of a larger astro-alchemical pattern hidden throughout Western history.

Fulcanelli is telling us that the Last Judgment is based on an astro-alchemical process, and that the designers of the Philosopher's Church [Notre Dame de Paris] were aware of this fact.

Following this thread of alchemical apocalypse led us back to first-century C.E. Alexandria and the gnostic mysteries that emerged from the ruins of ancient cultures such as Egypt. At the core of this gnostic current was a belief in the Great Return, a form of eschatology that, when merged with a Judaic stream to become Christianity, created the idea of Chiliasm. It was Chiliasm, an obscure but not heretical belief within Christianity, that preserved the secret and then revealed it in the thronging symbolism of Notre Dame's Great Porch.[11]

It is worth mentioning that *A Monument to the End of Time* implicates Tarot, Sufism, Black Madonna cults, Knights Templar activities, the Grail mythos, and the Kabbalah of Jewish mysticism as other repositories of the great secret. In their various ways they all encode information about the transformative cross that manifests at the end of our historical cycle to renew the earth, for better or worse.

By way of summary, the Hendaye cross contains clear references to the four Yuga periods of precession, which Fulcanelli also discusses in his *Dwellings of the Philosophers*.[12] Eclipse symbolism is also embedded into the cross, but the eclipse nodes seem to have two meanings—the node of Sun and Moon yes, but on a higher level the node of ecliptic and galaxy. (This ecliptic-galaxy node is none other than the Mayan sacred tree, or crossroads, located in Sagittarius and Gemini.) Equinox and solstice symbology, the return of Jesus, the Day of Judgment, Tarot, and Kabbalah—all of this is wrapped into the monument to pinpoint an equinox eclipse in 2002 as the prophesied Day of Judgment, when a double catastrophe will burn the Northern Hemisphere. And the only place of refuge will be the high plateau of Peru.

One obvious effect of the inscription on the Cross at Hendaye is that many people interested in symbols and the occult would translate it and then head off for Peru. This group of chiliasts, or believers in the coming apocalypse, if they are still active in the Andes, would then sift through the many travelers and visitors and contact those that they thought worthy. In this way, they would be slowly gathering a group of

Figure 5.8. The cross at Urcos, Peru.
Photo by Jay Weidner

enlightened souls from around the world into one spot. With the knowledge of the secret tunnel system, this group of seekers would be safe even during a disaster of celestial magnitude. This group of self-elected souls would be the cultural, spiritual, and physical seeds for the world to come. The inscription is attempting to tell the few who will understand to come to Peru and become part of the coming Golden Age.[13]

The ancient cross located in Urcos, Peru, is thus believed to be a key to the Hendaye mystery.

Including LaViolette's theories gives scientific credence to the idea of a double catastrophe, but leads unavoidably to more complicated questions regarding the relationship between LaViolette's hypothetical superwave and the factual equinox-galaxy cross. It also urges that ancient beliefs about an alignment-defined cataclysm should be empirically proven, so that we might believe in them ourselves. But the implications of all of this might lead us into a metaphysics of transformation that hinges upon the alignment but that does not require an empirical mechanism in order to awaken us and have meaning.

At the end of our magical mystery tour we are left with a compelling seventeenth-century monument, Fulcanelli's revelation, and the faithful reconstruction of the monument's meaning by Weidner and Bridges. We are being led deeper south and further back in time. The esoteric information carved into the cross at Hendaye has a close relationship with certain medieval doctrines, such as Kabbalah and alchemy, that were introduced into Europe through Islamic and Jewish influences in southern Spain. It is a well-known fact that Persian and Islamic science stimulated the European Renaissance, anticipating many advances in knowledge that we often attribute to European thinkers. Especially in the arena of astronomy, Arabic thinkers were far ahead of contemporary Europeans and on a par with Hindu astronomers. In fact, Persian astronomy of the late first millennium—in ancient Iran and Iraq—shares many concepts with India. This milieu, led by Arabic astronomers like al-Bīrūnī in the eleventh-century A.D., partook of ancient traditions from the regions of ancient Sumer and Babylon—home of esteemed astronomers and astrologers some 3,500 years ago.

Another clue to lead us onward is that the lunar nodes and eclipses are involved in these cosmological questions. When were these astronomical concepts discovered? Does astrological tradition have anything to say about them? Our journey into the esoteric context of the cross at Hendaye is leading us in a specific direction; if we follow the path that opens before us, without knowing exactly where it leads, we might be surprised at what we find.

It is beyond the scope of this book to do a thorough survey of Babylonian, Sumerian, and Persian metaphysics. Readings in Sufi teachings, the works of Henry Corbin (*Cyclical Time and Ismaili Gnosis* and *Temple and Contemplation*), Seyyed Hossein Nasr (*An Introduction to Islamic Cosmological Doctrines*), and others would illuminate our understanding and stimulate our appreciation of Middle Eastern science and mysticism. Instead of exhaustively exploring this field, I will simply share one item of evidence that points right to the Galactic Center in a very compelling and thought-provoking way.

SIX

Islamic Astrology
and the Lunar Dragon

An intriguing, unpublished essay by Ananda K. Coomaraswamy can be found in the Princeton Archive in New Jersey. Entitled "Early Iconography of Sagittarius," the essay existed in three separate versions that I had to piece together. Coomaraswamy's subject included references to provocative iconography related to the part of the sky that houses the Galactic Center. These references were unpronounced in Coomaraswamy's interpretation, even though he quite clearly seemed to be grappling with something he sensed as profound, but just out of sight. I will explore the implications of this essay more fully in chapter 13, but I wanted to mention it here because it led me to another very significant article.

Coomaraswamy's essay referred to an article by Dr. Willy Hartner, published in the 1938 volume of *Ars Islamica*. It was clearly an ambitious piece by a thirty-three-year-old scholar who would later become president of the International Academy of the History of Science from 1971 to his death in 1978. "The Pseudoplanetary Nodes of the Moon's Orbit in Hindu and Islamic Iconographies" was dedicated to Coomaraswamy and Coomaraswamy's unpublished essay, reworked several times, appears to have been a response to the progressive interpretations put forward by Hartner. I sensed in Hartner's work the broaching of a truth that few might dare address—that the location of the Galactic Center was close to the degree in the sidereal zodiac at which the lunar south node (known as Ketu in Hindu astronomy) was exalted in the traditional astrological schemes of both Islam and India.

The lunar nodes are the points in the sky where the orbits of the Sun and the Moon intersect (see fig. 6.1), and they indicate the places where eclipses can occur. Generally, the Sun and the Moon both travel along the ecliptic, but their orbits are slightly skewed in relation to each other, other-

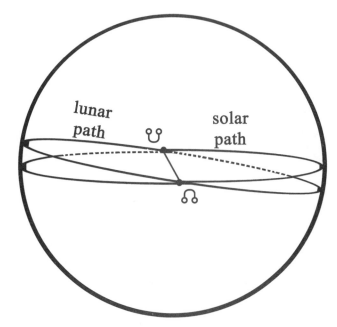

Figure 6.1. The lunar nodes

wise we would see two eclipses every month. Hartner refers to these intangible node points as "pseudoplanetary" because, although they are not planets per se, they were treated as such by most Arabic and Hindu astrologers. In Hindu astrology they are deified as the head and tail of a serpent-dragon and are called Rahu and Ketu, both of whom are involved in the Vedic Creation myth called the Churning of the Milky Ocean. Rahu was pictured as a monstrous disembodied head, while Ketu was portrayed as the knotted tail of a fish or serpent. The lunar nodes, like each planet, were associated with a specific sign of the zodiac, which was known as the planet's *domicile* or *house*. These house placements indicate the zodiacal sign where a planet's influence is most at home. So we have seven planets and two nodes: Sun, Moon, Mercury, Venus, Mars, Jupiter, Saturn, north node, and south node. In traditional astrology, the seven planets occupy the seven domains or planes of consciousness, a conception directly related to the seven chakras of a human being's subtle-energy body. The seven planets are associated with their "houses" as shown in figure 6.2. Notice that the central axis defines the house locations for each planet; for example, the houses of Venus are Taurus and Libra. Saturn is in the "highest" house at the Capricorn-Aquarius cusp, which corresponds to the winter solstice in

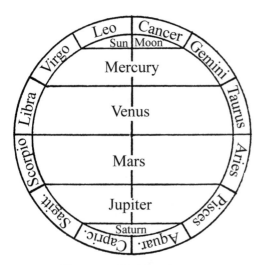

Figure 6.2. Planetary houses

the ancient calendar. At some point in the development of astrological doctrine the lunar nodes were included in this scheme, to make a total of nine planetary levels.

The house placements are only one set of signs to which each planet could be associated. A planet also had signs of exaltation and detriment, positions that oppose each other in the zodiac. The sign of exaltation was where a planet (or node) was especially enhanced, but the scheme of identification is different from the house placements. A model that became universal in Hindu, Arabic, and Greek Hellenistic astrology gives the following correspondences for planetary exaltations:

Sun	19° Aries
Moon	3° Taurus
Mercury	15° Virgo
Venus	27° Pisces
Mars	28° Capricorn
Jupiter	15° Cancer
Saturn	21° Libra

Notice there are five signs that are without planetary exaltations: Leo, Aquarius, Gemini, Sagittarius, and Scorpio, the latter two being adjacent in the sky. In fact, the cusp between Sagittarius and Scorpio is where the Galactic Center is located, and is precisely indicated by the arrow of Sagittarius and the stinger of Scorpio. As we shall see, prevailing Hindu and Islamic astrological doctrines placed the exaltation of the lunar south node in Sagittarius and the lunar north node at the opposite location, in Gemini. Notice that the table gives a specific degree of exaltation for each planet. This feature was implemented in ancient times to provide a more specific point of reference when a horoscope was cast. With this background, we can now look at what Hartner found.

In this 1938 article, Hartner identified *djawzahr* as the Arabic term for the lunar south node, referred to sometimes as "the eighth planet." He refers to a 1920 article by German scholar Ernst Herzfeld called "The Throne of Khusraw," where photographs were published of astrological information found on the pillars of the great bridge that spanned the Tigris River in the Iraqi town of Djazīrat ibn 'Umar. The pillars on this bridge, built in the late twelfth century, contain sculptures on eight pairs of columns, each pair showing the symbol for the planet next to its sign of exaltation. The Arabic term *sharara* (exalted in) is used. The associations are consistent with the traditional seven-planet model described above, except the Sun is shown with its sign of rulership, Leo. In addition, there is an eighth pair on the last pillar, which shows the lunar south node in Sagittarius (see fig. 6.3).

Figure 6.3. Bridge columns from Djazīrat ibn 'Umar showing the Moon's south node in Sagittarius

On the left in figure 6.3 we see a lunar dragon or snake with a knotted tail. Like the Hindu deity Ketu, this knotted snake's tail symbolizes the south lunar node. In comparison, the north lunar node, Rahu, is usually pictured as a grimacing monster or dragon's head. In the Hindu myth, the demon Rahu lost his head because he stole a sip of the soma nectar. Dissociated from his body forever, he seeks to devour the Sun during eclipses. Meanwhile, his tail—Ketu, the south node—is knotted, which represents the crossover node in which the lunar and solar planes intersect. Astronomically, this intersection point defines eclipse locations and is forever precessing backward through the zodiac, making a complete circuit once every 18.51 years.[1]

In the diagram, the knotted Ketu snake is paired with the astrological sign of the Archer, Sagittarius, confirming its place of exaltation. Conversely, the north node would be exalted in the opposite sign, Gemini. This opposition corresponds to the Sagittarius-Gemini axis of Galactic Center–Galactic Anticenter (hereafter GC–GA). We find this same nodal placement in other Islamic sources. For example, an illuminated sixteenth-century Turkish astrological manuscript in the Pierpont Morgan Library shows the exaltations of the head and tail of the eclipse dragon. The signs of both Gemini and Sagittarius are illustrated, and in figure 6.4 the Arabic inscriptions above them are given.

Figure 6.4. Exaltations of Ketu and Rahu. Translations: *left*, "The exaltation of the tail is in Sagittarius"; *right*, "The exaltation of the head is in Gemini."

Rahu (the north node) is the head, exalted in Gemini at the Galactic Anticenter or crown-chakra location. Ketu, the south-node tail, is exalted at the tail or root of the galactic-axis "dragon"—at the Galactic Center in Sagittarius.

So we have general evidence that the south node was exalted in Sagittarius. But we also have specific information that the south node was exalted exactly at 3° Sagittarius. Hartner tells us that Persian and Hindu manuscripts went so far as to identify a specific degree of exaltation for each planet and lunar node. In showing that the south lunar node's point of exaltation is 3° Sagittarius, Hartner cites manuscript evidence in the great Arab astronomer al-Bīrūnī's *The Book of Instruction in the Elements of the Art of Astrology* (written around A.D. 1029), in the writings of Abū Ma'shar (author of *De magnis conjunctionibus* [*Great Conjunctions*], from the ninth century A.D.), and in the work of contemporary and later Hindu astrologers. The Galactic Center is indirectly alluded to in these obscure doctrines—for the Galactic Center is located nearby at 6° Sagittarius in the sidereal zodiac!

Additional evidence helps us understand exactly what the nodal axis was intended to symbolize. Figure 6.5 shows the early-thirteenth-century Kalam Box, which has zodiacal sequences inlaid on its top.

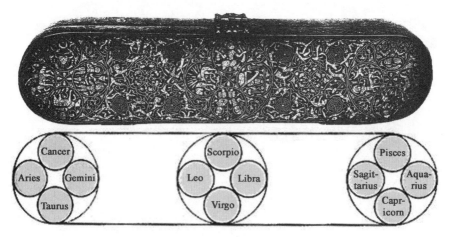

Figure 6.5. The Kalam Box zodiac

As much Celtic in design as Persian, the Kalam Box was made and inscribed by Mahmud ibn Subkur in A.D. 1212. As the diagram in figure 6.5 reveals, the arrangement of zodiacal signs allows interesting geometrical relationships to be drawn. For example, notice that Cancer and Capricorn are on opposite sides of the box in two senses, and Gemini and Sagittarius are along the central horizontal axis. Hartner makes a point about the atypical representation of the Gemini sign shown in figure 6.6. As expected we see the twins—but notice they are on either side of a column surmounted by a head. This staff head in Gemini is analogous to the monstrous Rahu head in the Indian Navagraha reliefs discussed in Hartner's essay (see fig. 6.8). The Rahu head thus indicates Gemini as the sign of the dragon head's exaltation. I must emphasize here that the vertical staff or axis, as a symbol of the World Axis, is usually targeted on the Pole Star and is thus associated with the polar axis. Here we have the ubiquitous axial symbolism, but instead it is applied to an axis that runs from Sagittarius to Gemini. This provides evidence for a shift in ancient times from polar-centered axiology to a galaxy-oriented one. The Gemini sign on the Kalam Box explicitly portrays the galactic chakra axis that runs from the root in Sagittarius to the crown in Gemini: the GC-GA axis.

Figure 6.6. Close-up of Rahu-Gemini   **Figure 6.7. Close-up of Ketu-Sagittarius**

The Sagittarian archer on the Kalam Box (fig. 6.7) is also somewhat atypical in that he is shooting his arrow into the mouth of a snakelike figure connected to his own tail. This reminds one of the ouroboros swallowing its own tail, a symbol of eternity and the cyclic nature of time. It also might suggest the dark rift in the Milky Way in Sagittarius—a "mouth" that is nevertheless closely related to the galactic root or "tail."

Tail and head are clearly associated with Sagittarius and Gemini, as well as the lunar south and north nodes, a scheme with ancient roots going back to India. Varāhamihira, an Indian astronomer from the sixth century A.D. who wrote the *Bṛhatsaṃhitā*, discussed the Rahu-Ketu myth in connection with the lunar nodes and the theory of eclipses. The Navagraha reliefs are eighth- and ninth-century sculptures that portray the seven planetary deities together with the additional eighth and ninth "planets"—the lunar south and north nodes, Ketu and Rahu. In figure 6.8 we can see, on the far right, the monster head, Rahu, and the half-fish snake-dragon Ketu with its coiled or knotted tail.[2] The coiled serpent tail here reminds us of the coiled serpent energy of *kundalini* residing at the base of the human spine, ready to spring forth and stimulate our spiritual growth. The south node's exaltation at 3° Sagittarius—the location of the Galactic Center—provides contextual evidence for a "galactic chakra" cosmology that we shall explore in chapter 23.

According to Hartner, there is an early Greek reference to the lunar nodes. Fifty years after Ptolemy, around A.D. 230, Tertullian mentioned the *anabibazon* and the *katabibazon,* which are the Greek terms for the ascending and descending nodes. Even so, the lunar dragon is surely of Eastern, not Greek, origin. In fact, the Rahu-Ketu myth, embedded as it is in the very ancient Vedic Creation myth called the Churning of the Milky Ocean, suggests that a Vedic knowledge of the nodes could go back thousands of years prior to the Greeks. As we shall see in part 3, ancient Vedic astronomy was indeed extremely advanced.

Hartner notes that information about the lunar nodes was sometimes intentionally left out of documents by early astronomers who openly mention them elsewhere. This might be, as Hartner suggests, because the lunar nodes were not widely accepted as "planets" eight and nine. Hartner writes, in fact, after surveying the obfuscating words of Maimonides, that in the twelfth century "the astrological doctrines of the Djawzahr [the south node] had by no means become a generally known matter but used to be treated as a secret by the initiated, in such a way that even a highly

Fiigure 6.8. Rahu and Ketu on the Navagraha reliefs

erudite scholar like Maimonides could make only a rather vague state-ment about it."[3] One could take this further and point out that by associ-ating the nodes with celestial spheres higher than the seventh planet, Saturn, perhaps a hidden, esoterically guarded knowledge is indicated. Our clue, the south node's exaltation in Sagittarius, is even specified as being located at 3° Sagittarius. Could it be that the plane of the galaxy was seen by high initiates as the trans-Saturn domain, which for the Greeks could only be accessed through Mount Olympus? After all, "planets" eight and nine, at 3° Sagittarius and 3° Gemini, would be located right on the plane of the galaxy.

Although the nodal doctrine may have been esoterically hidden, it was not unstable, for the 3° Sagittarian nodal exaltation remained consistent for some eight hundred years, from the early ninth-century reference by Abū-Ma'shar up to the compiling, translating, and printing of his writings in the sixteenth century, where the lunar dragon is portrayed appropriately between two intersecting circles in figure 6.9. I have added the exact degrees of the exaltation of the lunar nodes to figure 6.9 because that knowledge was contemporary with Abū-Ma'shar, and also to show that 3° Sagittarius is close to where the ecliptic-galactic crossing point (node) is located, which also closely identifies the Galactic Center.[4] Perhaps these intersecting circles can be read on two levels: the intersection of solar and lunar orbital planes, which define the lunar nodes, but also the intersection of galactic and planetary planes (the galactic equator and the ecliptic) that defines the Galactic Center–Galactic Anticenter axis. Hartner does not recognize this connection between the placement of the south node at 3° Sagittarius and the galactic node. Information in the Persian *Bundahishn*, however, indicates a conscious recognition of just such a connection. A passage from this ninth-century text reads: "The [nodal] Dragon stood in the middle of the sky like a serpent, its Head in the Two Images [Gemini] and its Tail in the Centaur [Sagittarius] so that

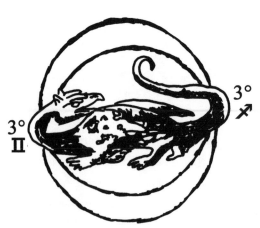

Figure 6.9. Lunar dragon of eclipses (from Abū-Ma'shar's *De magnis conjunctionibus* [Venice, 1515], a translation of his ninth-century writings)

at all times there are six constellations between its Head and Tail."[5] One assumes that a serpent "stands" on its tail, as do the serpents of Indian snake charmers. If so, then the *Bundahishn*'s explicit statement that the nodal serpent stands in the "middle of the sky" in Sagittarius identifies the Galactic Center region as a "middle of the sky." Another quote from the *Bundahishn* is striking in this regard: "This mark in the sky, which they call the Milky Way, is the brilliance of the [nodal] Dragon, the serpent which is in the firmament."[6] This indicates that the Milky Way is the "brilliance," the visible signifier, of the intangible or invisible nodal serpent. This can only be so if they are placed on top of each other, so to speak, with the tail of the nodal serpent placed at the crossroads of Milky Way and ecliptic in Sagittarius.[7]

Based on this evidence, can we simply dismiss the association of the nodes of the Sun and the Moon with the nodes of our galaxy and solar system as a coincidence? This would seem beyond coincidence, and we would be justified in suspecting that these astrological systems were put in place by people who thought of the Galactic Center as the tail of an enormous serpent or dragon—and this statement is probably overly cautious. Another point is that the lunar nodes precess backward through the zodiac, and thus they could have been compared metaphorically with the precession of the equinox and solstice points.

The intersection of lunar, solar, and galactic planes is certainly worth looking at, but even more astounding is the fact that the south-node exaltation targets the galactic-ecliptic node in early Sagittarius, within a few degrees of the Galactic Center. The iconography of the dragon's tail combined with this celestial location evokes an entire set of metaphysical concepts related to *kundalini*, the serpent power of evolution residing in the root chakra in the human being. In the macrocosm, the serpent power comes from the cosmic source and center, wherever we decide that may be. Here we encounter the "as above, so below" principle again, because human spiritual anatomy is a microcosmic reflection of the universe on a galactic scale!

Hartner cites evidence indicating that in some systems the tail of the dragon (Ketu) was exalted not in Sagittarius, but in Gemini. Could it be that the *djawzahr* exalted in Sagittarius is really the dragon's head, Rahu, rather than the tail? Perhaps. We should be aware of the celestial features in the region under consideration. Given the association of the dark rift with dragon's mouth iconography among the Maya, one might initially prefer to see the head of the nodal dragon in Sagittarius, as we find in at least one source cited by Hartner, but "tail in Sagittarius" actually seems better for the galactic chakra model that has the Galactic Center as the root (*muladhara*) and the Pleiades (in Taurus-Gemini) as the crown (*sahasrara*). In addition, we might be looking at an overlay of symbols going back thousands of years to previous alignments in precession, fragmented survivals of earlier cosmo-conceptions. Thus, the majority of tail and head placements for Ketu and Rahu that Hartner found do seem appropriate from this perspective.

We might also suppose that the oppositional symbolism, as with all locations that metaphysically transcend dualisms, could be mapped in either direction. The cosmic tree is often portrayed as inverted, for example, rooted in and descending from the celestial center rather than growing upward from the earth. In the end we are left with a large amount of evidence that the tail of the nodal dragon was thought of as exalted at 3° Sagittarius, the Galactic Center.

What should be emphasized is that the lunar nodes (formed by the intersection of two orbital circles) and the Galactic Center (targeted by two *different* orbital circles) are basically cospatial. In the Arabic astrological manuscripts surveyed by Hartner, the lunar south node is exalted at 3° Sagittarius, which is basically coincident with the "galactic-ecliptic" intersection node. It is difficult to conceive that this could be a complete coincidence. But we might be willing to entertain the implications.

If the lunar south node is most enhanced when it is in alignment with the galactic node—when cosmological dimensions align that unite the solar, lunar, solar-system, and galactic planes—larger cycles of time are indicated. Eclipses in alignment with the Galactic Center–Galactic Anticenter axis will occur every 9.25 years. At those times, the locations of the Sun and the Moon will identify the higher opposition between Galactic Center and Galactic Anticenter. The apocalyptic associations mentioned by Hartner (for example, the Revelation of Saint John the Divine) seem related to the even more rare occurrence of solstice eclipses in alignment with the Galactic Center. Incredibly, after many millennia of celestial shifting, it is in our current era that solstice eclipses will occur in alignment with the Galactic Center–Galactic Anticenter axis. What else could define our era as being more astronomically rare and unusual? The solstice eclipse on June 21, 2001, was the closest empirical unification of the multiple planes of Moon, Sun, and galaxy in over 12,000 years. On that day, Ketu, the tail of the lunar dragon, sat exalted on the tail of the galactic serpent, while the sun made its solstice turnabout.

The solstice-galaxy alignment was calculated by the U.S. Naval Observatory to have occurred in late 1998. If eclipses represent the quicker "second hand" of the precessional clock, then 2001, as foreseen by Stanley Kubrick in his movie *2001: A Space Odyssey*, may indeed have triggered the ingress of something truly strange into our historical experience.[8] I don't imagine that the world will end, but the rarity of the alignment should, at the very least, give us pause.

It seems that a very ancient doctrine relating to the spring-equinox node's movement with precession was later coopted into the nodal "planets" of Rahu and Ketu, thus allowing the apocalyptic imagery—as well as a great deal more—to make better sense. At least we can say that Sagittarius—3° Sagittarius in ancient Islamic sources—is the location of something quite amazing, something that, over the centuries, was kept secret. Hartner's article is all we need to include Islamic cosmology in the growing list of traditions that utilized the Galactic Center—and the alignments to it—in their esoteric doctrines.

SEVEN

Mount Olympus
and the Fall of Troy

J ohn Michell has almost singlehandedly elaborated the nature of sacred topography in the British Isles. The primary intention of this practice was to map the heavens into the landscape—what Michell calls "enchanting the landscape." Michell's further research in his *Twelve-Tribe Nations* explores the larger global context of this tradition, surveying evidence from Madagascar to Australia. Michell's coauthor, Christine Rhone, also translated Jean Richer's *Sacred Geography of the Ancient Greeks: Astrological Symbolism in Art, Architecture, and Landscape*, which reveals how the Greeks encoded the heavens into their environment.

Richer's research, reasoning, and breakthrough findings are significant and should rightly stimulate a revolution in how we understand the esoteric preoccupations of the Greeks, cherished as they are as the intellectual prototype of Western civilization. Richer's main points bear directly on the question of the Galactic Center's location in Greek sacred geography, although, as with Michell, this implicit connection is left unspoken. As we shall see, and as we should expect, the Galactic Center is mirrored in Greek terrain on the lofty throne of Zeus, Mount Olympus, symbol of the winter solstice and the gateway of the gods.

Richer's book on Greek sacred geography was followed by books on Roman sacred geography and the Greek sites of Delphi, Delos, and Cumae, both of which await translation into English. Richer successfully decoded the astronomical preoccupations of the Greeks and revealed how they mapped the heavens onto their world. He accomplished this by tuning in to the evidence spread out before him, all of it right there for anyone to see. As he said of this intuitive process, "It has long been my firm conviction that all the religious and poetic experience of peoples and individuals of the past is, at certain special moments, available to whoever can recapture it."[1]

Richer's work with Greek sacred architecture and geography began with a dream he had in 1958. He had been living for some time in Athens near the Parthenon, and was pondering a strange anomaly: Why was the sanctuary to Athena Pronaia placed at the entrance to Delphi such that visitors could not avoid seeing it? In Richer's dream he was looking at a *kouros* statue—similar to Apollo, the god of light—from behind, and it slowly rotated to face him. Upon waking, still half asleep, the image seemed to him somehow to link Delphi, where the Apollo sanctuary is located, and Athens, where the dream occurred. He found a map and traced a line between Delphi and Athens. Then he extended it farther and found it passed through Delos, the legendary birthplace of Apollo, and on to Camiros in Rhodes, to the site of the oldest Apollo sanctuary on the island!

This dream-derived discovery provided Richer with the key: There are lines of orientation (similar to ley lines) between widely separated sacred sites all throughout Greece and the islands that could be discovered and mapped. The reasoning behind this was transparent enough and was supplied by Greek tradition itself. Greece was divided by the gods into a circle of twelve precincts, each ruled by its own astrological deity; Zeus ruled the twelve gods from his throne on Mount Olympus. As demonstrated by Michell, this system of division evolved into a practical way of political governance used throughout the ancient world.

When looking at a map, this twelve-way division appears as a zodiacal wheel. Several Greek zodiac wheels centering on Delphi, Delos, Athens, and other important sites were eventually identified by Richer. One thing that Richer himself didn't realize with this system—it took his brother Lucien to bring it to international attention in 1977—is that these Greek hubs are strung along an axis that begins at Mount Carmel in Israel and extends through over a dozen Saint Michael shrines throughout Europe to end at the Skellig Michael shrine on the tip of southwest Ireland. In figure 7.1 site number 1 is Skellig Michael in Ireland and site number 14 is Mount Carmel in Israel.

This phenomenal occurrence was described in *Twelve-Tribe Nations*, and it suggests a deep and mysterious esoteric stream in European religious consciousness. It also indicates that Richer had tapped into something very profound, involving ancient traditions that are only now coming to light.

Figure 7.1. Michael line from Ireland to Jerusalem

Richer understood that a significant Greek zodiacal wheel would be centered on Delphi, the Greek omphalos, or navel. Over the years Richer visited many Greek sites and mapped out the correspondences. To situate the zodiacal regions correctly around a given hub, he found valuable evidence in regional coin iconography, which provided each region's "totem" astrological symbol. He also drew from Greek myth, which encodes zodiacal relationships and places events in specific geographical settings.

Of all the Greek zodiacal wheels, the one centered on Delphi is of most importance to us because it is the one involving both Delphi and Mount Olympus. A close look at figure 7.2 reveals a primary axis running from Mount Olympus in the north, through Delphi, to Cape Taenarum in the south. Richer's correlation of various regional traditions with the mythological adventures of certain deities led him to identify this axis as the Capricorn-Cancer axis. Notice the twelve zodiac signs in the diagram. The sign of Capricorn is identified with the "north" and thus has an association with the Pole Star and the semimythical land of Hyperborea. Mount Olympus is in the northern section of this zodiacal wheel centered on Delphi, and thus also symbolizes the polar center.

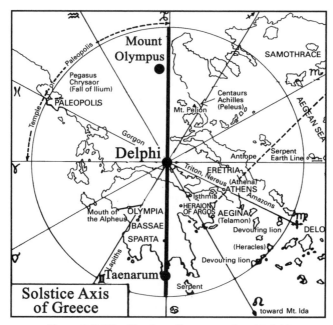

Figure 7.2. The Greek zodiac centered on Delphi

Mount Olympus lies in the sign of Capricorn because of the necessary orientation of the zodiacal wheel as it maps onto the terrain. The evidence for how this zodiacal wheel should be oriented comes from coin iconography, sanctuary locations, and geographical references in Greek myth. For example, Mount Pelion, to the east of Mount Olympus, is in the Sagittarius sector, which makes perfect sense because it is the home of the centaurs (half-horse, half-man archers) who symbolize Sagittarius. So if Mount Olympus occupies the realm of Capricorn in the zodiacal wheel, and the Greeks identified Capricorn with the northern polar center, why should a Capricorn-Cancer axis be analogous to a north-south polar axis? Richer has a ready answer, because he was well acquainted with the work of René Guénon, who wrote about the conceptual mapping of the yearly cycle onto spatial topography. Guénon says it best:

> "The vertical axis, in so far as it joins the two poles, is obviously a north-south axis; in the [transition] from polar to solar symbolism, this axis must somehow be projected onto the zodiacal plane, but in a way that maintains a certain correspondence, we might even say as exact an equivalence as possible, with the primitive polar axis. Now, in the annual

cycle the solstices of winter and summer are the two points which correspond respectively to North and South in the spatial order, just as the equinoxes of spring and of autumn correspond to East and West. The axis which fulfills the desired condition, therefore, is that which joins the two solstitial points; and it could be said that this solstitial axis will then play the part of a relatively vertical axis."[2]

The reasoning is that within the yearly cycle of the zodiac, the solstice axis is conceptually equivalent to the north-south "vertical" axis that connects the earth's geographical poles. Furthermore, Capricorn is the location of the Sun at winter solstice, the extreme "rebirth" point in its annual cycle. Capricorn is thus, in this sense, the central emanation point for the entire yearly cycle. Conceptually speaking it is analogous to, in the spatial order, the northern pole in the sky. Thus, the solstice axis serves as a temporal *axis mundi* representing the spatial *axis mundi* connecting the earth's poles.

This solves the problem and seems to serve the purposes of Richer's map well enough, but there is something else going on here. Guénon was writing about a shift in cosmological thinking from a polar-oriented model to a solar-oriented one. This polar-to-solar shift is evident in many traditions, is sometimes identified with a quasi-historical shift from a Hyperborean tradition to an Atlantean tradition, and is embedded in the shifting symbolic functions of certain constellations. Without doubt, the evolution of cosmological thinking that underlies these changing orientations is related to the precession of the equinoxes. The polar-to-solar shift took place in some remote era when eight circumpolar constellations were mapped into twelve signs on the ecliptic path of the Sun—thus the new "solar" track. In his article "The Boar and the She-Bear," Guénon cites evidence that the seven stars of the Big Dipper were mapped onto the seven stars of the Pleiades.[3] The Big Dipper is polar whereas the Pleiades are on the ecliptic path of the Sun—thus, polar to solar. This is not the full story, however. Here we must uncover another layer of the mystery.

In my research on Mayan cosmology I discovered that many traditional cultures have seen an opposition between the Pleiades and Scorpio-Sagittarius—often perceived as the tail and head sides of a giant celestial snake. The snake in this conception is the Milky Way, because the Milky Way runs right by the Pleiades on one side of the sky, and runs through

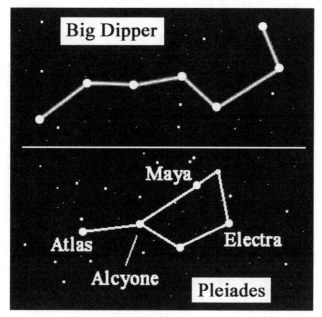

Figure 7.3. The Big Dipper and the Pleiades dipper

Scorpio-Sagittarius on the other side. Since the Galactic Center is near Sagittarius, the implied axis is actually a conceptual south-north axis on a galactic level that runs from the Galactic Center near Sagittarius, through the earth, and out toward the Galactic Anticenter region of the Pleiades. Thus the shift from the polar stars of the Big Dipper to the Pleiades indicates not only a polar-to-solar shift in cosmological orientation, but a polar-to-galactic shift.[4] In this sense, the ancient Hyperborean tradition remains polar and northern while the fabled Atlantean tradition can now be understood as not simply solar, but galactic and southern. It is southern because the bright and wide bulge of the Galactic Center moves through the southern skies as viewed from latitudes north of the equator. What we have here is the key to understanding the polar-to-solar shift that René Guénon sought to elucidate, which we shall examine more closely in chapter 12.

These questions of cosmic centers and reorientations bear directly upon our understanding of the Capricorn–Mount Olympus relationship and are essential for clarifying the true celestial reference of the Capricorn-Cancer axis. The final problem arises with the fact that Mount Olympus, as symbol of the throne of the galactic pole, is placed in Capricorn rather than Sagittarius. Of course, Capricorn borders Sagittarius, so the issue may seem trivial, but we should address it nonetheless.

First, the Capricorn-Cancer axis in the zodiacal wheel centered on Delphi is intended to be both temporal and spatial. In the temporal sense, Capricorn represents the winter solstice because 2,500 years ago that is where the winter-solstice sun was located. In the spatial sense, Capricorn is intended to symbolize both the Galactic Center and the polar center of the older Hyperborean system. But the Galactic Center is in Sagittarius, so how to explain this Capricorn-Sagittarius overlap? Consider this: *When the winter-solstice sun was in Capricorn during the Greek heyday, some 2,500 years ago, Sagittarius was observed rising heliacally (ahead of the Sun) at dawn.*

If this sounds contrived, the Greek writer Macrobius said in his *Commentary on the Dream of Scipio* that the "gates" of Capricorn-Cancer were really located "where the Zodiac and the Milky Way intersect."[5] I agree with the authors of *Hamlet's Mill* that the Greek skywatchers were more interested in what was rising heliacally than in the Sun's precise location.[6]

Associating Mount Olympus with Sagittarius rather than Capricorn seems to contradict Richer's map, but in fact there is abundant mythological data associating Zeus and Olympus with centaurs and Sagittarians rather than sea goats and Capricorn. For example, Richer notes that Zeus was associated with Sagittarius: "One must first remember that Zeus took the form of a swan (that is, the animal that represented the celestial region opposing Gemini in the old zodiac . . .) to couple with Leda and to father Castor and Pollux."[7] The swan connects Zeus with Sagittarius according to older Greek zodiacal symbolism, and Castor and Pollux are the twins of Gemini (at the Galactic Anticenter position). This is a clear statement about Zeus residing at the "top" of an axis that runs from Gemini to Sagittarius. Of course, either side can be the "top," depending on how one chooses to view the symbolism.

Centaurs are associated with Scorpio and Sagittarius, and according to Richer there are texts that relate them to the winter solstice. This may be explained by the heliacal rise of Sagittarius on the winter solstice. In the following narrative by the Greek writer Teucer we see that the solstitial gateway of the gods—supposedly "in Capricorn"—is actually a gate in Sagittarius: "The soul, soon after crossing the 'Acheron sea,' meets a centaur on the way, who is Sagittarius in the zodiac. . . . This corresponds to the exit of the soul through the 'gateway of the gods.'"[8] This quote places the gateway of the gods not in Capricorn but among centaurs in Sagittarius. Note that the text reports the soul's after-death journey and its meeting with the Archer (Sagittarius) at the gate of the gods, associated with the winter solstice. Richer states, "This gateway of Capricorn is associated with Mount Olympus in sacred geography."[9] Richer explicitly states that the gateway of the gods is associated with Capricorn and with Mount Olympus in the Greek topographical zodiac. While he adjusts the gate to Capricorn, the myth literally points to Sagittarius.

These conflicting identifications are less of an issue than one might suppose, because the symbolic roles of each constellation will shift with the dawn of a new age, and these traditions go back through at least three zodiacal ages. In the astronomical references to "gates," however, we are dealing with an unmoving sidereal location—imagery associated with the dark rift and the Galactic Center. Perhaps we can explain this with what I mentioned earlier: Sagittarius was rising heliacally—the dark-rift "gate" was open on the horizon—when the solstice sun occupied Capricorn 2,500 years ago.

Richer confirms that the place where the soul ascends into heaven indeed seems to be the sanctuary of the gods on the summit of Olympus; it is the trans-Saturnian "gateway of the gods" that we shall have occasion to discuss more deeply in relation to Vedic cosmology and Mithraism. Many Greek legends, even modern ones, vouch for the mysterious nature of the upper plateau of Mount Olympus. According to Lucian, who probably had direct experience for what he was saying, "the assembly of the gods took place on the heights of Olympus at the time of the winter solstice."[10] And yet the gate in the story by Teucer is near the Archeron Sea, guarded by a Sagittarian centaur.

The Scorpion men and the Sagittarian archers who defend the gate to heaven against interlopers are motifs that Ananda Coomaraswamy explored, for they reveal the metaphysical dimensions of these cosmographical adventures. Sacred topography, even if it is anchored to a real geography, can also represent the inner landscape of the soul's after-death journey. These metaphysical implications will be explored more deeply in part 3.

In general, we are safe in concluding that Mount Olympus, as gateway of the gods, has a direct association with nearby Sagittarius. Zeus even has a relationship with Scorpio: "In Greek, Scorpio was called the Claws of the Scorpion, but the earlier symbol for this sign was the Eagle. . . . The zodiacal eagle then became identified with the eagle of Zeus."[11] Richer notes that, according to Alexandre Volguine in *L'Ésotérisme de l'astrologie*, "the substitution of the Eagle by Scorpio is linked to the superimposition of an eight-part division of the zodiac over twelve signs." Volguine writes: "The fixed signs of the zodiac: Taurus, Leo, Scorpio, and Aquarius . . . have a very special importance," and he notes that the symbols for these signs are equivalent to the four animals of the Apocalypse and also represent the four Evangelists.[12]

Finally, we can look at another Zeus myth: "The serpent Typhon represents the World Axis and is simultaneously associated with Cancer. The Cancer-Capricorn opposition is often symbolized by the combat of Zeus, whose throne is at Olympus, and Typhon."[13] But Typhon, as symbol of the Milky Way serpent, runs through Sagittarius-Scorpio and Gemini-Taurus.

The mixing of the zodiacal imagery of Capricorn with Sagittarius and even Scorpio, giving them all a loose association with the Galactic Center–Mount Olympus region, would appear to be caused by three factors: the combining of signs when shifting from an eight- or ten-sign zodiac to a twelve-sign zodiac; overlapping symbology through several zodiacal ages; and the heliacal rise of a constellation versus precise solar alignment.

Figure 7.4. The Scorpion archer: guardian of paradise?

There is another function of the Capricorn-Cancer axis that can be mentioned here, as it relates to our earlier discussion of the pseudoplanetary nodes in Islamic astronomy. Richer identified alignments in latitude between sites, each corresponding to planetary levels. The seven planetary planes are mapped upward from Taenarum to Delphi, and are mirrored again northward to the Galactic Center at Mount Olympus. According to Richer's findings, the descent of souls along the Cancer-

Capricorn axis occurred in the following order through the spheres of
(1) Kronos, (2) Zeus, (3) Ares, (4) Apollo, (5) Aphrodite, (6) Hermes,
(7) Selene. And the ascent of souls took place in the reverse order, start-
ing from Delphi, the center of the earth, and rising northward to Mount
Olympus. In general the Delphi axis unites seven planetary levels extending in two directions, north and south, which encompass the "three
worlds" of sky, earth, and underworld.

If we refer to the north-south axis in the map of Greece in figure 7.2,
we can see how the Taenarum–Delphi–Mount Olympus axis is the planetary chakra axis, with each successive latitude corresponding to a planet
and chakra. Richer, however, does not mention nodal symbolism; perhaps
the eighth and ninth "planets" could only be accessed from Mount Olympus, where the portal to the higher, trans-Saturnian realm was located.

Despite the complexity of Richer's study of Greek sacred geography,
his conclusions are unequivocal:

> The system of cosmic references is thus complete: Taenarum is the
> nadir, Delphi the center, and Olympus the zenith. The six directions of
> space and the center are present; the remnants of the planetary lines give
> the zodiacal diagram greater vitality and meaning. The mystical signif-
> icance of the Cancer-Capricorn axis is confirmed by the Pythagorean
> texts that have been mentioned. . . . The existence of Delphi and the
> alignments of sanctuaries is, however, much earlier than Pythagore-
> anism, which only took up and revealed far more ancient doctrines.[14]

Because Richer bases his identification of Capricorn with the solstice
on Guénon's work, we can more easily understand the misplaced emphasis on Capricorn. But this is not necessarily a mistake; the two perspectives might already have been seen as one as long ago as the time of
Pythagoras (550 B.C.), because Sagittarius (the Galactic Center area) was
even then rising heliacally when the winter-solstice sun was in Capricorn.
The combining of symbolism is understandable, but the references to
Sagittarius are numerous, and we should understand that *the combined
symbolism suggests that Mount Olympus represents the winter-solstice sun
aligned with the galactic node in Sagittarius.* The intended reference is clear,
and the necessary adjustment or enlargement of the parameters is allowable. Greek sacred geography was intended to reflect celestial geography;

time cycles and alignments dance around this unmoving center. We don't need to rethink Richer too much here, nor Guénon, we just need to understand that the Capricorn-Cancer reference and symbolism "bridges the distance," so to say, between Capricorn and Sagittarius. The heliacal rise, 2,500 years ago, of Sagittarius during the Capricorn winter solstice made those two constellations intimate enough for their symbolism to be intertwined. As a result of the precession of the solstice axis, the alignment of Sagittarius with the winter solstice has become even more unified, such that Mount Olympus has now become perfectly aligned, conceptually and in terms of sacred cosmology, with both the Galactic Center and the winter-solstice sun!

The Greek doctrine that the soul passes along the Milky Way was inherited from earlier Orphic and Pythagorean ideas. Souls are believed to pass to and from the higher world through two gates, one in Capricorn and one in Cancer. As Guénon suggests, these gates correspond to the solstices, a temporal location in the seasonal cycle, but Macrobius offered a specific sidereal location as well, which provides further clarification that the "signs" of Capricorn and Cancer correspond to the constellations (the actual sidereal locations) occupied by Sagittarius and Gemini. The notion of a celestial gateway is also found in the writings of Porphyry, based upon the earlier writings of certain Stoics and Mithraists such as Numenius and Chronus.

Concerned as he was with determining which gate was descending and which was ascending, Guénon's writings on the galactic gateways confuse the issue somewhat, but he also clarified the question of how the temporal, seasonal quarters of the year should be mapped topographically. A confusion also arises from thinking of the solstice "signs" of Capricorn and Cancer as actual sidereal locations; precession has shifted the conceptual signs away from their original corresponding constellations. In addition, as we have seen, a one-sign adjustment even in the Greek writings is required, because in any era the constellation observed rising during the solstice is actually the one next door to the constellation occupied by the sun. Thus, with a minor adjustment in Guénon's writings we can understand, as Macrobius did, that the solstice gateways (in his era as well as ours) are "close enough" to the two crossroads formed by the Milky Way and the ecliptic (the zodiac) to be considered the same. I say "close enough" because even though a precessional shift of almost thirty degrees has occurred since the time of Macrobius, the gateways then were seen rising heliacally on the solstices, whereas in our era the solstices are precisely aligned with the gateways. Thus, a perception of correspondence between the two can be argued for both eras, one apparent and one actual.

The celestial gateways appear as a theme in classical Greek literature and mythology. For example, in the myth of Er reported by Plato, we read of a near-death journey of a Greek soldier who was believed dead, but who revived on his funeral pyre to tell of his experience. After his soul left his body, he traveled with many other departed ones to a beautiful place. He saw two openings in the earth, and opposite them two others in the sky. Judges sat to the side, reviewing the deeds of the souls, who were then dispatched either downward or upward through the portals. Er was told to observe all he saw, as he was chosen to return to Earth and tell others. Through one of the Earth openings newly judged souls were dispatched, but from the other travel-stained souls emerged and turned aside to camp in a meadow and rejoice with old acquaintances. Likewise, the sky gates offered coming and going passages, with some souls descending clean and bright. Some spoke of their sorrows in purgatory, which lasted a thousand years; others told of the joy experienced in heaven above and incredible vistas of beauty.[15]

Big Dipper Falling: The Fall of Troy

Hamlet's Mill explored the Greek material relating to the galactic gateways, but a recent book takes one Greek legend to a new level of understanding. Florence and Kenneth Wood's *Homer's Secret Iliad* deals not only with the myth and history of the Trojan War but also with the encrypted astronomy within Homer's famous epic. The story of how the book itself came to be written is worth sketching.

As a young girl living in Kansas in the 1930s, Edna Johnston was fascinated by the stars. Even as she grew up and studied for a master's degree in literature at the local college, her astronomical interests never diminished. Romantic poets like Keats and Tennyson influenced her approach to the Greek classics, and understanding Homer and Greek mythology became her passion.

When World War II ended, Edna married John Leigh and relocated with him to England. During the 1950s she grappled with Homer's *Iliad* in her spare time, trying to identify a key that she felt would unlock its secrets. Eventually she identified "the general subject matter of Homeric epic as astronomy."[16] In the mid-1960s she developed a correspondence with the authors of *Hamlet's Mill*, Giorgio de Santillana and Hertha von Dechend, who were so impressed with her work that in one of their letters to her they wrote, "Please count on us as a pair of your devoted admirers."[17]

Unfortunately, Edna Leigh was never able to publish her work; her many notebooks and drafts were left to her daughter, Florence Wood, to sort out. Working with her husband, Florence organized and applied her mother's research over many years, eventually publishing *Homer's Secret Iliad* in 1999. It is at once an homage to her mother's persistence and a solid contribution to decoding precessional astronomy in Homer's many-faceted epic. Special emphasis is placed on the events of era 4400 B.C., one-quarter of a precessional cycle ago. Although it wasn't made explicit in the book, this was the era during which the equinox axis aligned with the Milky Way.

The *Iliad* ostensibly describes the fall of Troy, perhaps around 2200 B.C., which led to the rise of Greece. But what bothered Edna Leigh was that the story seemed to be secretly saying a lot more. After identifying astronomy as the key, she was then able to identify some general principles that Homer used to encode astronomy. Briefly, the warriors and military regiments listed in book 2, the "Catalogue of Ships," are stars and constellations. Seasons and Sun and Moon positions are specified given that different geographical territories referred to different regions of the sky. Also, in a way similar to how Vedic literature encoded precessional eras, the *Iliad* documents zodiacal ages that shift every 2,160 years, going back some 7,000 years.[18]

Most astonishing is the chapter entitled "The Changing Heavens and the Fall of Troy," in which the demise of Troy is an allegory for the precession-caused "fall" of the Big Dipper in the sky (see fig. 2.1). This interpretation has a parallel in Mayan cosmology. In *Maya Cosmogenesis 2012*, in the section devoted to early Izapan astronomy, I noted that the precession-caused movement of the winter solstice sun toward the Milky Way is counterposed in the north by the movement of the Big Dipper away from the North Celestial Pole. I also identified how this astronomical process was encoded into Mayan mythology: the "fall" of Seven Macaw (the Big Dipper) out of his tree symbolizes the precession-caused movement of the Big Dipper away from the polar center—movement that accelerated around 1000 B.C.[19] I had never encountered this concept before, and its presence in Homer lends credence to my own reading of Mayan precessional cosmology as something any perceptive skywatcher was likely to notice and find significant. It indicates the unorthodox ways that ancient cultures incorporated precession into their evolving mythologies, and should stimulate a revolution among historians of science, literature, and astronomy. But I have the sneaking suspicion that, despite being beautifully written and clearly presented—as well as undeniably true—Edna Leigh's legacy may not get the recognition it deserves.

The Lion of Kea

Returning to Richer's research, we find compelling evidence that pushes our search back to before the time of the Trojan War. Richer alluded to the great antiquity of the traditions that he found in the Greek landscape. A sphinxlike monument he identified possibly leads to the Egyptian sources of Greek sacred geography. The Lion of Julius on the island of Kea (fig. 7.5) is a great enigma, and resembles the Sphinx at Gizeh.

The island of Kea is near the coast of Attica but is not part of the ordinary tourist circuit, so visiting its stone lion requires at least four days of travel and great desire. Richer had the definite impression that the six-meter-long lion was extremely old, based on the erosion and weathering visible along its sides. In fact, the oldest recorded lore from the island, going back some 2,500 years, reveals that the existence of the gigantic

Figure 7.5. The lion-sphinx on the island of Kea.

statue was already at that time inexplicable for the inhabitants. A traveler named Brönsted published a description of the statue in *Voyages dans la Grèce* (1828), which inspired Goethe to comment, "The Lion of Kea is the only prehistoric trace of a vanished civilization that was great geographically and remained so psychobiologically, that of Atlantis."[20]

Richer examined the lion's orientation very carefully, which revealed that it may have played a role in the creation of the Delphi–Mount Olympus axis to the northwest. Lengthwise, the lion is oriented almost northeast-southwest, meaning it is more or less oriented to the summer solstice sunrise. But since its head is turned perpendicular to its body, rather than facing straight ahead, it gazes toward the sunrise above a hill at the time of the winter solstice. Richer assesses the deep significance of this alignment: "An astronomer could undoubtedly date it precisely according to this [solstice alignment]. . . . As for the lion's body, it seems to indicate the direction of Acria on the south coast of the Peloponnese, where, according to Pausanias, stood the most ancient sanctuary of the Mother of the Gods."[21] Since it faces the solstice and it obviously symbolizes the constellation Leo, Richer suggests that the Lion of Kea indicates the era in which the summer solstice sun was in Leo—4400 B.C. to 2200 B.C. This makes the lion contemporaneous with the early culture whose traces have recently been unearthed and dated on Kea, and with the first recorded Egyptian dynasties. In fact, the Egyptian calendar is thought to have been inaugurated in 4200 B.C. The Lion of Kea indicates the era in which the summer-solstice sun was in Leo, and when the summer solstice sun entered Leo, circa 4400 B.C., the spring equinox was entering Gemini. Figure 7.6 shows a symbol identified by Richer of the spring equinox in Gemini.

Both the Gemini symbol and the Lion of Kea point to the era when the equinox axis was aligned with the Milky Way—an

Figure 7.6. Equinox in Gemini (previous galactic alignment of era 4400 B.C.)

era of galactic alignment. This rare precessional alignment was much labored over in the book *Hamlet's Mill*, where it is presented as nothing less than the fabled Golden Age. But the true reference might actually go back to an earlier alignment in precession.

The Egyptian Sphinx, which faces east, is believed to symbolize the era during which the spring equinox coincided with Leo—roughly 10,800 B.C. Summer solstice in Leo, one-quarter of a precessional cycle later, would have represented a "reanimation" of the Sphinx because it marked the first time since 10,800 B.C. that a seasonal quarter occupied Leo. The Lion of Kea, facing the solstice sunrise rather than the equinox sunrise, differentiates the solstice from the former equinox axis. Leo is a critical marker sign for these periodic galactic alignments because when it aligns with an equinox or solstice, this indicates that either the solstice axis or the equinox axis is aligning with the Milky Way and Galactic Center. For example, we are just entering the age of Aquarius, which means that the fall equinox is in Leo—this is also a way of indicating the solstice axis aligned with the Milky Way!

Richer surmises that the Lion of Kea was part of a very old zodiacal wheel probably centered on Trachis that was transferred later to Delphi, indicating the existence in a distant era of a system that symbolically described the first known calendar, possibly deriving from Egyptian traditions. Amazingly, that distant era of galactic alignment was when the summer solstice was in Leo. Richer has this to say about the origins of the Lion of Kea: "One is thus in the presence of a series of consistent indications, and it may be concluded that the Lion of Kea represented the zodiacal guardian of the sign of Leo during a time that seems indistinguishable from the very origins of the calendar. And it is certainly not a coincidence that the lion is looking towards Egypt."[22]

On our way to Egypt we shall pause to explore Mithraism, an important Greco-Roman tradition that provides a link between Europe and an older Persian mythology. More important, the Mithraic cosmology has as its highest initiatory revelation the doctrine of the ascent and descent of souls through the galactic gateways. Mithraism is a religion that arose as a result of the "discovery" of precession by Hipparchus in 128 B.C., and, without a doubt, it points the way to a Hypercosmic Sun above the abode of Saturn-Zeus on Mount Olympus.

EIGHT

The Galactic Mysteries of Mithraism

ithraism was a mystery religion that arose in the first century B.C. and for four hundred years spread through Europe, North Africa, the British Isles, and parts of West Asia. It was the state religion of the Roman Empire until it succumbed to Christianity at the end of the fourth century, when all "heresies" were condemned. In underground sanctuaries the aspiring seeker was led through seven grades of initiation corresponding to the seven planetary spheres. The central altar of Mithraism portrayed a bull-slaying scene called a tauroctony, which was usually surrounded by zodiacal signs, torchbearers, and other symbols. Only by studying many such scenes have scholars been able to understand the esoteric astronomy within the tauroctony, and the identity of the central figure, Mithras. The origin place of Mithraism has been identified, as well as its astronomico-religious doctrines.

The scholarly study of Mithraism is still recovering from seventy years of going down the wrong path. It promised to get a good start, because in 1869 the German scholar K. B. Stark proposed that the figures of the tauroctony were arranged to tell a story about stars and constellations. Unfortunately, French scholar Franz Cumont, writing in the 1890s, flatly rejected such a thesis, and instead argued for the merely historical derivation of Mithraic ideology from Iranian myths. As a testimony to academia's inability to overcome internal biases, Cumont's approach dominated the field until the 1970s, when the astronomical content of Mithraism could no longer be denied.[1] At the First International Congress on Mithraism in 1973, Roger Beck resurrected Stark's theory, showing how the tauroctony figures represent constellations lying between Antares and Aldebaran—the primary stars in Scorpio and Taurus. The sequence of constellations on the celestial equator runs from Canis Minor the dog, to

Figure 8.1. The Mithraic tauroctony (from Maarten Vermaseran, *Corpus Inscriptionum et monumentorum religionis mithriacae.* The Hague: Martinus Nijhoff, 1956)

Hydra the snake, Crater the cup, Corvus the raven, and Scorpio the scorpion.[2] There are other astronomical symbols in the tauroctony. For example, the bull's head on the upper right is Taurus, the ever-present scorpion on the lower left represents Scorpio, and the wound in the bull's shoulder is where the Pleiades are located. Instantly, Mithraic symbolism could thus be placed on the Galactic Center–Galactic Anticenter axis; however, recognition of this fact was not forthcoming.

Roger Beck, John Hinnells, and Robert Gordon clarified the astronomical content of Mithraic tauroctonies through the 1970s and 1980s and explained the many variations in Mithraic symbolism.[3] Before we take a closer look at a typical tauroctony scene from a Mithraic sanctuary in London, we need to understand where Mithraism originated and how its essential teaching involves the ascent and descent of souls through the celestial gateways.

David Ulansey's *Origins of the Mithraic Mysteries* shows how Mithraism arose as a result of the discovery of precession. In 128 B.C. the Greek astronomer Hipparchus wrote a paper on the shifting of the vernal point, and thus proved that the sphere of stars, believed to be eternally fixed, actually slowly moved. Later Greek writers admitted that this information was known to the earlier Babylonians and Egyptians, but Hipparchus definitively revealed it to the Greek world and without a telescope. It is interesting to note that he was comparing his own star observations with recorded star data that was only 170 years old. Hipparchus's "discovery" was based on this parameter, which yields a precessional shift of only two and one-half degrees (the space of five full moons). This helps us understand how relatively easy it is to notice precession, and we can imagine a similar circumstance among the Olmec and Izapan skywatchers who preserved star positions and rising times for at least a thousand years.[4]

The effect of the discovery of precession on the Greek world must have been dramatic. In 67 B.C. Plutarch wrote that Mithraic rites were being practiced by Cilician pirates, and Ulansey shows how the discovery of precession and the origins of Mithraism are intimately related. The figure of Mithras appears to be derived from the Perseus cult in the town of Tarsus, the capital of the province of Cilicia in southeastern Turkey. In Hellenistic and Roman times, Tarsus was home to an important intellectual community known as the Stoics. The Stoic Aratos of Soli (315–240 B.C.) was best known for his astronomical poem *Phaenomena*. Strabo, Cicero, Athenodorus, and Zeno were either Stoics or influenced by them, but the most influential Stoic philosopher was Posidonius (135–50 B.C.). Stoic philosophy is characterized by astronomical knowledge and a belief in a "cosmic sympathy" through which everything in the universe is connected. Even before Hipparchus, a Great Year of time was recognized that was believed to schedule the destruction of the world in a great conflagration (ekpyrosis), followed by its regeneration (palingenesis) in a new cycle. The durations of the Great Year proposed by various writers indicate precessional knowledge lurking in the shadows.

At Tarsus, the intellectual community of Stoics was also active in local politics. Posidonius was such a philosopher-king, and his ideas appear in the work of Cicero and Seneca. A polymath like Pythagoras before him, he taught the astrological doctrines of the Stoics without reserve and even built an orrery, a mechanical model of the cosmos with seven planets and celestial spheres. Given his interests, and as the dominant intellectual figure of his age, Posidonius looms as a prime suspect in the establishment of Mithraism. He was the leader of the Stoic school when Plutarch mentioned Mithraic rites in 67 B.C. Significantly, the Cilician pirates who practiced Mithraic ceremonies at that time came from Tarsus. A fleet of roving seamen 20,000 strong, they knew how to navigate by the stars and would have seeded Mithraism, like the later Romans did, in their outlying enclaves throughout the Mediterranean. According to Ulansey, this is how Mithraism arose in Tarsus following the discovery of precession.[5]

Scholars have been able to reconstruct a great deal about Mithraism by examining the symbolism in many surviving Mithraeum (Mithraic sanctuaries), often well preserved in underground chambers or natural caves. Although there is scant historical information on the doctrinal beliefs of Mithraism, a central tenet of Mithraism is described in the writings of Porphyry. In his *De antro nympharum* (*The Cave of the Nymphs*), Porphyry tells us that the Mithraic cave symbolizes the cosmos. For the doctrine of two doorways in the cosmic cave through which the soul ascends and descends, he draws explicitly from the neo-Pythagorean philosophers Numenius and Cronius. The soul is believed to descend into manifestation (genesis) through the gateway in Cancer and ascend to the transcendent realm (apogenesis) through the gateway in Capricorn.

The doctrine of the celestial gateways is essential to understanding Mithraism. Notice, however, that Porphyry places the gates, like all Greek writers after him, in Cancer and Capricorn, as that was the position of the solstice axis in his day. Macrobius clarified for us how the gates are viewed rising heliacally (before the Sun) during the solstices, requiring that we relocate them to Sagittarius and Gemini. The main axis portrayed in Mithraic tauroctonies is between Scorpio and Taurus, which is one further sign removed. How do we explain this? First, we need to be clear that the sidereal location of the gateways is defined by—as Macrobius wrote—the crossing point of the Milky Way and the ecliptic. Now, the crossing point is located near the arrow point of Sagittarius, but the way that Scorpio's tail loops underneath makes Scorpio also a viable candidate. The north gate is, for all intents and purposes (and especially in the context of naked-eye stargazing), located at the cusp of Sagittarius and Scorpio. More significantly, on the other side of the axis, Taurus contains the all-important indicator of the other gateway, the Pleiades. As previously discussed, the Pleiades are not exactly opposite the Galactic Center–north gate, which places them without question deep in the constellation of Taurus rather than at the Taurus-Gemini cusp. This situation explains why the Mithraists chose to encode the Galactic Center–Galactic Anti-center axis with Scorpio-Taurus symbolism, and Mithras literally spans the horizon, linking the two.

Mithras is also identified with the equinoxes—not just one equinox, but both, suggesting he is the equinox axis. Ulansey argues that Mithras represents Perseus because he is aligned over the body of Taurus, and therefore represents the era during which the equinox was in Taurus (4400–2200 B.C.). This is relevant because then the tauroctony also represents the age of the previous galactic alignment, when the equinoxes were aligned with the galaxy. This age ended in 2200 B.C., and the bull-slaying scene would thus signify the end of the Golden Age described in *Hamlet's Mill.* In the complex astronomico-religious symbolism of Mithraism, a few things are now clear:

★ The gateways through which the soul ascends and descends are located in Scorpio and Taurus—the Galactic Center–Galactic Anticenter axis (also identified by the two crossing points of the Milky Way and the zodiac).

★ Mithras is Perseus, but something more, for as the equinox axis, he spans the sky from horizon to horizon, uniting two opposed constellations.

★ Mithraism was concerned with the precession-caused end of the previous galactic alignment, and thus may also have been concerned with projecting forward to the next time an alignment like this would occur.

This last point brings up an interesting consideration. Because the Mithraists viewed the gateways rising heliacally on the solstice in their era, perhaps they believed they were living at the dawn of the next alignment era. Of course, this requires a double standard on the part of the Mithraists as to how the alignment is conceived, stretching it to suit their needs, but such a rationale is not uncommon in the establishment of religious beliefs. Secret teachings within Mithraism might have been about the end of the previous Golden Age, long ago, and the impending dawn of a new one. The grades of Mithraic initiation led the seeker through the seven planetary spheres to the abode of Pater (Saturn), associated with Capricorn. Beyond the seventh level, a secret teaching reveals an eighth "house" where the Hypercosmic Sun was located, accessed through a celestial doorway that appeared when the Sun was in Capricorn.

The implications of this line of interpretation are astounding, but we mustn't get ahead of ourselves. Let's take a look at a typical tauroctony to see how the galactic mysteries of Mithraism are secretly encoded. In figure 8.2, notice the overall zodiacal circle, typical of tauroctony scenes. The central scene is, of course, the bull slaying, symbolizing the end of the Age of Taurus, but a great deal more is going on here.

The bull obviously symbolizes Taurus; its head even points up to Taurus on the surrounding zodiacal circle. The bull-Mithras axis is skewed to a two o'clock angle. The animal figures, from left to right in the lower area, are snake, scorpion, dog. According to Ulansey, they represent Hydra, Scorpio, and Canis Minor—constellations lying along the celestial equator. The dog, more specifically, probably represents the brightest star in Canis Major, Sirius, the Dog Star. Roger Beck offers an alternative to Hydra.[6] In examining the zodiac in the Mithraic sanctuary at Ponza, Beck noticed that the snake stretched from one side of the sky to

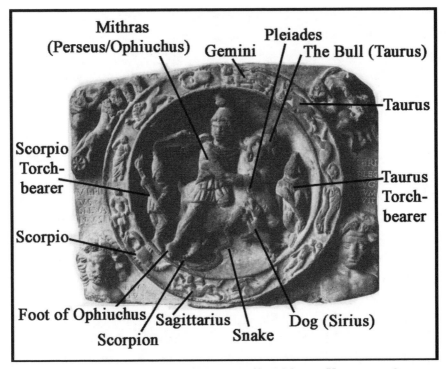

Figure 8.2. Galactic framework of Mithraism (from Maarten Vermaseran, *Corpus Inscriptionum et monumentorum religionis mithriacae*. The Hague: Martinus Nijhoff, 1956)

the other, from Capricorn to Cancer. He proposed that the snake is the lunar dragon whose body, like Mithras, stretches from one side of the zodiac to the other. As we discovered earlier, the south node of the lunar snake (the tail) is exalted in Sagittarius, but the Sun in Capricorn reveals it on the eastern horizon.

There may have been multiple meanings for each of the scene's figures. For example, the torchbearers on the left and right are associated with the equinoxes, but they are often shown wearing the emblems of Scorpio and Taurus. Their torches symbolize light, or soul-fire, and one points up while the other points down, which refers to the two gateways and the ascending and descending paths on the two sides of the tauroctony zodiac. The apparently conflicting symbology can be interpreted as the equinoxes in Taurus-Scorpio aligned with the celestial gateways.

In the tauroctony scenes Mithras always stabs the bull in the shoulder just below the neck. Blood and sometimes ears of wheat pour from the wound, which the snake and the dog are eager to lap up. This motif is symbolic of the descent of souls into manifestation, for sustenance is essential to birth and growth. The dagger is similar to the sword that Perseus uses to cut off Medusa's head. Knowing that the bull is Taurus, we should look more closely at that constellation to get a sense for what is being portrayed.

As Ulansey points out, the Pleiades are located precisely where the dagger slays the bull (see fig. 8.3). What can we make of this? First off, it identifies the Pleiades as a significant pole in the Mithraic tauroctony, associated with the Taurean gateway that leads the soul into manifestation (genesis). We have already described how the Pleiades are the general marker of the Galactic Anticenter. Now, the dog in the tauroctony represents Sirius, and he is lunging wildly at the wound that locates the Pleiades. Significantly, Sirius is on the same meridian as the Galactic Anticenter—that is, it passes through the southern meridian at the same time as the Galactic Anticenter, although it is lower in altitude. Likewise, the snake feeds on the blood, and the lunar snake's head (Rahu) is exalted at 3° Gemini—also an indicator of the Galactic Anticenter.

The other action in the tauroctony occurs, not surprisingly, at the opposite side of the sky, where the foot of Mithras, the snake's tail, and a scorpion all meet. Like the snake of the lunar nodes, Mithras conceptually stretches from horizon to horizon; he is Perseus on one side of the

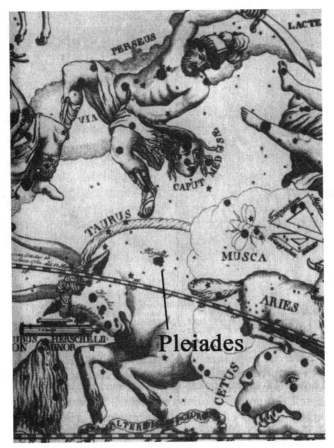

Figure 8.3. Taurus with the Pleiades on its shoulder

sky, but his leg actually belongs to the oppositional counterpart to Perseus: Ophiuchus. Mithraic scholars have not, to my knowledge, suggested this link. Taking a close look at the grouping of astrological symbols in the lower portion of the tauroctony, and knowing where the foot of Ophiuchus is located in the sky (see fig. 8.4), such an interpretation seems not only possible, but hard to deny.

The clearest evidence for the presence of the Galactic Center in Mithraic symbolism is the fact that in the tauroctony the foot of Mithras (as Ophiuchus) converges with the arrow of Sagittarius and the stinger of Scorpio on the outer zodiacal circle. The snake's tail contributes to the reading, as the lunar south node is exalted at the Galactic Center (3° Sagittarius). Complementing the Pleiades at the Galactic Anticenter as the gateway of genesis is the Galactic Center, the gateway of apogenesis

Figure 8.4. Close-up of the galactic root of the tauroctony scene

where the soul exits the cosmic cave to meet the Hypercosmic Sun.[7] Mithraism is fundamentally about the soul's passage through the galactic gateways that open during eras of galactic alignment. As far as I am aware, this is a new perspective in understanding the galactic parameters of Mithraism.

It is quite astounding that Mithraism, as the state religion of the Roman Empire for several centuries, contained initiatory knowledge that involved the Galactic Center–Galactic Anticenter gateways. Of course, the religion that replaced Mithraism, Christianity, has its own encoded reference to the solstice-galaxy alignment, most notably in Revelation, but this topic is beyond the scope of this book.

After the death of the Golden Age—the killing of the Bull and the passage out of the age of Taurus—human beings fell into deeper manifestation or, we might say, deeper materialism. Mithras is celebrated as the high deity or demiurge who turns the wheel of precession, the implicit "secret" information being that another galactic alignment looms. The Greek Stoics of Tarsus who devised the Mithraic mysteries may have adjusted the perspective to give the impression that it was *their* age that would experience the next galactic alignment—not that of the equinox axis with the galactic gate-

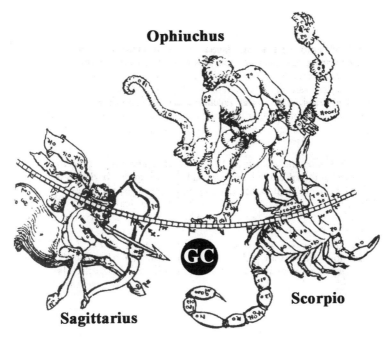

Ophiuchus

Sagittarius

GC

Scorpio

Figure 8.5. Scorpio, Sagittarius, and Ophiuchus at the Galactic Center

ways, but the solstice axis. This was accomplished through "fudging" one sign and observing the constellation rising heliacally on the solstices. The new equinoctial age of Pisces, born out of the early Christian ferment and astronomically timed to occur around the first century A.D., was probably seen by early Christian gnostics to be the age of the new alignment, comparable to the Golden Age of Taurus, which ended when Mithras stabbed the Pleiades. We know that the solstice-galaxy alignment doesn't precisely occur until the era of A.D. 2000, but who, two thousand years ago, would argue with the dramatic initiatory revelation of the galactic gateway rising just before the December solstice sun? It thus must have seemed that the approaching dawn of the Age of Pisces was significant. The tauroctony scenes aren't explicit with Piscean symbolism because they are focused instead on solstice symbolism and the constellations associated with the galactic gateways—in Taurus and Scorpio.

The Mithraic tauroctony scenes encode the dual process of human spirituality—incarnation (manifestation/genesis) and transcendence (involution or sublimation/apogenesis). These processes occur, according to Stoic and Hellenistic astrology, at the celestial gateways in Capricorn and Cancer. A reevaluation of the description of these gateways given by Porphyry and Macrobius and in the Avestan *Greater Bundahishn*[8] reveals that the gateways should be understood in a twofold sense: In the annual seasonal cycle they are the solstices; in the sidereal zodiac they are in early Gemini (or late Taurus) and early Sagittarius (or late Scorpio). The former is the gateway into earthly genesis and incarnation; the latter is the gateway out of the "cave" of the manifest cosmos.

We could continue to speculate on this complex symbolism of the Mithraic mysteries, but we have already uncovered much new information. We should rest for a moment with these new perspectives, and ponder Ernest Renan's observation on the flukes of history and the fate of Western civilization: "If Christianity had been stopped at its birth by some mortal illness, the world would have become Mithraic."[9]

NINE

Abydos and the Sphinx: Egyptian Alignment Eras

Despite the hundreds of academics who will argue until their last breath that Greece is the source of all Western civilization, the fact is that Egypt pioneered, developed, and realized scientific and religious traditions that Grecian giants like Pythagoras, Socrates, and Plato borrowed from after being initiated into the ancient Egyptian mystery schools. In his *Timaeus*, Plato preserves a legend derived from Egyptian sources of Atlantis, somehow mixed up with Egyptian prehistory, dating back nine thousand years from the time of his writing. This places the existence of an advanced civilization thriving around the time of the previous solstice-galaxy alignment, 10,500 B.C. But more accessible evidence testifies to Egypt's astronomical sophistication and its role as elder brother to Greece. The Greek neoplatonist Proclus, who studied at Alexandria in the fifth century A.D., reported that it was the Egyptians and not the Greeks who discovered precession: "Let those, who believe . . . the stars to move around the poles of the zodiac [precession], as Ptolemy and Hipparchus before him, [let him] know . . . that the Egyptians had already taught Plato about the movement of the fixed stars." [1]

Through selective citation, modern scholars dismiss the larger body of evidence for Egypt's genius as anomalous, apocryphal, or downright fictional. Much of this bias has its roots in the nineteenth century when the "strange and alien" Egyptians were soundly denounced as primitive, pre-Christian heathens. More recently a fascination with and respect for ancient Egypt's accomplishments has grown in the public mind. This welcome development, however, has been coopted by the popular media and its emphasis on treasure hunting, human sacrifice, and mummification rituals. But the multidimensional metaphysical knowledge of ancient Egypt does have its champions.

Egyptian Mysteries of Isis

The arguments for an Egyptian knowledge of precession are now ubiquitous in the literature. R. A. Schwaller de Lubicz found evidence for precession in his work at Luxor and Karnak, Jane B. Sellers shows as much in her book *The Death of Gods in Ancient Egypt*, and Robert Bauval and Adrian Gilbert's *The Orion Mystery* provided new insights into this question. This aspect of Egyptian cosmology is critical to understanding how the Galactic Center and galactic alignments were known to the ancient Egyptians. New insights into the symbolic identity of Isis supports this view, and Vincent Bridges's new interpretation of the early site of Abydos provides an important key.

This is not the place to review all that's been written, speculated, and proven about Egypt. In general, Peter Tompkins eloquently summarized the history of Egyptology and dozens of other aspects of Egyptian pyramid science in his *Secrets of the Great Pyramid*. Egyptian sacred science is now recognized as a metaphysical system of ideas centered on geometrical principles that are universal and manifest in all realms of nature. In his monumental *The Temple of Man*, Schwaller de Lubicz reconstructed this sacred science, showing how the square roots of 2, 3, and 5 were used in Egyptian architecture and sculpture to represent the forces in nature that create, sustain, and evolve life. De Lubicz, over decades of research in Egypt, was able to penetrate the ancient Egyptian mind frame and reconstruct a metaphysics of human becoming—a sacred science—unsurpassed even in modern times. In his own words, he compares the brilliant symbolic expressions of Mayan and Egyptian sacred science: "Very certainly there is a kinship in the expression of the knowledge of the old traditions among the Maya and the same pharaonic tradition, but presented in ideogrammatic fashion that is always more difficult to decipher than the always mere hieroglyphic writing."[2]

The findings of de Lubicz also have a strong astronomical component, in that cycles of time define a cosmic alchemy pursued by the enigmatic Hru Shemsu school, from which the Hermetic teachings of Hermes Trismegistus are believed to derive. It is well known that Egyptian gnosis filtered down through the millennia to emerge in Pythagorean tradition and the Orphic philosophies of the early Greek thinkers. Perhaps less well known is how the Egyptian Isis cult and its profound mysteries survived in the image of the Virgin Mary and in Black Madonna cults in southern France.[3] Even to this day, the Mother of God is emphasized in Latin American churches and other variants of Christian worship. The wisdom behind this continued interest in the Great Mother deity involves the identification of Isis with the Milky Way, specifically, with the center of the Milky Way as the mother of all stars, including our own sun. A general argument, as well as a specific one, suggests that Isis may represent the Galactic Center.

First, Sharron Rose advocates for the relationship between Isis and the serpent power that awakens seekers through their dancing embodiment of the Goddess energy.[4] Having studied sacred dance in India on two Fullbright scholarships, Rose realized that dance movements told complex stories and in fact encoded lost wisdom. When she began studying Egyptian sacred dance and the rituals associated with Isis, she noticed similarities with the Tantric practices of India, in which the latent serpent power at the base of the spine is awakened to rise and unfold into the seeker's life. Similarly, Isis is the mother power at the root of the world that awakens and transforms (she resurrected Osiris). Thus, Isis performs a similar function to *kundalini,* the creative force at the galactic root that manifests as the *muladhara* chakra within the human microcosm. Second, if Isis does indeed correspond to Sirius, then we can recall that Sirius occupies the same meridian as the Galactic Anticenter—they both pass through the southern meridian at the same time, although Sirius is lower in altitude. My idea here is speculative, though astronomically very true. Further research may show more clearly how Sirius may have been a marker for the galactic axis that emanates from the Galactic Center.

The rebirth of the sun is aptly depicted on an Egyptian fresco, where the sun is placed near the birthplace of Nut, the sky goddess who may represent the Milky Way (see fig. 9.1). In Egyptian mythology, Nut is the night sky; she swallows the sun at dusk, it passes through her body all night, and she gives birth to the sun at dawn. The metaphor operates on the daily level as well as in larger cycles. In Mayan cosmology, the Milky Way's dark rift, as a kind of "cosmic vagina" near the Galactic Center, is the place where the sun is reborn at the end of the age. In the myth of the resurrection of Osiris, Plutarch reports that Osiris was tricked into being interred in a coffin that was then sent downriver to the sea by way of the Tanaitic Mouth. Symbolic of the death of Osiris and the commencement of his underworld journey, the Egyptians said that this event took place

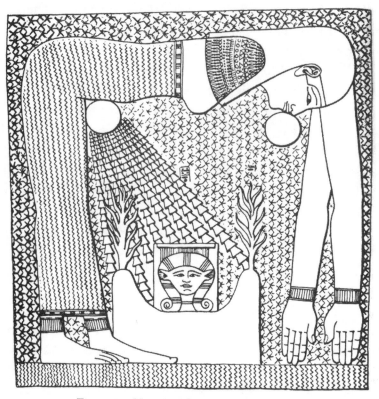

Figure 9.1. Nut, the Milky Way sky goddess
(from Isha Schwaller de Lubicz, *Her-Bak: The Living Face of
Ancient Egypt* ([New York: Inner Traditions International, 1978], 216)

on the seventeenth day of Athyr, when the sun was in Scorpio (near the dark rift).[5]

The Egyptian ankh scepter is suggestive of the crossroads formed by the Milky Way where it crosses over the ecliptic, and the dark rift near the Galactic Center. A form of it was held by Isis, and it later became the astrological symbol for Venus. As seen in figure 9.2, the ancient ankh of Isis is the template for sacred symbols in many traditions down through the ages, including (from left to right) Kabbalah, sacred architecture, and early Christianity.

In astrological symbolism, the Isis image was applied to the constellation Virgo, which is 90° away from the Galactic Center–Galactic Anticenter axis. (In fact, Spica, the main star in Virgo, is almost exactly 90° from the Galactic Anticenter in Gemini.) As we shall see in chapter 16,

Figure 9.2. The many forms of the ankh

this complication derives from using the equinox rather than the solstice to indicate each zodiacal age; thus the important solstice reference is actually three signs away. In other words, we might say "the Age of equinox in Aquarius" is equivalent to the "Age of solstice in Scorpio." Since Pisces is the twelfth and last sign of the zodiac, the end of the Age of Pisces—which is where we are now—indicates the end of an entire 26,000-year precession cycle, or *manvantara* in Vedic terms. But it is the alignment to the Galactic Center that serves as the anchor of this shift, which could be conceived as a reappearance of Isis. The relationship between Isis and the Hindu *kundalini* goddess also evokes a connection to Kali, who appears at the end of the *yuga* cycle, wisely trampling under her dancing feet the fragmented remnants of degenerate humanity so that earth's flowering can start anew.

My interpretations here are speculative, and a great deal more work needs to be done to uncover the galactic level within the symbolism of Isis. Moira Timms, an expert in the esoteric dimensions of Egyptian symbolism, tells me that Isis should not be equated with Kali in her destructive aspect. She also points out that the Zep Tepi or "First Time" of Egyptian cosmogenesis refers to the dawn of time long before 11,800 B.C., the date suggested by Robert Bauval and Graham Hancock. However, in my opinion the doctrine of World Ages requires periodic re-creations of the world, and thus a "First Time" can occur at each successive commencement of each new World Age. Her questioning of whether the Galactic Center should be conceived of as expelling energy or attracting energy introduces an important area for discussion: Is the Galactic Center the top of the tree or the root? Timms' work deserves greater attention, especially her pioneering insights into the relationship between the Egyptian *djed* pillar and the Galactic Center (see the bibliography).

At any rate, Isis symbology is just one facet of Egyptian gnosis, a knowledge that extends far into the dim mists of prehistory. Schwaller de Lubicz made the observation that erosion on the Sphinx was caused by water rather than wind and therefore seemed to indicate a greater age than archaeologists had given it. John Anthony West, in his *Serpent in the Sky*, picked up this thread decades later and enlisted the expertise of geologist Robert Schoch to rally evidence for an extreme age for the Sphinx—going back perhaps 10,000 years. Their critics, scientists and archaeologists alike, have not been able to refute convincingly the facts they present. More significantly, astronomical evidence seems to suggest that the Sphinx, whether or not it was built a long time ago, at least seems to pay homage to a specific era of precession that some researchers equate with the Egyptian Zep Tepi, or "First Time."

The Orion Mystery

Robert Bauval's *The Orion Mystery* made the simple points that the three Gizeh pyramids reflected the three belt stars of Orion, and that the so-called air shafts were really sight tubes to Sirius and other stars. In addition, these sight-tube alignments were accurate only in specific eras of precession. Beyond these findings, controversy over the age of the Sphinx led Graham Hancock to restate Jean Richer's idea that the Sphinx represented the constellation Leo. Based on this, Hancock took the next step and pointed out that the Sphinx faces directly east and therefore might pay homage to the time when the vernal equinox was situated in Leo—10,800 B.C.

In their *Message of the Sphinx*, Robert Bauval and Graham Hancock describe the heart of the mystery. They integrate the north-south precessional oscillation of Orion with the ecliptic precession to describe what they call the First and Last Times—10,800 B.C. and 2400 A.D. During these times Orion reaches its lowest and highest meridian transit while at

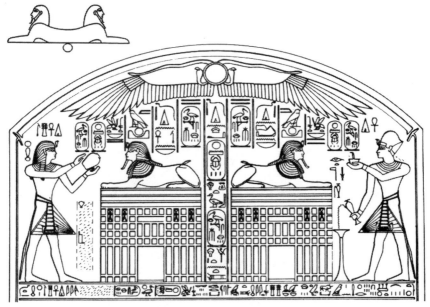

Figure 9.3. Balancing the cosmos: solstice sun on the galactic equator.

the same time the solstice sun sits on the Milky Way. Bauval and Hancock do not, however, place the solstice sun right on the Milky Way (the galactic equator). Instead they refer to when the sun reaches *the other side* of the Milky Way—the western edges. But if we adjust a few hundred years to reach precise alignment, whether or not precise alignment was intended by the ancient Egyptians, then we reach an adjusted First and Last Time, corresponding with the solstice-galaxy alignments of circa A.D. 2012 and 12,800 years ago. According to my current understanding, this is when the skies are "balanced" by the sun's alignment with the galactic plane, corresponding roughly with the southern and northern extreme meridian transits of Orion.[6]

In figure 9.3, the image in the upper left symbolizes the concept of "balancing the skies," but, as the larger scene below it shows, this symbol is also part of a larger cosmological schema. The balance of the skies portrays the midpoint of the sun's journey through the *duat* (underworld), and the winged disk (at the top) is Horus at noontime. But I feel that the idea of balance depicted applies to the daily and yearly cycles as well as larger cycles. We should remember that the galactic alignments of 10,800 B.C. and era 2012 are often indicated in the body of evidence by the Age of Leo and the Age of Aquarius. These ages frame the times when the solstice axis aligns with the plane of the Milky Way. One-half of a precession cycle ago the summer-solstice sun aligned with the part of the Milky Way containing the Galactic Center. Today, it is the December solstice sun that aligns with the Galactic Center. But what about the alignment in between, when the equinox axis aligned with the Milky Way, some 6,400 years ago? We should expect that this, too, was important for the Egyptians. In fact, Egyptian dynastic history begins around this date, and the equinox-galaxy alignment of era 4400 B.C. may have stimulated a remembering among the Egyptians of what the Sphinx, already an ancient eroding monument by that time, was meant to represent. One early Egyptian site provides some answers.

Abydos and the Galactic Alignment of Era 4400 B.C.

An early Egyptian site called Abydos lies along a hairpin curve of the Upper Nile, hundreds of miles south of the Gizeh plateau. Abydos, or Abedju, can be loosely translated as "heart of the world axis," suggesting the same idea as the Greek omphalos (earth navel), like the one at Delphi. Archaeological evidence indicates that the earliest temple at Abydos was dedicated to a pre-Osiris dog deity named Khent-Amenty, which means something like "head of the west." Since the entrance to the underworld was believed to be accessed through a gap in the Libyan hills to the west of Abydos, Khent-Amenty was obviously a guardian of the underworld gateway leading into the land of the dead.

The original Khent-Amenty shrine was situated in the center of Abydos and was in use well before 3000 B.C. At that time, Osirian funereal objects begin to appear in the archaeological record, and eventually the Egyptian ruler Seti I built a cenotaph (ritual temple) over an old shrine at the site. Vincent Bridges, in his research essay on Abydos, writes that the cult of Osiris appropriated and distorted the original doctrines of Khent-Amenty, and a glimpse of the original knowledge can be identified in Seti I's Osirian cenotaph.[7] The entire Thinite necropolis that houses the Osiris shrine (the Osireion) is aligned to the gap in the Libyan hills on a southeast-northwest axis, such that sunlight from the setting sun on the summer solstice illuminates the complex. Likewise, sunrise at the December solstice illuminates the necropolis from the other direction. Abydos has the same primary solstice-axis orientation as Izapa.

Bridges points out that Khent-Amenty, the dog-headed deity, is a variant of the lion deity and, like the Sphinx or the Lion at Kea, represents the constellation Leo. Aligned as it is to the solstice axis, the Thinite necropolis probably relates to the birth and death of the solar cycle, when the sun is reborn at winter solstice, and reaches its apex at summer solstice, only to begin "dying." This is what the solstice orientation suggests. But beyond this, a precession-specific era is indicated with the Leo symbolism—we seem to have an indication of the solstice in Leo that occurred one-quarter of a precessional cycle after the Sphinx's equinox in Leo alignment. Solstice in Leo occurred in era 4400 B.C., precisely when the cult of Khent-Amenty was under way at Abydos, and indicates when the equinox axis aligned with the galaxy—the Golden Age described in *Hamlet's Mill*.

Even more compelling is the fact that murals inside the Osireion (known as the Book of Caverns) describe the metaphysical usage of the astronomical alignments. In a summary of his findings, Bridges writes:

> With this in mind, we can glimpse the greater pattern of precessional astronomy behind all of Egyptian sacred science. The Aker or horizon of the Sphinx marks the half round, every 13,000 or so years, rising of Leo on the equinoxes. The Aker/horizon of Abydos—and there is a curious sphinx-like Aker shown in the Osireion's Book of Caverns—marks the quarter cycle with the summer solstice alignment of Leo. Thus using Leo, or more precisely the cusp of Leo/Cancer, which would allow the maximum visibility of Khent-Amenty through the gap, it is possible to track with great accuracy the turning of the seasons in the Great Year.
>
> The importance of the Book of Caverns information must be stressed. Here, the creation drama is taken over to form the mythology of the salvation of the Prisoner in the Underworld. This unusual viewpoint forms the basis for a kind of Gnostic shamanism that lies at the core of Egyptian sacred science . . . the mystery of Osiris's resurrection, the mystery of immortality, is also the mystery of time itself.[8]

That all seasonal quarters served as anchors in this precessional cosmo-conception is unavoidable and a natural conclusion. For the Golden Age denizens of the alignment of 10,800 B.C., a projection forward to the next alignment era, beginning in 4400 B.C., must have been a much-anticipated feature of their eschatological doctrine. Given that it involves the secrets of cyclic time and resurrection, however, this aspect of the doctrine probably would have been more esoterically guarded than anything else. Perhaps this is why the secretive Hru Shemsu school was formed. The need to make the secret teachings obscure to the uninitiated is probably why the World Age concept in Western astrology is anchored to the equinox axis, and thus encodes the solstice "alignment" as an equinox "cross." Abydos, like the Sphinx and the Great Pyramid, was intimately involved in calibrating alignments in precession. We can only begin to wonder at the consistent obsession among the Egyptians with these alignments to the galaxy. Also, we may begin to question how old this knowledge is, and where it came from.

The Sphinx: The Time and Place of the First Time

The evidence at Abydos for an awareness of the equinox-galaxy alignment of era 4400 B.C. is intriguing, and ties in to the suggestive comments

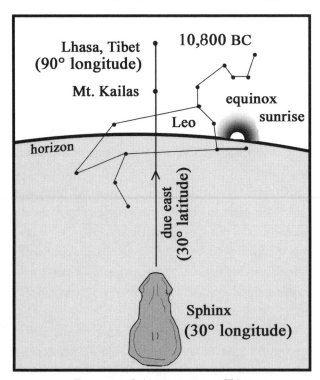

Figure 9.4. Sphinx pointing to Tibet

on the Egyptian origins of Greek sacred geography by Jean Richer quoted in chapter 7. It would not be surprising if Greek sacred topography was based on earlier Egyptian ideas, and that a metaphysical knowledge of alignments within the precessional cycle filtered down to Greece but became obscured as a more materialistic consciousness arose, leading to the birth of rationalism among the Greek philosophers. The "as above, so below" principle is alive and well in the findings of Richer, most notably in the geographical pointers formed by temple alignments and the directions faced by certain monuments, such as the Lion of Kea. Richer speculated that the Lion of Kea not only faced the winter-solstice sunrise but also was looking over at Egypt, hundreds of miles away. It faced not only a time (the solstice), but *a place*, the place in fact from which "it came"—or where its encoded wisdom originated. Perhaps we should take this seriously, and look again at the Sphinx, for deeper and more ancient mysteries may be lurking there.

Graham Hancock has maintained that the Sphinx, facing directly eastward, points to the time of the Zep Tepi, the Age of Leo. (Although the term Zep Tepi refers in Egyptian Creation texts to the dawn and creation of the universe, it is used in this context as a more recent "rebirth" event.) This was the fabled Golden Age of gods walking on Earth, of wisdom available to all, and when the current cycle of manifestation got its start: 10,800 B.C. And so we have the time, but why should we assume that Egypt was the place? Perhaps the Sphinx is pointing not only at the time of the fabled Golden Age, but the place as well? If we look at a world map and note the latitude of the Sphinx, and trace a line eastward across Saudi Arabia, Iran, and beyond, we pass by Mount Kailas, the sacred mountain of the Himalayas, into the upper plateau of Tibet, ending up precisely at Lhasa, the ancient capital of Tibetan religion and culture! Could Tibet, 10,800 B.C., be the time and the place of the Golden Age (see fig. 9.4)?

According to widely held beliefs, central Asia is the crucible of civilization out of which sprang the human peregrinations of the current cycle of history. Tibetan culture is believed to be one of the most ancient in the world, and shamanistic cultures to the north of Tibet, in Siberia, central Asia, and Tuva, preserve traditions that are at least 10,000 years old. Vedic culture in India to the south, as indicated in the Vedic literature, migrated from northern regions beyond the high mountains of the

Himalayas. In India and central Asia we find a vast repository, a living voice, that can trace a history going back 10,000 years. And, like Egypt, Vedic civilization has its own doctrine of a long-gone Golden Age, as well as a profound knowledge of the cycles of time, the descent of consciousness, and the unavoidable terminus and turnabout of history that we, of all generations, are currently experiencing. The Egyptian Sphinx, without a doubt, points us to India.

Despite the evidence in major European and Middle Eastern traditions surveyed thus far, we can still hear the call coming from further back in time, and from farther east—India. This is one of the few places that can compare to Egypt in the scale and scope of its vision and claim to an ancient lineage going back to the previous solstice-galaxy alignment of 10,800 B.C. In the Vedic conception of World Ages, as recorded in the Laws of Manu, we find detailed evidence for a knowledge of the Galactic Center and the role played by galactic alignments. We also find much more than compelling facts that indicate an ancient galactic gnosis; for in India we encounter a primordial tradition and a profound galactic metaphysics of spiritual transformation.

PART THREE

Vedic India and the Primordial Tradition

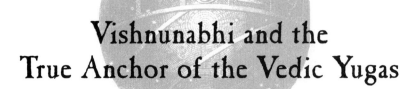

TEN

Vishnunabhi and the True Anchor of the Vedic Yugas

Our understanding of the true age of the ancient Vedic civilization has recently undergone a well-documented revolution. Feuerstein, Kak, and Frawley have shown conclusively (see their *In Search of the Cradle of Civilization*) that the long-accepted age of the Vedic culture—erroneously dated by scholars to roughly 1500 B.C.— is much too recent. Evidence for an older date comes from geological, archaeological, and literary sources, as well as the astronomical references within Vedic literature. The corrected dating was made possible by recognizing that precessional eras are encoded in Vedic mythology and were recorded by ancient Vedic astronomers. As a result, the Indus Valley civilization, dated conservatively to 7000 B.C., appears to be a possible cradle of civilization. There are layers upon layers of even older astronomical references, however, and legends persist that the true "cradle" might be found farther to the north, in Tibet or nearby central Asia.

The work of Feuerstein, Kak, and Frawley shows that, next to the Australian aborigines, the Vedic civilization is perhaps the oldest continuous living tradition in the world. Its ancient doctrines and insights into human spirituality are unsurpassed. We might expect that Vedic cosmology and its science of time has been as misunderstood as its true antiquity. In looking closely at Vedic doctrines of time and spiritual growth, at its calendars and astronomy, we shall see that the idea of our periodic alignment to the Galactic Center plays a central role. In addition, according to these ancient Vedic beliefs, the galactic alignment we are currently experiencing heralds a shift from a millennia-long descent of deepening spiritual darkness to a new era of light and ascending consciousness.

Vishnunabhi and the True Anchor of the Vedic Yugas

One of the oldest writings in Vedic literature is attributed to a mythical god-man called Manu. René Guénon pointed out that Manu belongs to a family of related archetypal figures that includes Melchezidek, Metatron, Saint Michael, Gabriel, and Enoch. As an angelic inspiration for the rebirth of humanity at the dawn of a new era, or *manvantara,* Manu is the primal lawgiver, and his laws were recorded in the ancient Vedic text called the Laws of Manu. Much of its contents describe moral and ethical codes of right behavior, but there is a section that deals with the ancient Vedic doctrine of World Ages, or *yugas.* Manu indicates that a period of 24,000 years—clearly a reference to precession—comprises a series of four *yugas* or ages, each shorter and spiritually darker than the previous. In one story this process of increasing limitation is envisioned as a cosmic cow standing with each leg in one quarter of the world; with each age that passes a leg is lost, resulting in the absurd and unstable world we live in today—a cow balancing on one leg.

According to the information in the Laws of Manu, the morning and twilight periods between the dawn of each new era equal one-tenth of their associated *yuga,* as shown in the following:

DAWN ERA DUSK TOTAL	NAME
400 + 4000 + 400 = 4,800 years	Satya Yuga (Golden Age)
300 + 3000 + 300 = 3,600 years	Treta Yuga (Silver Age)
200 + 2000 + 200 = 2,400 years	Dwapara Yuga (Bronze Age)
100 + 1000 + 100 = <u>1,200</u> years	Kali Yuga (Iron Age)
12,000 years	

In Vedic mythology, a fabled dawn time existed in the distant past, when human beings had direct contact with the divine intelligence emanating from Brahma—the seat of creative power and intelligence in the cosmos. This archaic Golden Age (the Satya Yuga) lasted some 4,800 years. After the Golden Age ended, humanity entered a denser era, that of the Silver Age, lasting only 3,600 years. In this age, humanity's connection with the source was dimmed, and sacrifices and spiritual practices became necessary to preserve it. The Bronze Age followed, and humanity forgot its divine nature. Empty dogmas arose, along with indulgence in materialism. Next we entered the Kali Yuga—in which we remain today—where the human spirit suffers under gross materialism, ignorance, warfare, stupidity, arrogance, and everything contrary to our divine spiritual potential.

As the teachings tell, Kali, the creator-destroyer goddess, will appear at the end of Kali Yuga to sweep away the wasted detritus of a spirit-dead humanity, making way for a new cycle of light and peace. The process described in the Manu text takes us from the pinnacle of light to the ultimate end point—the darkness and dissolution of Kali Yuga. Notice that the four ages, when the overlap period is added, amount to only half of the 24,000-year period of the Vedic *yuga* cycle. This points to an obscure aspect of the doctrine that a Hindu master, Sri Yukteswar, sought to clarify.

Sri Yukteswar's Update

Sri Yukteswar was a Hindu saint active in the late 1800s and early 1900s. He was the master of the famous Yogananda, founder of the Self-Realization Fellowship and author of *Autobiography of a Yogi*. Yukteswar was interested in contemporary scientific advances and in showing parallels between Hindu religion and Christianity. His book *The Holy Science* is primarily about these correspondences. It was written in the mid-1890s at the behest of his teacher, Mahavatar Babaji; its introduction contains an intriguing clarification of the World Age system of the *yugas*.

Although the exact timing of the Kali Yuga's beginning is subject to debate, no one argues that we are deep into it. Unfortunately, the cycles and year-counts of Hindu chronology are subject to gross exaggerations and manipulation—the sorry effect of scholars trying to reconstruct the ancient doctrines. These errors have been inserted into doctrines as long ago as the fourth century A.D., and have been passed down to unsuspecting students as a kind of conventional wisdom. However, it strikes me that Sri Yukteswar got closest to the true intention of the *yuga* doctrine. Yukteswar based his "updated *yuga* model" on the Laws of Manu as well as other traditions in Vedic and Hindu astronomy and mythology. In the tradition he describes, "the sun, with its planets and their moons, takes some star for its dual and revolves around it in about 24,000 years of our earth—a celestial phenomenon [precession]. . . . The sun also has another

Figure 10.1. Jnanavatar Swami Sri Yukteswar Giri
(photo courtesy of Self-Realization Fellowship)

motion by which it revolves around a grand center called Vishnunabhi, which is the seat of creative power, Brahma, the universal magnetism. Brahma regulates dharma, the mental virtue of the internal world."[1] In reading an account like this, it is immediately apparent that things could be worded more clearly. But there is a huge grain of wisdom inside Yukteswar's description, and it is worth looking at closely. Let us see if we can read between the lines and get a sense for what Yukteswar is really referring to.

We have an important identification of the "grand center" as Vishnunabhi or Brahma, the seat of creative power. Vishnunabhi is the navel of the god Vishnu, the emanation point of the cosmos, and modern Vedic scholar David Frawley identifies Vishnunabhi with the Galactic Center. In his 1990 book *Astrology of the Seers* he writes, "The galactic center is called 'Brahma,' the creative force, or 'Vishnunabhi,' the navel of Vishnu. From the galactic sun emanates the light which determines the life and intelligence on Earth."[2] Without mincing words, it is clear that the ancient Vedic skywatchers were aware of the Galactic Center, and, indeed, considered it to be the center and source of creative power in the universe. Again, as I've argued for the ancient Mayan skywatchers, recognizing the Galactic Center as an important place along the Milky Way is completely within the possibility of naked-eye observation (although that may not have been the only method used).

Yukteswar suggests that the Sun "takes a star for its dual" and revolves around it in one precessional cycle. Clearly, the reference is not to an actual orbital period, such as the Moon orbiting around the earth, but is rather to the *precessional shifting* of the Sun around the zodiac. If the sun's dual is a fixed star against which the Sun's precessional motion is measured, then we can understand this more clearly. Now, in order to measure the precessional motion of the Sun, the ancient astronomers would have needed to identify a specific "sun," or solar position, in the seasonal cycle—for example, the vernal-equinox sun or the summer-solstice sun. This specification will anchor the Sun to a seasonal quarter so that the "orbital" motion referred to by Yukteswar (which is really precessional shifting) can be measured against a fixed sidereal location, the Sun's "dual." Aldebaran might be a candidate, but the real fixed "dual" against which the cycle of precession is tracked in this Vedic description may actually be Vishnunabhi—the Galactic Center.

Yukteswar also mentions "another motion" of the Sun around the Galactic Center, which is probably its actual orbital period—a huge cycle of some 225,000,000 years. Although it is striking that he mentions this (writing back in the 1890s), this larger cycle applies to the meaning of multiple precessional cycles and is not relevant to the immediate question under consideration. Yukteswar goes on to say that "when the sun in its revolution around its dual comes to the place nearest to this grand center, the seat of Brahma (an event which takes place when the Autumnal Equinox comes to the first point of Aries), dharma, the mental virtue, becomes so much developed that man can easily comprehend all, even the mysteries of the spirit."[3]

The precessional movement of "the Sun" closer to "the grand center" causes the full expression of a Golden Age of light, a time indicated in Vedic traditions as occurring a dozen or so millennia ago. As such, it must be the precessional motion of the June solstice sun around the grand center that is indicated, because the June solstice sun was "closest to" the Galactic Center roughly 12,000 to 13,000 years ago. I should emphasize that this "closeness" is in terms of alignment (as viewed from Earth), not distance. Unfortunately, Yukteswar attempts a precise dating based upon a 12,000-year period for one-half of a precession cycle. As a result, he backdates to the time of the fabled Golden Age (which he later gives as 11,501 B.C.) by using an autumnal equinox point in Aries that is in error. Yukteswar's diagram (fig. 10.2) preserves the important insight of a descending phase and an ascending phase of the precessional cycle, but the timing of the shift from descending Kali Yuga to ascending Kali Yuga must be adjusted.

The outer wheel shows the descent of time clockwise from the Age of Leo at the top, when the June solstice sun was closest to the "grand center." The shaded wheel indicates the equinoctial age of precession according to the unadjusted Western zodiac. The inner wheel shows the actual sidereal position of the solstice axis. Why the need for an adjustment? Sri Yukteswar wanted the end of descending Kali Yuga to correspond to his historical understanding—based on a nineteenth-century education—of the European Dark Ages and his belief in the elevation of human consciousness beginning around A.D. 500. He cites scientific advances and Europe's slow emergence from the Dark Ages to support this, but in my opinion, technology has thrust us deeper into material dependency and spiritual darkness. Yukteswar's scenario is Eurocentric and ignores Islamic and Chinese civilization. In addition, his elucidation depends on certain astronomical details of the ancient doctrines that, by his time, had eroded into semantic vagaries. Finally, he was writing before modern science had rediscovered the Galactic Center. Although I have changed Yukteswar's reading, my conclusions—and corrections—are fairly straightforward.

Let's look at it this way: Yukteswar writes that the Golden Age ended and we began our descent into spiritual darkness in 11,501 B.C. This was roughly 13,500 years ago. Now, Yukteswar also said that this Golden Age occurred when "the Sun" was close to Vishnunabhi (the Galactic Center). And the context of his description is solar movements within the cycle of

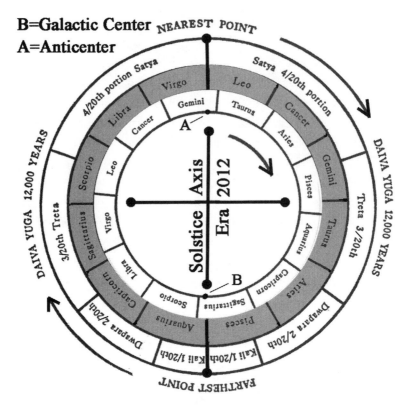

Figure 10.2. Yukteswar's *yuga* model, adjusted. Yukteswar's original diagram assumes
A.D. 500 as the commencement of the ascending Kali Yuga. This adjusted version
places it on the solstice-galaxy alignment of era A.D. 2012.

precession. Now, the question we must ask is this: what kind of precessional alignment between the Sun and the Galactic Center happened roughly 13,500 years ago, *the reverse of which happens one-half of a precession cycle later?* The answer is readily apparent—the Golden Age shift is timed with the alignment of the June solstice sun and the Galactic Center. The opposite event is the alignment of the December solstice sun with the Galactic Center, and we can get a true bearing on the timing of this event, as modern astronomy has calculated it. We must shift these timing parameters to accord with solstice-galaxy alignments, and therefore we have two dates: era A.D. 2000 and era 10,800 B.C. There are actually several factors and features involved in the timing issue that enrich our understanding of what these galactic alignments might mean to us. (I shall address the issues and parameters of the current galactic alignment in part 5.)

An important implication in this material is that the Golden Age mentioned by Yukteswar represented the culmination of the previous ascent phase and the shift to the descending phase, the archaic "fall of man" scenario. The flip side—the shift to the ascending phase—therefore occurs at the astronomically opposed event (ca. A.D. 2000): "After 12,000 years, when the sun goes to the place in its orbit which is farthest from Brahma, the grand center . . . [then] dharma, the mental virtue, comes to such a reduced state that man cannot grasp anything beyond the gross material creation."[4] This is the Vedic doctrine, clearly based in astronomy, that underlies René Guénon's belief that modern people are unconscious degenerates with little resemblance to the full human potential that our ancient ancestors manifested. Furthermore, as we shall see shortly, it underlies and defines the end of the Kali Yuga that Guénon (without being specific) foresaw occurring very soon.

The Galactic Dimensions of Vedic Astrology

Vedic scholar and teacher David Frawley has further clarified Yukteswar's model: "When the Sun is on the side of its orbit wherein its dark companion comes between it and the galactic center, the reception of that cosmic light appears to be greatly reduced. At such times there is a dark or materialistic age on Earth."[5] I would add that the June solstice sun's "dark companion" could be the December solstice sun, the day of greatest darkness in the solar year. In this scenario, the June solstice sun continually revolves around (in opposition to) the December solstice sun. Whether or not there is an actual occulting of the June solstice sun in terms of energetic radiation may simply be beside the point; the metaphor points us to the astronomy involved in this doctrine and the Vedic belief system woven through it.

The critical information encoded in Yukteswar's book—written decades before the Galactic Center was "officially" discovered in the 1920s—is that the ancient Vedic *yuga* doctrine was calibrated with the periodic alignments of the solstice sun and the Galactic Center. If we do sense that the Vedic wisdom speaks a truth to us (nothing less than a lost science of the galactic influences on human evolution), the words of David Frawley may help us understand the importance of our impending "harmonization" with the Galactic Center:

An important cosmic event is occurring now. The winter solstice is now at a point in conjunction with the galactic center. . . . This should cause a slow harmonization of humanity with the Divine will as transmitted from the galactic center. . . . By the accounts of thinkers like Plato, the flood that destroyed Atlantis (and probably ended the Ice Age) occurred about 9300 B.C. (9000 years before Plato). This appears to have been when the summer solstice was in conjunction with the galactic center—a point completely opposite to the one today.[6]

In fact, Frawley believes that all of Vedic astrology "orients the zodiac to the galactic center" as the source of creative intelligence, mediated to human beings by the fixed stars of Sagittarius and the guru planet Jupiter, the divine teacher.[7] Frawley gives an astronomically accurate sidereal location for the Galactic Center: 6°40' Sagittarius. This corresponds to 28° Sagittarius in the unadjusted tropical system, wherein the December solstice is nearby at 0° Capricorn (by definition). Again, the precise parameters of the galactic alignment will be explored later.

The lunar mansions of Vedic astrology indicate the Galactic Center region as a "root" place. The *nakśastra,* or lunar mansion, corresponding to the 13°-wide lunar "sign" that embraces the Galactic Center is called *mula,* which means "root." The mansion that occurs before "root" is called "the eldest," suggesting that this spot in the sky is the end-beginning nexus in an ancient concept of the zodiac, which would be understandable given the precessional importance of the Galactic Center as a "root" or beginning point for time. This material augments the Hindu and Islamic information about the lunar south node being exalted at 3° Sagittarius.

There are compelling events in Hindu-Vedic mythology that are associated with the Galactic Center, Sagittarius, the theft of soma, and the solstices. These events compose a Vedic metaphysics of spiritual transcendence. However, many eras of overlapping symbology make it difficult to sort out the original meaning with certainty. The head of the horse, the Aśvin twins, and the Churning of the Milky Ocean myth are all involved. The head of the horse and the head of the *simśumara* crocodile (or *makara*) could very well be the bulging area of the nuclear bulge with the dark-rift mouth. The story of the Aśvin twins is symbolically identical to the Hero Twins in the *Popol Vuh:* they facilitate the resurrection of their father, the winter-solstice sun.

According to Frawley, there do appear to be mythologically descriptive references in the Vedas to precessional eras in which the solstice point was in a constellation that would indicate a dating of 7000 B.C. The records are found in stories in which the lunar mansion occupied by the full moon during the solstice is mentioned, thus providing a 13°-wide lunar mansion position for the solstice point. These references seem to confirm that Vedic astronomy and cosmology is much older than scholars have been willing to allow.

The Gnostic Circle and Patrizia Norelli-Bachelet

My work to reconstruct Mayan cosmology led me to understand its galactic nature. Specifically, I discovered overwhelming evidence that the Maya intended their 2012 end-date to mark the alignment of the December solstice sun with the Milky Way and the Galactic Center. After showing how the Maya encoded this knowledge into their Creation myth, king accession rites, and the sacred ball game, I wondered if this knowledge was present in other traditions. My hunch was confirmed when I came across *The Gnostic Circle* by Patrizia Norelli-Bachelet.

Norelli-Bachelet is a disciple of Aurobindo and his spiritual partner, known as the Mother, and in 1968 was involved in the building activities at Auroville, a spiritual center in India. She worked closely with the Mother on the design and symbology of the Mátrimandir, a temple shrine designed to replicate the godhead on Earth. It was strategically situated at 12° north latitude in India so as to synthesize the local zenith-passage date with the grand center. Immediately this jumped out at me as a reflection of what the Maya did at Chichen Itza, when they unified the zenith-Pleiades cosmology with the galactic cosmology. Briefly, the Matrimandir was built at the latitude at which the Sun passes through the zenith on August 22; on that date the Sun is at 29° Leo, passing into 0° Virgo. These degrees are exactly opposite 29° Aquarius and 0° Pisces, which indicate the present location of the equinox axis as we move into the new Age of Aquarius. As with other systems we've described, the implied (and more important) reference here actually involves the solstice axis, 90° away, which will therefore be at 0° Capricorn-Cancer—or 6° Sagittarius-Gemini when we adjust for the actual sidereal position. This position is the Galactic Center–Galactic Anticenter axis. Simply stated,

Figure 10.3. The Matrimandir

the Matrimandir indicates the zenith center and the Galactic Center at the same time. In addition, polar symbolism is also integrated into descriptions of its meaning. Thus, as with Mayan cosmology, three cosmic centers and axial directions were combined into one fully integrated conception.

According to Norelli-Bachelet, while the Matrimandir was built at the spot intended, the design specified by the Mother was altered by the builders at Auroville. Critical geometrical relationships were changed and a subversion of the original design occurred, thereby rendering the initiatory chamber useless. Norelli-Bachelet emphasizes that the wisdom of the Mother's specific requirements were ignored by the builders, and her book *The New Way* explains the issues involved. Unfortunately, this misguided appropriation of a spiritual vision seems to occur when a higher-dimensional perspective is downloaded into a more limited framework of conceptualization. In a similar way, modern physical sciences are but pro-fane shadows of the ancient sacred sciences. But Norelli-Bachelet, in service to the Mother's original vision, defends and gives voice to the original design of the Matrimandir.

The Gnostic Circle is a deep, intuitive, and complex work. Norelli-Bachelet draws from a great reservoir of Hindu wisdom, obviously com-bined with personal insights into the nature of time and human spirituality. It contains an almost matter-of-fact description of the evolu-tionary implications of our periodic alignments with the Galactic Center:

> There is the mysterious centre that keeps all the stars in orbit around itself. This Centre, that Science knows so little of as yet, is located with respect to our Sun and planet in the direction of the Constellation Her-cules or the zodiacal sign Capricorn, and slowly, at the rate of 12 miles per second . . . our sun orbits around and moves closer to this Solar Apex, as it is called. That is, at the end of December each year, the Earth is directly behind the sun with respect to this great Void; our solar sys-tem with our planet is being drawn ever closer to this colossal Magnet.[8]

As with Yukteswar's description, one must read this one very carefully to determine what is being described. Here we are again confronted with the question of whether the statement refers to the Sun's literal orbital cycle around the great center, or whether the reference is to the Sun's pre-cessional motion around the zodiac. As with Yukteswar, Norelli-Bachelet's intention is the latter. In fact, later on in *The Gnostic Circle* we get a clarification on this point. In discussing the shifting of the poles caused by precession, she writes, "The shifting of the poles themselves . . . is connected with the movement of our solar system around the galactic centre. . . . Our solar system, the Sun with all its orbiting bodies, is slowly being drawn into this Centre—or is moving ever closer into the sign of Capricorn, we could say."[9] This demonstrates that the Sun's "orbit" around the Galactic Center is actually the apparent motion of the Sun around the zodiac, caused by precession.[10]

The spiritual importance of our changing relationship to the Galactic Center is elucidated by Norelli-Bachelet:

At this time, we are given the means whereby we can know the so-called esoteric truth of our System and its evolution, and the part the Earth plays therein, as well as each of its inhabitants. We can go so far as to know that there is a great Centre to which we in our System are related and which determines our course, because it is this Centre that finally holds the key to the Precession of the Equinoxes. It is this Centre that makes of the axis Capricorn and Cancer the Evolutionary Axis of our planet. And through our study we can know that in ourselves, in our very bodies, we can find the exact reproduction of this Galaxy which then gives us the revelation of the Supreme Herself.[11]

The Evolutionary Axis described between Capricorn and Cancer is the Galactic Center–Galactic Anticenter axis. I have described this as the galactic chakra axis, and during alignment eras the *shakti* or evolutionary energy emanating from the root chakra—the Galactic Center—awakens all of the consciousness centers along the axis, including Earth and the Pleiades. Elsewhere Norelli-Bachelet writes that evolutionary avatars (like Aurobindo and the Mother) incarnate on Earth every 6,480 years, and we are in one of these evolutionary periods right now.[12] The span of 6,480 years clearly refers to one-quarter of a precessional cycle. Four times every precessional cycle, one of the seasonal quarters lines up with the Galactic Center. We are currently in the precessional window in which it is the December solstice that lines up with the Galactic Center. The profound integrative conclusion to be grasped is that this situation heralds the shift from descending Kali Yuga to ascending Kali Yuga.

The Gnostic Circle anticipated my explication of a similar galactic cosmology among the Maya, yet I was unaware of Norelli-Bachelet's work until 1999. In chapter 7 we found the concepts of the solstice gateways and the Capricorn-Cancer axis in Jean Richer's work on the sacred geography of the Greeks. There, we saw how the polar *axis mundi* was mapped onto a north-south axis centered on Delphi that symbolically corresponded to a Capricorn-Cancer "solstice" axis. The topographical axis Richer reconstructed stretched from the temple site of Taenarum in the south (Cancer), through Delphi (the navel or omphalos), to Mount Olympus in the north (Capricorn). Notice that Olympus, abode of the gods, where a convocation was held every winter solstice, symbolically occupies the Capricorn or Galactic Center position. As was the case with the Capricorn-Sagittarius conflict evident in Richer, Norelli-Bachelet may have derived her Capricorn location from Guénon's work, particularly his *Formes traditionnelles et cycles cosmiques,* or other writings on Vedic symbolism.

It is by now quite apparent that these ancient Vedic doctrines point not only to a spot in the sky, but also to specific times within the precessional cycle. The solstice at 0° Capricorn is eternally fixed by definition within the unadjusted zodiac still used by Western tropical astrologers. In that system the Galactic Center is at 28° Sagittarius, or 2° from 0° Capricorn. Now, precession has shifted the artificial frame of the zodiacal signs some twenty-two degrees such that the true sidereal position of the solstice meridian is actually in early Sagittarius, in alignment with the galaxy. Thus, the *place* of importance is the Galactic Center (in early Sagittarius). And the *time* is now.

Fragments of Ancient Wisdom

Looking further afield, there is a bizarre and obscure literary work that bears mentioning here, as it indicates that the importance of the Galactic Center's sidereal location at 6° Sagittarius has been floating around in esoteric circles since the early 1900s. Valentia Straiton's *The Celestial Ship of the North,* published in 1927, is a seductive but frustratingly oblique ramble on occult topics, with many references to astronomy. Sources are often lacking, and the presumption is that what is being shared is a body of esoteric knowledge operating behind the scenes of conventional science and religion. And some of the material anticipates the scientific discovery of the Galactic Center, not to mention the galactic cosmology. In one passage we read: "The 6th degree of Sagittarius is perhaps the most remarkable in the Southern Hemisphere, and of equal importance is this same 6th degree of its opposite sign in the north, which corresponds to the magnetic pole of the ecliptic of the heaven."[13] This statement describes the Galactic Center–Galactic Anticenter axis. And yet no mention is made of the center of the galaxy, apart from occasional reference to the "spiritual sun." The sacred ogdoad of the early Christian Gnostics might be the same as this occult spiritual sun, and it is said to be "the sun behind the Sun"—possibly meaning the Sun in alignment with the Galactic Center. Even more bizarre is a secondary reference in *The Celestial Ship of the North* to a quote by one Edgar Conrow—who I have been unable to locate anywhere.[14] One assumes the following statement is from a public talk or personal correspondence with Straiton and occurred, at the very latest, in the mid-1920s. Astoundingly, Conrow directly associates the "North Gate" with the pineal gland:

> The Pineal Gland is the "North Gate." This, in man, is the central spiritual creative center. Above in the heavens, it is found in the beginning of this sign Sagittarius, and is the point from which spiritual gifts are given. It is called "Vision of God," and is the Light within, a gift to the pure in heart, who verily may "see God," but to the impure or those who abuse this great gift the consequences are terrible.
>
> This North Gate, the creative center in man, the most interior center in the body, has become atrophied, and redemption or regeneration means its restoration to creative ability, by having the electrical or positive and the magnetic or negative forces restored in equal balance in man or woman.[15]

Notice that the Galactic Center is never named directly, which may be reminiscent of archaic prohibitions against saying the true name of the deity. While the identity of these sources is mysterious, the true mystery is that this information doesn't appear in the literature more often, as anyone could see it, simply by looking at the sky.

Somehow the ancient galactic knowledge has filtered down through the ages, preserved in occult circles and in compelling statements in obscure sources. Or perhaps the universal wisdom is reentering the ongoing discussion by way of a renewed higher-dimensional contact. Nevertheless, two celebrated scholars—René Guénon and Ananda Coomaraswamy—have also been drawn into the same mystery. Guénon came to the topic from various angles, most notably in the context of exploring traditional symbolism and the Vedic *yuga* doctrine. Coomaraswamy's essays and books on Oriental iconography and metaphysics leave little doubt as to the true location of the "north gate," which is the "Sundoor at World's End"—the solar gateway leading into the next world.

ELEVEN

Coomaraswamy and Guénon Point the Way

I n my exploration of Vedic scholarship and the issues of the solstice-galaxy alignment, I was led to the writings of Ananda Coomaraswamy and René Guénon. As the primary exponents of the Traditionalist school of thought, these scholars provide the keys to understanding the temporal dimension of the Primordial Tradition. And their lives prove to be as interesting as their work.[1]

Ananda Coomaraswamy

Ananda Kentish Coomaraswamy was born in Ceylon, August 22, 1877. His father, Sir Mutu, was a prominent member of the legislative council in Ceylon, and, while visiting England, he met Elizabeth Clay Beeby. They married in 1876 and moved into a mansion in Columbo, Ceylon. A year later Ananda was born. Mother and child returned to England the following year and were to be followed by Sir Mutu. He died unexpectedly, however, on the day of his departure for England; Ananda was two years old.

Growing up in England among his mother's relatives, Coomaraswamy developed an interest in the natural sciences. By age twenty-five he had received a bachelors in geology and botany from University College in London, having spent a year studying geology in Ceylon. After graduation he returned to Ceylon with his new wife, Ethel, and undertook geological field research, publishing maps while discovering deposits of mica, graphite, corundum, and other minerals. Over the next decade Coomaraswamy traveled throughout India, collecting Indian art treasures, and became friends with the poet Rabindranath Tagore as well as activists in the Ceylonese Social Reform Society. These were the days of

India's rebellion from the tyranny of British rule. At the time, Indian art was considered by the standard-bearers of art history to be degenerate, clumsy, and crude, in service to anti-Christian idolatry. In 1908 Coomaraswamy's photographic collection, *Mediaeval Sinhalese Art*, demonstrated that Oriental art matched and often exceeded, in its subtlety and skill of craftsmanship, the best in classical Greco-Roman forms.

Returning to England several times between 1908 and 1916, he wrote and published various papers and criticized the death of traditional crafts as mass production divorced people from an age-old connection with creative meaning and self-sustaining craft. In his view, a person's craft represented a connection to an ancient life current and was a way that people participated in ancient folk customs and the higher spirit of religion. Mechanized production was perceived as a threat to humanity's daily connection to the spiritual root of life, destroying the idea of work as a yoga, a way of connection to the divine. As his interest in religious forms and traditions grew, he mastered Sanskrit, Latin, and other languages. While overcoming conventional views he became well known as an insightful commentator on both Oriental and Occidental mythology and iconography. Many of his books, among them *What Is Civilization?*, *The Dance of Śiva, and Hinduism and Buddhism,* are still considered classics. In 1916 he immigrated to America, where he became a curator at the Boston Museum of Fine Arts. He contributed hundreds of pieces from his own collection to the museum's already extensive holdings, and engaged in several art-collecting journeys to India. In the 1920s he settled into life in America and entered into a third marriage, his first two having ended in divorce. His essays and articles during this period reflect his focus on art history, displaying comparative skill but ignoring the symbolic content of the metaphysical and religious symbolism. Toward the end of the 1920s, however, his third marriage dissolved, and Coomaraswamy underwent a transformation, one that generated a greater interest in the religious content of art. As his thinking evolved between 1928 and 1932, the geologist turned art historian became an academic metaphysician. Ratiocination intact, intuitive senses finely honed, his purpose became subsumed into a higher call to elucidate religious and metaphysical symbolism and wisdom.

In 1932 Coomaraswamy was appointed Research Fellow at the Boston Museum of Fine Arts, a position he held until his death in 1947. In the early thirties he also encountered the work of René Guénon, and they developed a professional relationship and a mutual appreciation for each other's work. Their correspondence is not extensive, but they frequently quoted from each other's work and developed similar attitudes to the ancient doctrines and motifs they were exploring "together at a distance," Coomaraswamy in Boston and Guénon in Cairo. The interpretive paradigm they developed gave voice to the same universal wisdom—an eternal and universal wisdom that became known as the *sophia perennis et universalis,* or the Primordial Tradition. This point is important, because both writers knew that their function was to serve the higher wisdom, to act as midwives to its reemergence into human consciousness. They both avoided personalizing labels and shunned being identified as spiritual teachers.

The years between 1932 and 1947 saw the writing of Coomaraswamy's most important essays. Most of these were collected into two volumes, published by Princeton University Press in 1977. The themes of the essays range widely, but most important for our present discussion are the Scorpion Men who guard the gates of paradise; the clashing cliffs that, as in the Argo's narrow escape, present a do-or-die moment of quick decision to the seeker; the story of the theft of soma; and the cycles of time in Vedic cosmology. Also, Coomaraswamy explored the distinction between sacred and secular power as a fundamental cause of modern civilization's inability to connect with the transcendent realm.

Many other essays were partially finished and never published, and we will explore one of these, "Early Iconography of Sagittarius," in chapter 13. Coomaraswamy influenced many twentieth-century scholars, including Heinrich Zimmer, Joseph Campbell, and Alan Watts.

Coomaraswamy died unexpectedly in 1947, several weeks after his seventieth birthday. He was planning on retiring with his wife to northern India, to end his days in spiritual contemplation of the truths he had intellectually mastered. It is not possible to overestimate Coomaraswamy's great contribution to reconstructing the lost artifacts of the Primordial Tradition. Other writers who share or have shared in the milieu of the Primordial Tradition include Julius Evola, Frithjof Schuon, Henry Corbin, Martin Lings, and Seyyed Hossein Nasr. But it is in the work of René Guénon that we find not only a colleague and contemporary of Coomaraswamy, but a match for his ability to make sense of both ancient wisdom and our modern crisis.

René Guénon

René Jean-Marie-Joseph Guénon was born on November 15, 1886, in Blois, France. The son of an architect, he had a traditional Catholic upbringing. Although a sickly child, at school he excelled in philosophy and mathematics. When he was twelve he entered Notre Dame des Aydes, a secondary school run by priests that was equivalent to a junior seminary. He mastered his subjects quickly and was considered a brilliant student, often standing first in his class. At age fifteen, however, he left the school following an incident in which he fell ill after quarreling with a teacher who poorly graded one of his essays. He entered another college in 1902 and continued to excel as a student of Latin and philosophy. After graduating with high regard from his teachers, he moved to Paris to continue his studies, but poor health rendered him unable to attend many classes. He had taken a room in the Latin Quarter, but the rowdy student atmosphere was distracting, so he located a quiet apartment on the Isle Saint Louis where he could devote himself entirely to study. He lived there for twenty-five years, up to the moment he left for Egypt in 1930. His poor attendance at the university caused him to fall behind "the examination standard," so he voluntarily terminated his university studies.

In 1907, Guénon was twenty years old, and Paris was a world of esoteric and occult schools in full ferment. Societies devoted to spirituality ranged from respected Oriental lineages to "table raisers" and Ouija board dealers. Guénon's activities during this period are unclear. He seems to have run in different circles at the same time, though early on he was initiated into the Shivaite line of Advaita Vedanta by a Hindu teacher visiting Paris. We have no details as to the time or place of this initiation, but the encounter appears to have been both providential and intense. Contact with his Hindu teachers ended definitively in a year or two. Thereafter, Guénon was involved with the Hermetic School, which published a journal called *L'Initiation* in 1909. In his various associations with spiritualists, he came to criticize their efforts to evoke spirits from the "subconscious" as well as the way that certain fly-by-night teachers designed their own teachings as a hodgepodge amalgamation of authentic living traditions. He particularly criticized Blavatsky and the Theosophical movement as a pale reflection of the Hindu teachings that, if one truly studied and understood them, made the ad hoc "modernized" versions unnecessary. In fact, the modern derivations could be seen as being essentially deceptive and misleading, evidence that the intellect in our modern age distorts truth.

Here we encounter the crux of Guénon's critique of Western civilization: Modern civilization has become divorced from the transcendent realm, which in former ages was consciously integrated into daily life. The modern world fails to understand the meaning of the word *transcendent* as well as the meaning of the word *intellect*. In the traditional usage—which corresponds to the Sanskrit word for mind, *buddhi*—*intellect* means the perception of transcendent realities, the faculty that can perceive the activity of the higher worlds. Notice that this doesn't correspond to the modern idea of being "intellectual" or "smart." We can see here that the intellect is a faculty for perceiving, directly, our relationship with higher realities rather than something someone acquires through study and schooling. It is ironic that modern civilization effectively erodes the original *buddhi* mind of pure intellection that is the birthright of everyone, even while it educates and indoctrinates us. In addition, the myth of progress allows modern civilization to masquerade as the most sophisticated in all of human history. For Guénon and the other Traditionalist writers, however, this is a reversal of the true situation: modern civilization is not the result of progress, it is the civilization of the Kali Yuga, the darkest age, in which humanity, obsessed with materialism, has been completely removed from a direct experience of connection with the higher source.

Martin Lings, translator of Guénon's *East and West*, writes that Guénon may have experienced some kind of direct intellectual illumination at an early age.[2] France was in tumult during World War I, Guénon was thirty years old, and he knew that the world was heading in the wrong direction. After the war, antireligious sentiment among the French intelligentsia indicated that new levels of decadence were imminent, and for Guénon this meant a further distancing of humanity from its traditional roots. After a stint teaching in Algeria, he returned to France, and in 1921 his first book, *Introduction to the Study of Hindu Doctrines*, was published, followed in 1925 by his classic *Man and His Becoming According to the Vedanta*. During this time he contributed essays to *La Gnose*, *Regnabit*, and *La Voile d'Isis*, as well as the journal that would eventually be called *Études Traditionnelles*. His collected essays were published after his death in the book *Fundamental Symbols: The Universal Language of Sacred Science*, only recently available in English. The 1920s also saw the publication of some of his most important works, including *East and West* (1924); *Theosophy: History of a Pseudo-Religion* (1921); *The Esoterism of Dante* (1925); *The Lord of the World* (1927); and *Crisis of the Modern World* (1927).

As the 1920s drew to a close, Guénon lost his wife of sixteen years, Berthe Loury. They had no children but had raised a niece whom Guénon had loved "as his own daughter and spoiled . . . greatly."[3] Decisive events unfolded that led Guénon to take a trip to Egypt in 1930, and he never returned to France. In Islam Guénon found a living tradition that was, in many respects, halfway between East and West, Oriental yet Western. His transformation into a practicing Muslim took place at the same time as Coomaraswamy's shift to a scholar-metaphysician, mentioned earlier. And around this time they first encountered each other's work. Guénon lived in Cairo unobtrusively, wishing to have little contact with his former life and the "outside world" in general. Speaking flawless Arabic, he adopted the customs of his new country, integrated himself into the rhythms of Islam, and became known not as René Guénon but as Sheikh 'Abd al-Wahid Yahya. In his first two years as an expatriate, Guénon completed his books *Symbolism of the Cross* and *Multiple States of Being*. His most important book of his later years was *The Reign of Quantity*, an insightfully argued critique of the fundamental errors of modern civilization, published in 1945.

While performing devotions at a local mosque, Guénon became friends with his future father-in-law. In July 1934 he married, and seven years later he and his wife, Fatma, were surprised when they had the first of their four children. Guénon's integration into Islamic society was complete when he had a friend send him his remaining belongings from France in 1935, and after his father-in-law died he moved with his wife to a greenery-sheltered little cottage in a quiet district just ten minutes from downtown Cairo. He called the home Villa Fatma, out of affection for his wife. Here Guénon studied, prayed, corresponded, and wrote articles and books, most notably for the French journal *Études Traditionnelles*. He was seen by his neighbors as an honorable sheikh, and they had no knowledge of his true identity. In fact, one neighbor who was an appreciative reader of Guénon's books was shocked when he died in 1951 and she realized that the devotional and kindly old Muslim gentleman down the street was Guénon himself![4]

Guénon's *Reign of Quantity and the Signs of the Times* is his final word on the causes of modern civilization's downward spiral. But the collected essays in *Fundamental Symbols* reveal Guénon as a premiere symbolist philosopher and the primary exponent of the Traditionalist school of thought. That Guénon collaborated with and influenced the brilliant scholar Ananda Coomaraswamy reveals enough about his qualifications as a scholar. He also influenced Julius Evola, Frithjof Schuon, and Mircea Eliade. Although he is barely known in the United States and his books, though reprinted recently, cannot be found in mainstream bookstores nor often in college libraries, as a committed devotee of the perennial wisdom, his works have perennial value.

Coomaraswamy and Guénon are twin spirits who strove to elucidate the Primordial Tradition according to their own abilities, which essentially complemented each other. Guénon's intellect was razor sharp, and he concerned himself with abstract metaphysical concepts; rarely did he venture into aesthetics, and never did he emotionally proselytize. Coomaraswamy, on the other hand, was both an intellect of high standing and a talented photographer. His aesthetic interests led him to acquire precious art pieces from all over the Orient, which he bequeathed to the Boston Museum of Fine Arts. They had dialectically opposed styles, and, as one writer put it, "if they agreed about their main conclusions, as indeed they did, one can yet describe them as temperamentally poles apart."[5] This statement is all the more interesting when you look at the astrological birth charts of these two thinkers. Born almost exactly nine and a quarter years apart (Guénon the younger), their lunar nodes are exactly opposed. Astronomically, the lunar node positions indicate where eclipses can occur; they indicate the intersection of the lunar orbit and the solar orbit, which are slightly skewed in relation to each other. Astrologically, the lunar south node indicates one's past achievements and failings while the lunar north node indicates one's work in this life, one's mission or destiny—where one can contribute and grow. A parent and child will often have opposed node placements, which can result in strife and misunderstanding. That Coomaraswamy and Guénon realized they were not at odds with each other, but approached the same problems from different sides, testifies to their inherent greatness of spirit.

The challenge they both shared involved giving voice to the lost elements of the Primordial Tradition. Their work spans many fields of study and it is not possible to do justice or even to summarize here their respective monumental outputs. A little-examined area in the thought of Coomaraswamy and Guénon needs clarification, however, and it has to do with the timing of the end of Kali Yuga, a subject that threads its way through Guénon's writings. And the mythological motifs and astronomical references that come into play in this question are found in the most brilliant of Coomaraswamy's essays. Unfortunately, even though the *yugas* are related to precession and the solstices, and certain constellations are implicated, the precise timing mechanism of the *yugas* was never examined or even seriously sought, most likely because both Coomaraswamy and Guénon were more concerned with the metaphysical processes of spiritual transcendence—the dynamics to emerge during the terminal phase of Kali Yuga—than with pinpointing its precise astronomical timing. Perhaps the solution to the problem was too obscure for them; perhaps the astronomy involved was unclear. Still, Guénon wrote shortly before his death in 1951 that the end of Kali Yuga was not too far off, and another major Traditionalist writer, Frithjof Schuon, said in 1967 that it would be fifty or so years in the future—circa 2017.[6] The question is unanswered, and not central, in Traditionalist literature. Nevertheless, if it be deemed unwise to "predict" a precise year during which the dire events of the "end of the *yuga*" will unfold, we might at least be able to clarify the astronomical process involved, according to key motifs explored in Traditionalist thought, most notably: the Sundoor at World's End, the Clashing Cliffs, and the solstice gateways.

TWELVE

The Sundoor at World's End and the Clashing Cliffs

What is the Primordial Tradition? Aldous Huxley called it the "perennial philosophy," an ageless wisdom that comes from a transcendent realm. Coomaraswamy preferred to call it *sophia perennis et universalis*, the eternal *and universal* wisdom. It has come to be called simply the Primordial Tradition. Perennial means "eternally recurring or rebirthing." Thus, even though the ancient wisdom may be forgotten, it will inevitably resurface, for it is a wisdom based upon universal principles that operate whether or not human beings are directly aware of them. The universal principles within the Primordial Tradition are those found in ancient sacred sciences; for example, the geometrical cosmology of the ancient Egyptians, based on the square-root principles of 2, 3, and 5.[1] The Pythagorean school adopted a similar approach, but the advent of rationalist Aristotelian philosophy signaled the dawn of a profane science that would be out of touch with its metaphysical (transcendent) roots. The Primordial Tradition is thus not something invented by human beings. Based in eternal universal principles, it has always been what it is, being left for human beings to discover and integrate as a guiding principle in the creation of social, religious, and political institutions. As it is today, modern civilization is out of touch with the Primordial Tradition; its institutions are based in man-made ideals, and derive from a degenerate process of increasing alienation from our transcendent origin. It is this devolution that removes us from the intimate vicinity of our source and center to an extreme wasteland of alienation called the Kali Yuga.

The Primordial Tradition is a state of mind rather than a distant Golden Age or ancient location. As such, the Primordial Tradition is accessible to any person or culture, at any time or place, without the aid of direct transmission through a particular lineage or Atlantean antecedent. The current pop-culture quest to trace fragments of compelling "evidence" back to some Atlantean Ur-civilization misses the point, and is evidence of the overliteral preoccupations of Western "modern" consciousness. The deeper truth of our search for lost "artifacts" is our desire to make visible a knowledge or mind-set that is more comprehensive and fulfilling. As with the legend of Shambhala, which faded into invisibility as humanity lost the ability to see it, the Primordial Tradition fades but reemerges in places conducive to rediscovering and appreciating its profound depth and wisdom. This explains how the ancient Maya, in their isolation, independently tapped into the same doctrines also found in ancient Vedic and Egyptian cosmology. Transoceanic voyages are not required for this simultaneous nonlocal emergence.

In his *Mystery of the Grail,* Julius Evola cites sacred rulership as one of the defining characteristics of the Primordial Tradition. Also known as sacred kingship, sacred rulership represents the fusion of what today we distinguish as the religious and political functions. Within the dimension of the Primordial Tradition, the king demonstrates his ability to rule with power and wisdom when he attains high degrees of initiation into universal gnosis. Sacred knowledge is won or achieved by undertaking visionary journeys up the World Axis to the cosmic center. A ruler, having thus become fused with the divine source and emanating power of life and wisdom, constellates the beings and objects of lesser degrees. He becomes the locus of worldly life through succeeding in the difficult task of integrating high degrees of initiatory knowledge into his or her consciousness.

This feature of the Primordial Tradition is alien to modern Western mores because the separation of church and state is the antithesis of sacred rulership. The pope and the president have two very different functions. The pope has little effectiveness in the political landscape, apart from mass appeal and token respect from political leaders. A president does not attain office through demonstrating a deep understanding of the processes that create and sustain nations, cultures, and people, but through financial contribution, propaganda, promises, and business alliances.

Sacred kingship is usually associated with the term *theocracy,* which, far from being taken seriously, is usually framed as a political style in which the king arbitrarily makes all the rules. This may have been kingship in its later degenerative phase, but it doesn't reflect the doctrine of divine self-election in its original form. In fact, this corrupt state of theocracy and sacred kingship can be seen as the degenerate expression of a tradition that was at one time, prior to its fragmentation, aligned with healthy, collectively beneficial intentions.[2]

The achievement of sacred knowledge allows one to become a natural leader of others. This achievement comes through direct experience (what we might call degrees of initiation). Experience itself, however, is not enough, for one must also cultivate understanding.

Islamic scholar Seyyed Hossein Nasr once wrote, "The traditional universe is dominated by the two basic realities of Origin and Center, both of which belong to the realm of the eternal."[3] Everything emanates from the center and source, located in the sky and emulated by a terrestrial counterpart. Sacred sites were designed to mirror the celestial center, so that the geometry and wisdom of sacred sciences could manifest on Earth. The Maya, for example, were interested in knowing where the sacred center in the sky was located, but they encountered at least three compelling possibilities: the polar center, the zenith center, and the Galactic Center. At Izapa and in the Mayan Creation myth, we find evidence that the early Mayan astronomers abandoned the old polar god and shifted their cosmological framework to a new orientation, one centered on the Milky Way's Galactic Center. Likewise, in the development of Old World astronomy (out of Middle Eastern and Vedic roots) a shift took place away from the polar center. René Guénon identified the evidence for this shift in his essay "The Wild Boar and the Bear," and he called it a polar-to-solar shift.[4] The shift also seems to have paralleled the persistent mytho-historical transition from a hyperborean (northern) tradition to the Atlantean era (solar and southern). We need to look closely at Guénon's argument to understand why this shift would be better understood as a polar-to-galactic shift in cosmological orientation.

The Polar-to-Galactic Shift

The general idea of a historical shift in humanity's cosmic orientation is based in the knowledge that around the time of the *I Ching*'s creation—roughly 5,000 years ago—there were eight constellations organized around the Pole Star. Each corresponded to one of the eight primary trigrams used in the *I Ching* to generate the sixty-four hexagrams. At some point in history, the meanings of these constellations were shifted to star groups along the ecliptic, and four more constellations were identified, to make the total of twelve constellations that constitute the zodiac. The Pleiades or Ophiuchus are sometimes considered to be a lost thirteenth constellation, as both are near the ecliptic. This transition in astronomical thinking indicates an emphasis on the solar path (the zodiac) over the polar center, thus, a polar-to-solar shift. However, when we look closely at Guénon's contribution to understanding this shift, a new factor emerges.

Guénon's primary argument for a shift from a polar to a solar framework involves the transfer of the seven stars or seven sages (*sapta riksha*) of the Great Bear to the Pleiades. Both constellations have (or had) seven stars, and the Pleiades resemble a tiny dipper. (The number 7 also refers to the seven stages or rungs on the ladder of the cosmic pillar that the soul passes while ascending to the highest heaven.) A relationship between the Great Bear and the Pleiades is found in many stories. For example, the Pleiades are still referred to as the seven sisters, but there are now only six Pleiads. The Greek legend tells that one of the Pleiads, Elektra, was kidnapped by one of the seven kings (one of the stars in the Big Dipper, Alcor) and now accompanies him as a binary star companion. This myth is associated with the fall of Troy, which, as we saw in chapter 7, symbolizes the "fall" of the Big Dipper out of proximity to the North Celestial Pole, signaling a new World Age around 2200 B.C.

The Pleiads or Atlantides were the daughters of Atlas, and were therefore the children of the new Atlantean tradition. In addition, in Egypt the Big Dipper was called the "thigh of the bull," while the Pleiades are located in Taurus, right on the bull's shoulder. Guénon brings in linguistic comparisons as well, but the point is clear: The Pleiades symbolically replaced the function of the Big Dipper. This equation is rich in implications, especially when one considers that the Pleiades mark the direction opposite the Galactic Center. The cosmological framework that once revolved around the circumpolar constellation Ursa Major was transferred to the north pole of the evolutionary axis that extends from the Galactic Center to the Galactic Anticenter. The Pleiades are not precisely on the Galactic Anticenter, but then neither is the Great Bear precisely on the Pole Star. They serve as symbolic marker points at the crowns of their respective pillars.

Guénon writes that these two symbolic frameworks map onto each other and share the same astronomical references, making it difficult to identify the true intention of a given symbol, but the hyperborean (northern) tradition is probably older. Generally, however, the same set of ideas regarding the "cosmic center" was applied, in two different eras, to two different parts of the sky. The first is the hyperborean polar symbolism. The second is the solar or sun-centered symbolism that Julius Evola refers to as Olympian and others call Atlantean. Both locations occupy the summit of a cosmic axis and serve as centering points. Notice that the Pleiades are only solar in the sense that they are near the ecliptic and the sun passes by them once a year. Their true function, above being a solar reference point, is that they indicate the direction of the Galactic Anticenter, the crown of the galactic axis. In this way we can amend Guénon's reconstruction and call it, with good justification, a polar-to-galactic shift.

In the polar-solar-galactic equation there are three cosmic frameworks:

	POLAR	SOLAR	GALACTIC
north	Great Bear/ North Pole Star	Cancer/June solstice	Pleiades
south	South Celestial Pole	Capricorn / December solstice	Galactic Center

When the "seven lights" of spiritual growth were shifted to the Pleiades, a new framework was identified that operates on the level of the galaxy. This galactic level embraces the tree or axis that starts at the Galactic Center (the *muladhara* chakra of creation), extends through Earth, and proceeds outward toward the Pleiades (the *sahasrara* crown of creation) in the direction of the Galactic Anticenter (in Gemini). The Galactic Anticenter is the topmost point in this new framework, because it is the direction out of our galaxy, into transgalactic domains. The Pleiades, like the Great Bear, are a short distance from the highest point of the system, but nevertheless they serve as a mythic and symbolic indicator. By this reasoning it follows that the Galactic Center is analogous to the South Celestial Pole, and has special affinities with the Southern Hemisphere. In fact, from the viewpoint of the Northern Hemisphere, the Galactic Center always arches through the southern skies, and its highest altitude at meridian transit is related to one's latitude of observation. Farther south, the higher its altitude will be when it crosses the southern meridian (directly south, opposite the North Pole). The Pole Star (or North Celestial Pole) is located at an altitude above the northern horizon equal to one's latitude of observation. For example, at the 15° north latitude of Izapa, the Pole Star is 15° above the northern horizon. Because of precession, the relationship between the altitudes of the Pole Star and the Galactic Center as viewed from any given location depends on the era in which the observations are made. A question arises: At what latitude will the Pole Star and the Galactic Center reach the same altitudes, one to the north and one to the south? Perhaps such a "balanced" relationship was noticed by ancient skywatchers, and perhaps the unique latitude we might identify is significant. This question will be answered, in chapter 14.

Even though we have identified the galactic level in Guénon's Hyperborean-Atlantean shift, another unavoidable facet of this cosmological framework involves precession. The polar tradition tracks the polar precession while the solar-galactic (Atlantean) would presumably track the Sun's precessional slippage backward through the zodiac, in relation to the Pleiades. Or, in relation to the opposite point in the zodiac, the Galactic Center. These opposed points thus might be considered to be gateways in the sky—dusk and dawn markers for the precessional night and day phases. Here we begin to understand the true anchor points of the Vedic *yuga* system, which define seasonal epochs in precession, a concept that is in fact well known in Vedic thought.

The Solstice Gateways

We explored the Greek concept of the celestial gateways in chapter 7. It is an idea also found in the Vedic idea of dividing the year into ascending and descending phases. The ascending phase begins at winter solstice, which is called the *devayana,* or gate of the gods. The descending phase begins at summer solstice, which is called *pitriyana,* the gate of humanity. We can refer to the former as the portal of transcendence or ascension and the latter as the door to reincarnation or materialization. This model operates on smaller and larger levels of time. For example, the day "ascends" from midnight to midday (noon) and then "descends" through dusk to be reborn again at midnight. Likewise, the lunar month waxes and wanes in a period of 29.6 days. As noted, the solstices serve as the dividing line of the year into ascending and descending halves, and even

the precessional Great Year is divided by the solstice-galaxy alignment
into ascending and descending phases, as revealed in Yukteswar's reading
of the Laws of Manu.

The larger temporal level of the precessional Great Year is mentioned
by both Guénon and Coomaraswamy as the framework of the *yuga* doctrine, and they concur with early Greek writers that the solstice gateways
are located in Capricorn and Cancer. Neither seems to recognize, however, that two reference points are indicated here: The first is the solstice
axis, which constantly shifts with precession in relation to background
features such as constellations; the second is the Cancer-Capricorn axis,
which is a fixed sidereal backdrop. We should recognize that time is a factor in the manifestation of the "celestial gateways" when the larger "year"
of precession is considered; the doctrine implies both a temporal and a
spatial location for the gateways. Let's take a closer look at the sources of
this idea.

In his essay "The Solstitial Gates," Guénon attributes to the Greek
writers Porphyry and Numenius the placement of the solstice gateways in
Capricorn-Cancer. It is important to note that Numenius was writing in
the second century A.D., when the solstices were indeed in the constellations of Capricorn and Cancer. His statement was echoed in Porphyry's
Cave of the Nymphs, and must go back to an even earlier time, as the idea
of the solstices as gateways is alluded to in Homer's *Odyssey*. Guénon goes
to great lengths to identify which gateway is ascending and which is
descending, but the relationship between the solstice axis (which shifts
with precession) and the relatively fixed background of constellations is
not clear. The truth is that the unquestioned placement of the solstice axis
in Capricorn-Cancer really identifies a specific era of precession, one that
was valid up until the time of Numenius. And that placement was important because the Greeks were interested in the constellation that visibly
rose before the Sun on the solstices: as we explored earlier, these would
have been Gemini and Sagittarius. Macrobius, a contemporary of Numenius, also wrote that souls ascend to heaven by the gate of Capricorn and
descend into rebirth through the gate of Cancer. But since the Greeks
observed the constellation rising *before* the Sun, might he really mean
Sagittarius and Gemini? Confirming our suspicions, the authors of *Hamlet's Mill* clarify his intention for us: "Macrobius talks of *signs*; the constellations rising at the solstices in his time (and still in ours) were Gemini

and Sagittarius: the Gate of Cancer means Gemini. In fact, he states explicitly (*1.12.5*) that this 'Gate' is 'where the Zodiac and the Milky Way intersect.'"[5]

How much clearer can it be? And what better confirmation? The spatial gateways are located with the intersection points of the ecliptic (i.e., the zodiac) and the Milky Way, which target the Galactic Center–Galactic Anticenter axis and are located in Sagittarius and Gemini. A correction thus must be made to Guénon's overgeneralized use of Capricorn and Cancer: the solstices are indeed the gateways within the yearly cycle, but the sidereal background location of the gateways is Gemini and Sagittarius. Furthermore, although the gates were observed rising heliacally on the solstices some 2,000 years ago, precise alignment between the solstice axis and the galactic gateways occurs in our own era. The Maya marked this occurrence with their 2012 end-date.[6]

Guénon was satisfied with a loose reference to Capricorn and Cancer, but both he and Coomaraswamy examined star lore and constellation mythology relating to the gateways, much of which points at Sagittarius rather than Capricorn. For example, the "mouth" of the Vedic *siṁśumāra* crocodile "in Capricorn" may actually refer to the dark rift of the Milky Way near Sagittarius. We need to dig deep into the Traditionalist literature, and only in Coomaraswamy's unpublished essays will we find a compelling answer; but that must be saved for chapter 13.

Nevertheless, the doctrine of the celestial gateways involves the shifting solstice axis in relation to a background axis fixed to two important points along the zodiac. We might already suspect that the Pleiades and the Galactic Center serve as the crown and root of this sidereal framework.

The Symplegades

The Clashing Cliffs (or Symplegades) in the story of Jason and the Argonauts, like the motif of the rotating island-castle in the Grail Cycle, suggests a fleeting time of great opportunity during which a cosmic portal is open. In initiatory stories, it presents a final obstacle or test through which one must pass without hesitation before the door closes. It evokes, again, the precessional alignment of solstice and galaxy, which, of course, is the case for only a limited time. The Symplegades in the story of Jason are the treacherous Clashing Cliffs located in the Dardanelles. With the aid of a goddess the Argonauts slip through just before the rocks slam shut on the *Argo's* stern ornament. At the other end of the Mediterranean, the Pillars of Hercules conform to the Symplegades symbol in an especially profound way, which we shall explore later.

The Symplegades are a universal motif that Coomaraswamy suggests is older than the peopling of the Americas. In the Grail myth, the rotating island castle offers only occasional passage between the mundane and spiritual worlds. An Eskimo myth makes the Clashing Cliffs into icebergs that bar the seekers' way. Joseph Campbell, following Coomaraswamy, associated the Symplegades symbol with the parting of the Red Sea—the narrow passage opens briefly and the heroes can escape from the land of tyranny into the next realm. The "razor's edge," the "eye of the needle," and the "straight or narrow passage" are all related to the Symplegades symbol, and were explored individually by Guénon in his *Fundamental Symbols*.

Coomaraswamy's article on the Symplegades motif is, I believe, one of his most important. The motif occurs in geography and astronomy, but Coomaraswamy is concerned with its role in the quest for enlightenment. His esoteric interpretations draw primarily from celestial locations that are part astronomical, part metaphysical. In his interpretation, the "door in the sky"—that is, the north gate—is framed by the contrary "walls" of the Symplegades. In this sense, they guard the celestial gate from those who are unqualified to enter. The door to paradise is, in Coomaraswamy's words, the "Sundoor at World's End," and is always guarded by a being or a test that is meant to determine the spiritual attainment of the seeker. To get beyond the opposed grinding walls of the polarities that mark the "ends" of the manifest world of duality, one must transcend all notions of good and evil, of self and other. In the Christian tradition it is Saint Peter who has the key to the pearly gates; in the Hindu and Buddhist tradition, when one knocks on heaven's door and the voice bellows, "Who goes there?" the only worthy answer is: "It is you." In other words, to transcend this world of dualities, to exit the wheel of incarnation, all notions of selfhood and individuality must, so to speak, be left at the door. The soul thereby demonstrates its wisdom by merging with its infinite and eternal origin, and passes through the narrow gate of the contraries that bar passage to any unready interlopers.

In whatever legend or myth it manifests, at bottom we can understand that the Symplegades guard the north gate. We already have a sense for the location of the north gate, the gate of the gods. It is in Sagittarius, near all those astronomical features that play such an important role in the Mayan galactic cosmology, including the dark rift, the Galactic Center, and the Milky Way–ecliptic cross. The Symplegades mark the "crack between the worlds," the Eddic *gunungagap*, and even manifest as the dusk and dawn periods of the day cycle. We might think of the earth's equator as a Symplegades zone, as it divides the earth into two contrary hemispheres. Extending this analogy, we might imagine that the Milky Way divides the galaxy into north and south hemispheres, and thus the galactic equator represents the celestial Symplegades. In fact, this is without doubt the galactic meaning of the Symplegades, for the dark rift (which runs along the Milky Way near the Galactic Center) is framed by two white branches or "walls" of the Milky Way, and it is the solstice sun's successful passage through this forebidding zone that signals the ascending phase of precession. In South American Indian lore, the Milky Way is thought of as the great fissure of the "celestial brain," dividing the sky into two contrary zones. The two branches even look like white "pillars," beyond which lies the Galactic Center, the celestial heart and source of the world and all created beings. In this context, we can understand the Pillars of Hercules as Symplegades. If we map this pillared gateway onto the dark rift, bordered as it is by the two white pillars of the Milky Way, we can understand the Platonic legend that Atlantis lay beyond the Pillars of Hercules as a sky map to the Galactic Center, ultimately pointing to the Americas on the terrestrial level.

Based on these considerations, I venture a speculation that the galactic Symplegades are ultimately represented by the contrary forces on each side of the galactic equator. Thus the era in which the solstice sun aligns with this "null zone" between the opposites might be thought of as an era of collective initiation, or worse, collective judgment. In the biblical Revelation, the astrological signs symbolized by the four beasts of the Apocalypse mark the seasonal quarters during such alignment eras. It goes without saying that this identifies our own era as significant, during which the solstice doorway gives access, briefly, to the galactic door. But what is it that lies beyond the door? And why must it be guarded? The answer lies in Coomaraswamy's unpublished paper, which is the subject of chapter 13.

Symbolism of Domes

Houses, temple domes, and the shaman's tent are all quartered models of the cosmos, with a cosmic center at the topmost level. Often called the eye of the dome, this location is the abode of the high deity. The quadripartite cosmo-conception of the Primordial Tradition was encoded into sacred architecture in a particularly striking way, and this line of thought was explored by both Coomaraswamy and Guénon under the title "symbolism of the dome." We encountered this "as above, so below" principle in Michell's and Richer's accounts of sacred geography. Through this architectural symbolism we enter the realm of Christian sacred art, especially its forms during the Romanesque and Gothic phases that gave birth to Chartres cathedral (around A.D. 1200). It is now well understood that medieval Christianity retained close ties with the Hermetic tradition, and cathedral design during the Gothic period was intended to encode esoteric truths. Sacred geometry was utilized, somewhat after the fashion of ancient Egyptian sacred geometry, to create harmonious experiences inside cathedrals. In addition, murals and ornamental doorways depicting important scenes in Christian liturgy were placed in relation to the four directions so as to reveal profound truths to visitors willing to linger, listen, and contemplate. The general construction of many cathedrals and churches was quadrangular or square—oriented to the four directions— with a dome uniting the four directions in an apex or point to symbolize the highest spiritual zone, the doorway through which one exits this world and enters heaven or paradise. Viewed from above, a typical Gothic church depicts the same design as do Mayan pyramids—four directions united in a fifth, central direction, the apex of the pyramid.

In this way the apex of the dome is equivalent to the gate of the gods (in Sagittarius) through which the soul exits the mundane world. Coomaraswamy's analysis of the symbolism of the dome points out that the human body maps onto the architecture of sacred spaces, and the dome is likened to the human skull. Both Coomaraswamy and Guénon equate the apex of the dome (the north gate) with the cranial fontanel (the Brahmarandra), the highest spiritual chakra (*sahasrara*), associated with the pineal gland. This spiritual apex of the human being is thus equivalent to the uppermost central hole of the cosmic house, the north gate in Sagittarius, and can thereby be associated with the dark-rift "hole"

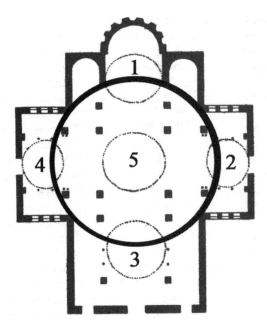

Figure 12.1. Gothic church, viewed from above
(from Burckhardt, *Sacred Art in East and West*)

and the nearby Galactic Center. One is reminded here of the earlier quote from Edgar Conrow about the celestial counterpart to the pineal gland being at 6° Sagittarius.[7]

The *axis mundi* in this model, which runs from the floor of the cathedral though the apex of the dome, corresponds to the evolutionary axis discussed by Patrizia Norelli-Bachelet (the Galactic Center–Galactic Anticenter axis). This in turn relates to the solstice gateways explained above, in that the solstice axis aligns with the evolutionary axis once every 13,000 years. We can imagine this to activate a kind of galactic awakening as we resonate with our deep galactic core (the *muladhara* or root chakra) and our extragalactic potentiality (Galactic Anticenter; *sahasrara*, or crown, chakra), which many esotericists equate with the Pleiades.

The symbolic formula is simple: The dome of the temple corresponds exoterically with the gate of the gods in Sagittarius and esoterically with the seventh chakra in the pineal gland. Nevertheless, I would like to take a quick look at the symbolism of the church doorway, which serves as a miniature reflection of the relationships encoded into the church as a whole.

The symbolism of doorways or "portals" of churches is almost self-explanatory: the door represents the entryway into divine space. "Above" the door corresponds to the apex of the dome, and sculptures located there depict activity or events happening at the gateway to heaven, often depicting Christ's apotheosis or ascension. The orientation of a church's front portal is usually toward the east, but on a symbolic level the door frame corresponds to the seasonal round in the way depicted in figure 12.2.

Based on the identification of the solstices as the "lowest" and "highest" points of the year, they lie on the vertical axis of the portal, with the winter solstice usually at the floor and the summer solstice at the top. The equinoxes are placed on either side of the door, such that the seasonal

Figure 12.2 Portal frame and seasonal placements
(adapted from Burckhardt, *Sacred Art in East and West*)

Figure 12.3 Royal Arch Masonry
(from Ovason, *The Secret Architecture of Our Nation's Capital*)

cycle moves clockwise around the door frame. This is in keeping with the ascending and descending movement of the larger precessional year. Since the winter-solstice gateway is called the gate of the gods, sometimes the placement of the solstices is reversed. For example, in Royal Arch Masonry, the winter-solstice gateway in "Capricorn" (meaning Sagittarius) is placed on the arch of the door. In this way we can see that the Christian themes placed above the door—whether Christ's birth, the Resurrection, or the Second Coming—occur symbolically at the north gate in Sagittarius. One wonders at what Masonic degree this information is revealed to the initiate.

The esoteric strategies of Gothic architects have become better known since the publication of Fulcanelli's *Mystery of the Cathedrals*. Historically, after the European plague and the rise of the Inquisition, Christianity moved into a dark phase that sought to abolish all forms of Hermetic and occult beliefs. The knowledge encoded into the cathedrals was forgotten, and sacred architecture went underground along with astrology, alchemy, and tarot. However, the opening up of the Americas provided an outlet for the repressed Hermetic symbolism, and sacred architecture thrived there for over two hundred years. In Guatemala, Peru, and Washington D.C., inklings of the galactic framework are preserved, and can still be found today.

In reexamining the concepts of the solstice gateways and the Symplegades, as well as Guénon's idea of a polar-to-solar shift, we have made a few amendments to the Traditionalist perspective, especially where it relates to the World Age doctrine and the true location of the gateways. First, we understood that Guénon's identification of an archaic shift from a polar framework to a solar cosmology actual refers to a polar-to-galactic shift; the old polar axis was mapped onto a new axis that runs from the Galactic Center to the Galactic Anticenter region near the Pleiades. Next, we were able to determine the Greek and Vedic conception of the placement of the solstice gateways in Capricorn and Cancer and thereby understand the true location of the gateways in the constellations rising heliacally, Sagittarius and Gemini. We also needed to distinguish between the solstice axis that constantly shifts with precession and the relatively fixed background axis of the gateways, which Macrobius identified with the two intersection points of the Milky Way and the ecliptic. Thus, specific eras in precession are implied in this information. Finally, we took a brief look at how the Symplegades motif operates, and how the spatial symbolism of cathedral domes and Royal Arch Masonry map onto the gateways and the spiritual centers of human beings. Now that we have a corrected framework of understanding as a foundation, we can go beyond the astronomy and venture more deeply into the metaphysics of spiritual transformation that awaits us on our approach to the galactic gateway.

THIRTEEN

Sagittarius and the Metaphysics of Transcendence

A s discussed in chapter 6, Coomaraswamy's unpublished "Early Iconography of Sagittarius" was clearly a response to Hartner's essay on the lunar nodes, the unstated implication of which was that Islamic and Hindu astrologers identified the exaltation of the south lunar node with 3° Sagittarius, coincident with the Galactic Center. Coomaraswamy quotes extensively from Hartner and takes the discussion into interesting areas. The galactic implications go unrecognized, however. The reader would need to know that the Galactic Center is located in Sagittarius for the full meaning of the essay to be clear.

The question that Coomaraswamy set himself was stated on the first page of his typescript: "The fundamental question to be asked will be *at what is the [Sagittarian] archer shooting?*" When I read this, knowing that the Sagittarian archer points his arrow right at the Galactic Center, I could scarcely believe what Coomaraswamy had written. The same paragraph emphasizes, however, that whatever astronomical references may be present, the mythological (or metaphysical) meaning is what will be of interest. In other words, Coomaraswamy intended to explore the metaphysical process of transcendence as it relates to the mythology of Sagittarius rather than belabor any implied or demonstrated astronomical features. Throughout the essay the Galactic Center is never mentioned, even though its composition occurred well after the Galactic Center's location had been identified by astrophysicists.

Coomaraswamy was not particularly interested in astronomy. As his metaphysical thinking evolved, and he transformed from a geologist to an art historian and iconographer, finally to become an academic metaphysician, he was drawn to several interrelated motifs: the Symplegades, the solstice doorways, the theft of soma, and the Scorpion men who guard the gate of the transcendent "Sundoor at World's End" that lies between the Clashing Cliffs, also called the north gate. Since his iconographic studies often touched upon cosmological beliefs, star lore, and the rich mythology of constellations, he eventually realized that all of these motifs pointed to Sagittarius. And whether he realized it or not, his trail led him right to the doorstep of the Galactic Center, the unspoken truth implied in his unpublished "Early Iconography of Sagittarius."

Following his own intuition, Coomaraswamy was drawn to Sagittarius as the location of unresolved mysteries in ancient cosmology and symbolism. Why his prized "key" motifs were located in Sagittarius had more to do, for him, with variations in and cross-comparisons in constellation mythology than with the fact that the Milky Way, the dark rift, the crossroads of Milky Way and ecliptic, and the Galactic Center are all located in that region. In fact, we can't even be sure that Coomaraswamy was aware of these facts. Ultimately, he was more concerned with the metaphysics of consciousness and the ancient doctrines that provided insight into the great voyage undertaken by the soul in its after-death journey to union with the transcendent realm, beyond this earthly plane of duality.

The image of the Sagittarian archer initiates Coomaraswamy's inquiry. The Archer points at the seeker who quests after a glimpse of heaven and a taste of the magic elixir of immortality. To attain this end one must overcome fear and doubt, and identify with the transpersonal realm at the root of all phenomenal manifestations. The Archer also points at the cosmic center, the Galactic Center, serving as a reminder of the goal. But his main function is to protect the heavenly realm from interlopers. This is why the defender seems like a dangerous guardian. The symbolism of the nearby Scorpion constellation is similar: the scorpion's tail contains a dangerous stinger and also points at the Galactic Center (see fig. 8.5).

Scorpion men play a role as guardians of the "western" gateway in the Sumerian epic of Gilgamesh. Like the Sagittarian archer, their role is to protect paradise from marauding interlopers or unworthy seekers. Gilgamesh is allowed through because he is recognized as being half divine. Coomaraswamy notes that in early constellation mythology the imagery of Scorpio and Sagittarius is often fused. Centaurs (half-men, half-horse beings) sometimes have a scorpion tail (see fig. 13.1; also fig. 7.4).

Sometimes the Sagittarian archer shoots into a mouth connected to his own tail, much like the self-devouring ouroboros symbol of infinity

Figure 13.1. Sagittarian archer with scorpion tail

(see fig. 6.7). Given that Sagittarius and Scorpio are located on either side of the Galactic Center, the astronomical reference should be clear.

In the use of both Scorpio and Sagittarius as attendants to the gate, a common image is repeated, that of the two guardians of the cosmic axis. On the other side of the sky, where the Galactic Anticenter passes through Gemini, the Gemini twins stand on either side of a staff, as we saw earlier on the Islamic Kalam Box (chapter 6). The two Babylonian gods who guard the portals of heaven are Tammuz and Ningiszida, identified with Castor and Pollux in Gemini. Semitic scholar Stephen Langdon wrote that "perhaps the Babylonians located the gateway of heaven in the constellation of Gemini, and placed the translated god Tammuz at this gate."[1] Indeed, that would identify the Galactic Anticenter as a celestial gateway of the Babylonians.

The cosmic doorway symbol can be mythologized in many ways. In Sanskrit the term *mukha* means "entranceway," "gate," or "mouth." The *kalamukha* (great mouth) is a motif found often in Hindu and Buddhist iconography. Grimacing lions' heads whose mouths hold door knockers, common in Asia, are architectural survivals of this ancient motif. Usually plants grow out of the mouth, suggesting it is a place from which life emerges. The immediate association is thus with a birthplace. Both Guénon and Coomaraswamy identify the *kalamukha* as birther *and* devourer and place it in Capricorn (really Sagittarius). I mentioned earlier that the astronomical reference of *makara* or *mukha* is probably to the dark rift in the Milky Way, which the Maya also identify as a monster mouth. The related monster mouth of the Vedic *simsumara* crocodile faces upstream and devours all unsuspecting seekers, preventing them from passing beyond the Sagittarian portal that it guards.

The monster head known as Rahu works just as hard to guard the gateway on the opposite side of the sky. Two ideas in Hindu myth connect a gorgonlike monster with the Gemini gateway. First, Rahu, as the lunar north node, is exalted at 3° Gemini. Second, a story illustrates the generation of a monster head called *kirttimukha* (the face of glory) from the mind of Śiva. Briefly, the tyrant Jalandhara challenged Śiva by sending the demon Rahu to demand that the goddess, Shakti, be delivered to him immediately. Śiva countered the challenge by generating from the spot between his eyebrows (the *ajña* chakra) a terrific burst of power that incarnated as the *kirttimukha*. As an embodiment of the righteous wrath of the Supreme Being, *kirttimukha* is popular in Southeast Asia as a door guardian and, as a grimacing monster head, is often placed over the doorways of homes and temples. What needs to be emphasized is that the

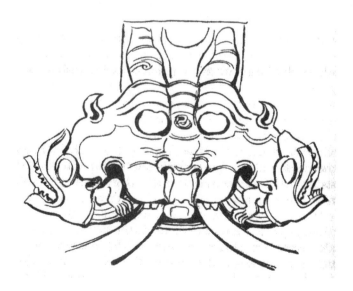

Figure 13.2. *Kalamukha*

kirttimukha, the face of glory, was projected from Śiva's third eye, where the vision of enlightenment is located, which is also esoterically equated with the pineal gland and the Pleiades. Since the Pleiades are the Galactic Anticenter indicator, and Rahu likewise directs our attention to that part of the sky, these adventures take place at one of the celestial gateways defined by the Galactic Center–Galactic Anticenter axis. These dynamics illustrate the motif of the defenders of the gate, which Coomaraswamy encountered in his examination of the iconography of the other gate, the one in Sagittarius.

At this point we can summarize the motifs discussed by Coomaraswamy. As we shall see, the entire mythological complex comes together in the story of the theft of soma. First, Sagittarius is the location of a celestial gateway that exists at the center and top of the cosmos. The doorway leads to higher worlds or offers an elixir that provides access to the higher worlds. The doorway is guarded by defenders, namely, Sagittarian archers and Scorpion men. Sagittarius, as the destination of the spiritual quest, presents a doorway that is guarded in two senses: by the defenders of the gate and by the Clashing Cliffs of the Symplegades. Therefore, the celestial doorway is framed by the universal contraries that one must transcend in order to enter the higher spiritual paradise. Lastly, the seeker either is desiring to sacrifice the individual identity in order to know Brahma or secretly plans to storm the heavenly gate, steal something that is valuable to the gods, and return to the world with enhanced power and advantage. That something, so cherished by the gods, is soma.

The gate of heaven must be protected because something very precious lies beyond the threshold: nothing less than the magical elixir of immortality, the nectar of infinite vision and wisdom. In Vedic literature, the nectar of paradise is called *amrita* or soma. With the introduction of soma into the discussion, some very interesting avenues open up. Ethnomycologist R. Gordon Wasson argued that the Vedic soma plant that bestowed heavenly visions on its users was the psychoactive *Amanita muscaria* mushroom.[2] Others have argued that *amanita*, the "pillar of the sky," is not reliably psychoactive and opt for the psilocybin species of mushrooms as the best candidate for soma. The operative chemicals in these sacred plants mimic certain neurotransmitters that regulate cognition and consciousness. The effects of ingesting these mushrooms are often described in terms such as "experiencing the immanent presence of divinity," "merging with the godhead," "experiencing eternity and a transcendent realm of infinite space." They can also bestow feelings of omniscience and omnipotence. At this point it is striking to note that serotonin and other neurotransmitters are regulated by the pineal gland, which is esoterically associated with the north gate at 6° Sagittarius. From the opposite perspective, the pineal can also be associated with the seventh chakra and the Pleiades, the south gate in Gemini (the Galactic Anticenter). In either case, the core axis of the universe is opened up to the seeker, the ideal result being the magnetic absorption of the lowest energy center into the highest. This upward union stimulates the experience of heavenly bliss, the imbibing of the soma nectar. In one sense, then, soma can be associated with a "nectar" of consciousness produced by an awakened seventh chakra or pineal center. But soma seems to be this and a whole lot more.

Soma is the "mainstay of the sky." It is perhaps a mushroom. In Vedic literature, the theft-of-soma story encapsulates the various aspects. Soma is a magical plant or elixir kept on the summit of Mount Meru, guarded by the gods. The gods are often portrayed as evil monsters who desire to prevent humanity from having the elixir of immortality, and sometimes soma is said to be kept in a bronze fortress. Indra, in his guise as the cosmic bird Garuda, flies to the top of Mount Meru and succeeds in stealing the soma. While escaping with the ambrosia, however, he is attacked by the archer Krisannau (Sagittarius), who shoots off one of his claws. This places the peak of Mount Meru in a specific zodiacal location—in Sagittarius near the Galactic Center. In this way the sacred plant or ambrosia was brought to humanity from the heights of the celestial regions by a bird who was Indra in disguise.

Coomaraswamy points out that the story is in essential respects equivalent to the rape of the Nagi serpent, who is the primal serpent goddess of life. In one version of this myth Indra receives the soma from the lips of the Nagi serpent goddess Apala. A reptile when Indra kisses the soma nectar from her lips, she is later purified and transformed into a beautiful bride. According to Coomaraswamy, the union of Apala and Indra is consummated in the heart, "where also the draught of Soma is really imbibed."[3] To drink soma with the selfish appetite for conquest brings negative results. There is a truth in the violence of the rape image, however, in that the serpent is eaten or subsumed into the higher principle of the bird deity. Like

Indra kissing Apala and facilitating her transformation into a purified bride by taking her poison as a nectar, the sublimation of the lower nature into the higher deity—serpent into bird or titan into angel—is the metaphysical meaning of the story. The soma can thus be a nectar or a poison, depending on how it is drunk. A defilement of the life principle and a consequent degradation of humanity occurs if heaven's door is approached with the intent of stealing the life nectar and returning with it to the earth plane, not unlike the way that Prometheus stole fire from atop Olympus. The result of this scandal is always detrimental for humanity, in the same way that Pandora's box, stolen from the gods, spewed disease and evil throughout the world after it was unwisely opened. This is why the soma center is guarded, for if an unprepared soul who still clings to earthly ambition succeeds in acquiring the soma nectar, the results are destructive, for that soul and for the world. But when a seeker approaches the portal of heaven with the intention of "dying to the world," Saint Peter willingly opens the gates to the higher spiritual realm.

Access to heaven is sometimes hard and at other times easy. The north gate opens and closes via the Symplegades, the contraries that one must transcend in order to survive the narrow passage. To die to the self and to transcend all worldly dualities of the mortal plane, one must merge with the higher self. Recognition of unity with the transcendent identifies an advanced soul. This is the path of knowledge, whereas the previously described path in which the soma nectar must be wrestled by force from the hands of deity is the path of worldly power and ultimately leads to self-destruction. The path of power is seductive, particularly in our own age of rampant materialism and instant gratification, but the path of knowledge, in which ego and worldly desire must be transcended, opens us to the higher planes of spirit.

In Finnish mythology, the theft of the Sampo (Runo 42 in the Finnish national epic, the *Kalevala*) parallels the Vedic theft of soma. The Sampo is a magical object in Finnish mythology, something like a magic mill capable of producing anything one wishes. Like soma, the Sampo is guarded by an evil being who may be a high deity in disguise; in the *Kalevala* she is Louhi, the witch of Northland. Like soma, the Sampo promises wealth, vitality, and fertility for its possessors. In Sanskrit, *soma* is written *somam*; in Finnish, *Sampo* is written *sammon*. Finnish scholars have identified the spinning mill of the Sampo with the celestial dome centered upon the Pole Star that, in the far north, is almost straight over-head. The Sampo has a "many ciphered cover" called the *kirjokansi* or "bright dome"—the night sky bespeckled with twinkling stars. In Finnish shamanism, the polar sky is the location of a high deity of wisdom and a totem of strength and immortality. It is the abode of Otava, the Great Bear (the Big Dipper), who climbs up and down the cosmic tree fixed to the Pole Star, the Nail of the North. The word *sampo* has been derived from the Sanskrit word *skamba*, "pillar." The cosmological framework of the Sampo is typical of Finno-Ugric and Siberian shamanism. It contains a central pillar and three, five, seven, or nine levels. There is a close par-allel with the Hindu chakra system.

The visual resemblance to the *Amanita muscaria* mushroom is more than a coincidence (see fig. 13.3). Among Siberian shamans, *Amanita* mushrooms with seven little white spots are especially prized, as they embody the seven stars of the Big Dipper. Thus, the inverted-bowl shape of the mushroom reflects the dome-shaped sky, the *kirjokansi* of the Sampo. In the Sampo, we find a cosmological model common to all Asian, Indian, and Siberian forms of shamanism as well as a picture of soma as mush-room. The model is even found in the Nordic mythology, where Yggsdrasil

Sampo Soma

Figure 13.3. Sampo model of stellar dome and the *Amanita* mushroom

is the cosmic tree. At the base of Yggsdrasil three goddesses, the Norns, can be found. They symbolize past, present, and future. These goddesses are deities of the magic tree, and offer travelers an elixir to refresh them on their journey. The Mordvin people of eastern Europe tell a story of a giant birch tree growing on a hill in the depths of the forest, the roots of which encircle the world. (The mycelial mat of mushrooms can stretch for miles, and *Amanita* prefers to grow in the roots of birch trees). The branches of this tree surround the heavens. Ethnographer Uno Holmberg reports: "At the root of the birch is a spring, roofed over with carved boards and white sheets, on its edge a red wooden can, in the can a sweet honey drink, and in the liquid a silver ladle, the bottom of which is decorated with the sun and the moon, the handle with smaller stars. . . . As the sun moves in the heavens, the handle of the ladle turns with it."⁴ The birch tree is the World Axis or cosmic tree. The ladle is clearly the Big Dipper; the red wooden can evokes *Amanita* itself; the sweet honey liquid therein is the sacrament; the roofed-over magic "spring" with boards and sheets is the little séance hut, where your friendly local wisewoman awaits your visit! Tales recall healings and passersby who drink of the tree's "magical sap" having been "refreshed," "satisfied," or even "strengthened ninefold." The scenario recalls the mushroom ceremonies of the Mazatec *curandera*, Maria Sabina. The witch/goddess/Norns at the base of the cosmic tree are equivalent to the Finnish Louhi, the turner of the milling stone and keeper of the Sampo. These are all equivalent to the goddess Kundalini at the base of the seven-layered spinal tree.

The theft of the Sampo, on one level of interpretation, involves the removal of the polar axis to another location, thus implying precession or perhaps even a pole shift. The pertinent passage from the *Kalevala* reads:

> *We will take the Sampo yonder*
> *And convey the ciphered cover*
> *To that misty point of land*
> *At the head of Foggy Island.*⁵

It is tempting to interpret the "head" of Foggy Island as the "top" of the Milky Way, and the polar Sampo's relocation there as being the Finnish equivalent of a polar-to-galactic shift. The Finnish legend of the theft of the Sampo is, like its Vedic counterpart, rich in symbolic associations on many levels: sexual connotations, cosmology, sacred plants, male-female dynamics, the spiritual quest—even intimations of precession—are wrapped into a seamless whole.

In the process of studying the *Kalevala* and editing Pekka Ervast's book *The Key to the Kalevala*, it became apparent to me that the "official" story was lacking, and the episode should be retold from the viewpoint of Louhi, the deity from whom the life-nectar was stolen. Coomaraswamy points out that the Garuda bird and Prometheus are celebrated as heroes from the viewpoint of mortals here on earth, but from the viewpoint of the gods they are condemned as demons or at least rascals, undeserving of the prize of heaven, who will get their due in the course of time. So too does Louhi condemn the "heroes" of the *Kalevala,* and then tries to prevent them from obtaining the Sampo. The problem is the tendency of human beings to steal wisdom rather than embrace it, compounded by the apparent "barriers" set up by heaven, which are actually barometers of a soul's preparedness.

Louhi, like all defenders of the gate, serves the higher purpose of heaven, and denies entry to those incapable of integrating the inner knowledge, for their own good and for the well-being of the true denizens of paradise. Unfortunately, it is still possible for unworthy interlopers to break through and seize the treasure, enslaving it to their earthly desires. But like the dragon who guards the gold and the virginal maiden, and can do nothing with either, so too the delusional hero will find the trophy spoiled and useless, bringing temporary rewards and ultimate misery. The choice of the path of power, a path leading to apparent success by the standards of earthly life, means nothing planted and nothing sown for the spiritual heart. Louhi refuses the nectar to those who cannot drink it with their spiritual hearts, for to enslave the life energy to the ambitions of ego is to close the door on divinity.

The path of knowledge and the path of power—one leads to higher spiritual planes and the other leads downward into deeper soul loss. In service to self or in service to other—a choice that occurs at the north gate in Sagittarius. Coomaraswamy's ultimate message goes deeper than this, however, to a paradox at the heart of all reality. He frames the two "paths" or positions as the Vedic conflict between the *asura* and *deva* spirits (the titans and angels), and helps us realize that both positions, ultimately, spring from the same source. They are therefore not mutually exclusive opposites, but, being united on a higher plane, complement one another. Like yin and yang, each pole contains the seed of the opposite, otherwise there would be no basis for relationship. Said another way, it takes both sides playing their roles in order for the nectar of consciousness to be generated. How the nectar is used or "imbibed" by each side is a function of their inherent natures. Ultimately, at the end of time the titans will be subsumed into angelic functions. It can't work the other way around, although during certain phases the titans are on the rampage.

In 1997 Princeton University Press republished some of Coomaraswamy's essays in a book called *The Door in the Sky*. The sun door of the title is illustrated on the book's cover with a painting by Hieronymous Bosch called *Entrance to the Celestial Paradise* (fig. 13.4). The image

Figure 13.4. *Entrance to the Celestial Paradise,* **by Hieronymous Bosch**

expresses well a passage from the Br̥hadāraṇyaka Upaniṣad: "He reaches the Sun, it opens out for him like a hole in a drum."[6] Even though the title and the cover art provide explicit clues, one might read the book cover to cover several times and not understand where the door is located and how it is opened. This door is the north gate activated by the solstice alignment with the Galactic Center, the "Sundoor at World's End" discussed at length in Coomaraswamy's work. But even when the door is open, welcoming all those desiring freedom, it still takes an act of self-sacrifice and active discernment for any soul to get beyond the defenders of the gate. Most of us cling too strongly to the world, to illusion. Like the flock of sheep who fail to leave the pen even when the gate is left open, the modern world has rendered human beings unconscious enough that even when the ultimate spiritual goal of human life is revealed for all to see, it yet goes ignored. The Symplegades open but briefly, and in that moment the fate of worlds is determined.

FOURTEEN

Galactic Alignment
and the Primordial Tradition

I n chapter 10 we reappraised the Laws of Manu following Sri Yukteswar's insight that the *yuga* doctrine of the World Ages, being
based in precession, should be divided into ascending and descending phases. The work of Frawley and Norelli-Bachelet confirmed that our
shift from descending Kali Yuga to ascending Kali Yuga is timed by the
solstice-galaxy alignment, which was most precise around 1998. Furthermore, in studying the work of Guénon and Coomaraswamy—respected
elucidators of the Primordial Tradition—it became very clear that the
solstice-galaxy alignment is also a central (though until now unrecognized) feature of the Primordial Tradition, especially evident in the Vedic
material. Based upon this collection of evidence, I have good reason to
offer the galactic alignment of era 1998 as the key to understanding the
temporal dynamics of the Primordial Tradition. The temporal manifestations of the evolutionary avatars, of Shambhala or Atlantis, and of the
Primordial Tradition itself, would seem therefore to be timed by the precessional cycle, specifically by solstice alignments to the Milky Way galaxy
that occur every 12,800 years.

The Primordial Tradition itself fades out of human consciousness and
reemerges in accordance with the same cyclic process it describes. In fact,
one of the primary ideas in the Primordial Tradition is that our connection with our source becomes increasingly obscure through time as human
beings adopt more materialist viewpoints until, finally, the end of
descending Kali Yuga brings renewal and a turnabout in the deepest seat
of consciousness. We might therefore say that the galactic alignment of
era 1998 signals the Primordial Tradition's resurfacing into conscious
awareness, like some long-submerged Ur-level of mind. This supposition
is based on the idea that the solstice-galaxy alignment of era 1998 signals

the end of descending Kali Yuga and our entry into the ascending phase of the precessional cycle. It is significant that we can now describe the Primordial Tradition (called the Perennial Philosophy by Aldous Huxley and Huston Smith) as being galactic in nature—the Galactic Center is its orientational locus and the transcendental source of the wisdom it encodes. Like a lost Atlantean dimension of the human soul, the Primordial Tradition now appears ready to make a dramatic reappearance on the stage of human history.

As we enter a new millennium by our own calendric reckoning, we can expect a respiritualizing (and dematerializing) of life on earth, to increase for another 12,800 years. The new "ascent" of galactic awareness should parallel the reappearance and eventual reestablishment of the Primordial Tradition. Such a scenario sounds like a nice ideal or philosophical metaphor, but why should we think of galactic awareness as beginning to rise? The answer comes from precessional astronomy. First of all, the December solstice's alignment with the Galactic Center indicates a "low point" in the precessional cycle, a new beginning in the same way that the December solstice functions in the solar-year cycle. That sounds fair enough, and we've already described this process at length. However, beyond this, a related "rise and fall" of the Galactic Center is keyed to the solstice-galaxy alignments, in the following way.

One summer evening several years ago, at 9,000 feet in the Rocky Mountains of Colorado, I noticed the Pole Star to the north and remembered how its altitude above the horizon is always equal to your latitude of observation. Thus, I reasoned, it was 40° above the horizon. Then, to the south, I noticed the Sagittarian archer and the stinger of Scorpio pass through the southern meridian. I knew that the Galactic Center is located right between them, and was surprised at the aesthetically compelling north-south counterpoint between the Pole Star and the Galactic Center. I realized that such a sight occurs almost every night, and would be especially pronounced around midnight during the summer months.

Thus began a series of questions that I answered with my astronomy software. One important question that emerged, mentioned earlier, was: At what latitude of observation do the Pole Star and the Galactic Center reach an equal latitude, thus "balancing" the skies? For our era, I found that the answer is 30° north latitude—the location of the Great Pyramids in Egypt. There, the Pole Star is, of course, 30° above the northern horizon, while every night the Galactic Center reaches an altitude of 30° above the southern horizon as it passes through the southern meridian. I also found that at 20° north latitude (Chichen Itza), the Galactic Center will be twice as high as the Pole Star, and at 15° north latitude (Izapa), the Galactic Center is three times higher. This was fascinating, but I knew that the skies change with precession, so I tracked backward, century by century, with my astronomy software.

As the earth wobbles on its axis, the North Celestial Pole shifts and traces out a large circle through the northern constellations. While this occurs, the Galactic Center, which is farther south and close to the ecliptic, moves higher and lower. Viewed from a location in the Northern Hemisphere, the effect is such that for 12,800 years the Galactic Center rises, then for another 12,800 years it falls. For example, if we go back to the time of the fabled Golden Age of the Vedas—one-half of a precessional cycle ago—we find that the latitude that "balances" the skies in that era is 53° north. This is the latitude running through Glastonbury in England.[1] There, 12,800 years ago, the Galactic Center could be viewed very high above the southern horizon, in fact, 53° high—the highest point it ever reaches. This would have been quite dramatic and, most significantly, this era of the Galactic Center's highest meridian transit was also the era of the previous solstice-galaxy alignment.

ERA	LATITUDE OF EQUALITY
10,800 B.C.	53°
6000 B.C.	45°
2000 B.C.	38°
2000 A.D.	30°

As the millennia passed, the Galactic Center has been falling lower and lower in elevation along the southern horizon. From the viewpoint of the northern latitudes, it has quite literally been "sinking" lower and lower until now, in our own era, the Galactic Center has reached its lowest meridian transit and cannot even be seen from the latitude of England, as it never quite makes it above the southern horizon (as mentioned, farther south, in Egypt, it can be seen 30° above the southern horizon). The Galactic Center has, in effect, sunk beneath the horizon, and today it has actually been submerged for almost a thousand years. This astronomical scenario might explain one of the most mysterious references in Greek literature: Could Plato's legend of the sinking of Atlantis—and its eventual reemergence—be rooted in this celestial process? At Greek latitudes, the sinking effect would have been the important phenomenon, even though the Galactic Center never fully disappears in Greece as it does at northern latitudes. More fascinating is the fact that since the Galactic Center reaches its lowest meridian transit in our own era, it will now begin to "rise" higher. And, *the eras of its "turnabout" are keyed to the solstice-galaxy alignment!* In other words, the solstice-galaxy alignments of 10,800 B.C. and A.D. 1998 signal the "fall" and "rise" of galactic consciousness, in a manner quite different from anything previously discussed.

The astronomical dynamic behind this phenomenon is based on the fact that the current Pole Star is on the far side of the ecliptic polar circle from the Galactic Center, as can be seen in figure 14.1.

One can only wonder if these processes were known to the ancient skywatchers. It seems to me that they were known, and were encoded into the world's oldest literature in ways that we are just now beginning to

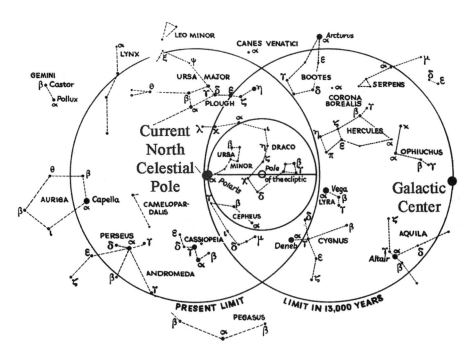

Figure 14.1. The farthest distance of the Galactic Center from the
North Celestial Pole is reached during the current solstice-galaxy alignment

decode and understand. According to the Vedic World Age doctrine, humanity descends into increasing spiritual darkness until we enter the *devayana* or ascending phase of the Great Year. Guénon himself subscribed to this as a personal belief. He saw the world bogging down deeper into mindlessness and materialism, and yet he also believed that the tide would eventually turn. And the Primordial Tradition, by way of the myth of the reemergence of the conscious kingdom (i.e., Shambhala), forecasts such a shift. The movements of the Galactic Center provide a deeper solution to the reason behind the ascent and descent of consciousness in the *yuga* cycle, keyed to the solstice-galaxy alignment.

Where to from here? We have covered a lot of ground and have made some fascinating discoveries. We traced the fragments of the archaic mono-myth backward through time and farther east, uncovering a mother lode of galactic gnosis manifested in many traditions. Many questions and lines of inquiry have been neglected, but we have discovered the core of the galactic cosmology in ancient Vedic India. The descent of history from that far-off Golden Age seems to have flowed westward, for the most part, and continues with the recent expansion of humanity across the Atlantic ocean. But where will it end? If the descent of consciousness has a temporal end and a turnabout in terms of precession, is there any geographical parallel occurring, sort of a "geography of precession" that identifies successive regions moving westward as significant, and specific locations as the "turnabout" zones on earth? If the sky maps onto the earth via the "as above, so below" principle, might *the movement* of the sky also be reflected on Earth? We unwound history back to the Golden Age in Vedic India, now lets rewind forward to see where it's all going.

PART 4

Unwinding and Rewinding History

FIFTEEN

The Geography of Precession

The sacred geography of England and Greece, as we saw in part 2, was perceived, named, and even molded to fit a larger celestial pattern. If we keep the underlying concepts of precession and galactic alignment in mind, a larger global pattern of sacred geography comes into view. What follows must simply be taken as an observation of facts and an identification of a pattern. As to who might have orchestrated these connections among far-flung cities on different continents over many millennia, there is no easy answer. Perhaps it was the invisible hand of the Great Geometer at work; perhaps it was our own collective unconscious, working out the secret so that it could eventually be manifested and beheld by our conscious minds; perhaps it is the same force that weaves crop circles and DNA, that grows ice crystals and river deltas. Whatever its origin, it brings our amazing journey of discovery full circle back to the modern-day Americas.

Figure 15.1 illustrates historical locations that have crystallized as important nodes of civilization and places that are landmarks to a deeper mystery. From left to right, the dots are:

- ★ 90° west longitude, mouth of the Mississippi River
- ★ 77° west, Washington, D.C.
- ★ 6° west, Pillars of Hercules
- ★ 12°30' east, Rome
- ★ 30° east, Egyptian Sphinx and Pyramids
- ★ 90° east, Lhasa, Tibet

Notice that the distance between the Pillars of Hercules and Washington, D.C., equals roughly 72° or one-fifth of the earth's circumference. From the Sphinx to Lhasa equals 60°, or one-sixth of the earth's circum-

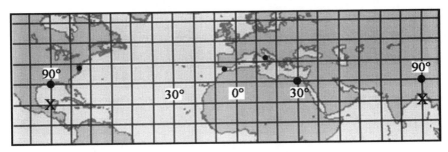

Figure 15.1. World map and the geography of precession

ference. From the Sphinx to the Pillars equals 36°, or one-tenth of the earth's circumference. There are two large Xs beneath the 90° longitudes. The X at 90° west marks the Pyramid of Kukulcan at Chichen Itza, a man-made mountain. Remember also that the apex of this pyramid symbolizes the rattlesnake's tail and the Pleiades, located in the Galactic Anticenter region of the Milky Way. The X at 90° east marks the mouth of the Ganges River. The Ganges symbolizes the Milky Way, and its mouth represents the dark rift near the Galactic Center region.

The two extremes of the map—at the 90° longitudes—display a double polarity. Two features at the 30° degree latitude are "mouth" (of the Mississippi) and "mountain" (Tibet). The two features slightly farther to the south, indicated by the Xs near 20° latitude, are the same but opposite: pyramid-mountain or "tail" (at Chichen Itza) and "mouth" (of the Ganges). In terms of space the astronomical reference is to the two extremes involving the mouth of the dark rift–Galactic Center and the tail of the Pleiades (the Galactic Center–Galactic Anticenter axis). More important, in terms of time the reference is to the extreme poles of the precessional cycle—the Golden Age of ancient Vedic India or Tibet that occurred one-half of a precessional cycle ago and the end of Kali Yuga occurring now that, in this model, is placed in the Americas.

In Western astrological terms, we are entering the Age of Aquarius; thus, these two extremes can be identified by the astrological ages of Leo and Aquarius. Tibet can be understood as representing the Golden Age and the start of the descent or fall of mankind, which occurred at the commencement of the Age of Leo, 13,000 years ago. America, centered on the Mississippi and the eschatological cosmology encoded into the Pyramid of Kukulcan at Chichen, locates the dawn of the Age of Aquarius and the beginning of the ascent phase. Clues throughout all of the Americas seem to signal our entry into a new age, and we shall explore evidence for this in Peru, Guatemala, and Washington, D.C.

This model of the "geography of precession" assumes a westward flow of history, an idea that is not new. That the process might be linked to precession is less well known, however, although the idea is explored in Norelli-Bachelet's *The New Way*. Still, it might seem coincidental that Tibet and mid-America are on opposite sides of the globe. But if we look more closely at the primary stage of Western history—the Mediterranean—we find intriguing pointers to the beginning and end of our current historical cycle. We can zero in on the Mediterranean to see how the two extreme ages—the dawn of time in Leo and the end of time in Aquarius—are honored there.

As figure 15.2 shows, there are two portals out of the Mediterranean, one at the eastern and the other at the western end. The Pillars of Hercules frame the Strait of Gibraltar at the western end, the doorway leading out of the Mediterranean into the Atlantic Ocean. At the eastern end, the Suez Canal leads to the Red Sea and ultimately the Indian Ocean. Monuments at these locations point to Tibet and America and indicate the ages of Leo and Aquarius.

As discussed in chapter 9, the Sphinx honors the dawn time by pointing eastward to Leo as it rises on the vernal equinox (see fig. 9.4). Graham Hancock and Robert Bauval have both argued for this, and it follows

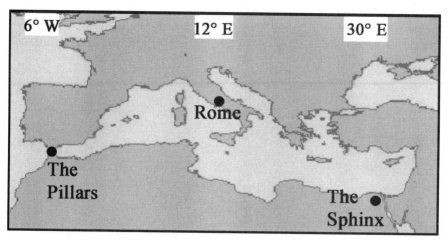

Figure 15.2. Map of Mediterranean and its gateways

from basic precepts in astrological symbolism, as well as the larger layout of the Gizeh plateau. The Sphinx is also, however, a geographical pointer along the 30° latitude line to Mount Kailas and, farther along, Lhasa in Tibet. In fact the Sphinx and Lhasa are separated by 60°, suggesting an interval of 4,300 years separating the founding of Egypt from the flowering of the Golden Age in India, Tibet, or central Asia. Following the westward flow of civilization (geographical precession), this places an ideal date for the Sphinx at 8,500 years ago. Geographical precession is not a precise mechanism, however, and we should understand these correspondences in general terms. The basic item of interest here is that the Sphinx honors not only the time of the previous Golden Age, but its geographical location as well.

All of classical Western history symbolically occupies the Mediterranean zone, and the flow of culture in this microcosm obeys the east-to-west pattern of the larger globe. As indicated in an ancient Greek map of the known world (fig. 15.3), the Mediterranean is prominently located, almost serving as a kind of pseudo-equator. In fact, *mediterranean* translates as "middle earth"—a dividing line between north and south. As such, it conforms, at a geographical level, to the Symplegades motif, dividing north from south. Rome, at 12° east longitude, stands out in history as a navel, or center. "All roads lead to Rome" was the ancient dictum, and in Christian cosmography Rome is placed at the center of the universe. London sits astride 0° longitude because of England's prominent role in the scientific revolution. We might think of London as the terminal point of European dominance, a phase begun decidedly in ancient Egypt and flowing through Greece, Italy, and western Europe. But Egypt honors Tibet as the older origin place, so it is compelling that London and Lhasa are 90° apart. Meanwhile, Rome was the launching point for a cultural style that went far beyond England, westward to a new world and a new country, whose capitol building was erected on a wooded hill known to colonists as New Rome, later as Jenkins Heights, and finally as Washington, D.C. Should we be surprised that Rome and Washington, D.C., are 90° apart? But the marvel doesn't end here, for we still need to identify the monument at the western end of the Mediterranean that is the counterpart to the Leo-Sphinx.

The portal at the western end of the Mediterranean is framed by the Pillars of Hercules. Ancient ideas about this natural gateway are found in

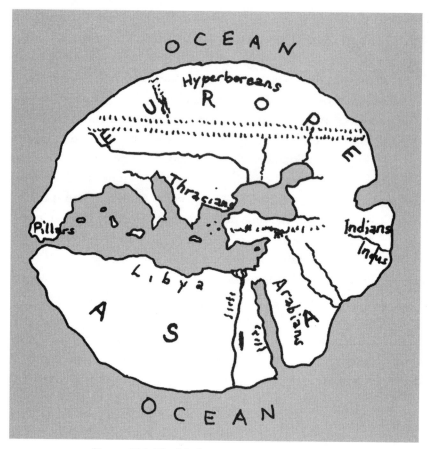

Figure 15.3. The Mediterranean as Middle Earth

Greek myths, and the Pillars are also portrayed on coins. As we might expect, the Pillars are a form of the Symplegades motif, uniting the opposite continents of Africa and Europe.[1] For ancient sailors traveling westward, the Pillars represented the end of the known world. According to Plato, beyond the Pillars lay the paradise island of Atlantis. On Greek coins the Pillars are portrayed as Ambrosia Petrai, rocks that drip the ambrosia of ecstasy, the waters of life. Some coins even place a tree of life between the pillars, whose fruits contain the elixir of immortality. As with the theft of soma, the key concepts in this symbology are "the end of the world" and the "waters of life" that cleanse and restore one to paradise. Given that the eastern Sphinx represents Leo, and considering all the motifs mentioned above, the Ambrosia Petrai of the Pillars of Hercules most clearly represent Aquarius, opposite Leo in the zodiac. Pisces is the twelfth or last zodiacal sign, and we are approaching its end, whereupon the Age of the Water Bearer will commence. Thus the western "end of the world" (the classical world) should point to the dawn of the Age of Aquarius. And indeed it does (see fig. 15.4).

There are several other profound associations that bring this identification home. As René Guénon wrote, certain Spanish coins portrayed a banner strung between the Pillars of Hercules and inscribed with the phrase *ne plus ultra*, which means "nothing greater beyond," or perhaps, "the ultimate lies beyond here." The ends of the earth—or time—come to mind. A version of the coat of arms of the Castile-León alliance that funded Columbus contains two pillars and a banner that reads "plus ultra"—obviously an appropriation of the ancient logo. Again, the "end" of Pisces—and the entire precessional cycle—is suggested. The reference is, of course, to the unknown "other side" of the Atlantic, but a double meaning does seem implied in Plato's Atlantis reference. When we remember that the Pillars are Symplegades, the metaphysical reading

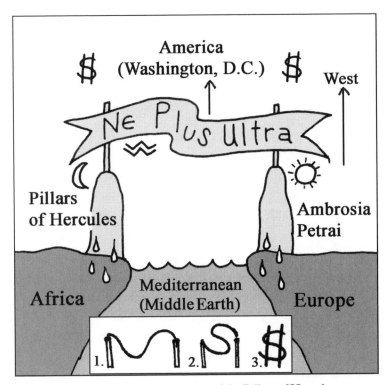

Figure 15.4. Esoteric meaning of the Pillars of Hercules

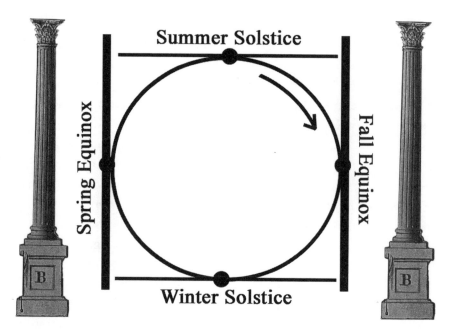

Figure 15.5. Why the Pillars symbolize the equinoxes

might be something like *beyond the contraries, the ultimate can be found, at the end of time.* In addition, the visual similarity between the wavy banner and the Aquarian "waves" symbol may not be insignificant. Also, the equinox axis is indicated by the upright pillars in the esoteric symbology (fig. 15.5) supplied by Guénon.[2]

In the circular representation of the yearly cycle, the solstices occupy the "highest" and "lowest" points by their very nature. Assuming the standard clockwise motion, the June solstice should be placed at the top, where the descent into decreasing daylight begins. It follows then that the equinoxes should be placed at the three and nine o'clock positions. Guénon points out that tangents drawn from the solstice points will be horizontal, and similar lines drawn through the equinox points will be vertical. If we think of the circle as a doorway, the vertical equinox lines become pillars that frame the sides of the doorway while the solstices become the archway and the threshold. This is the esoteric rationale behind how the seasonal quarters were mapped onto church portals in Gothic architecture. So, two vertical pillars symbolize the equinox points, which is another good reason for associating the Pillars of Hercules with the equinoxes.

This all provides a fascinating and rich symbology, but where is it pointing us? Guénon provides a further clue: The *ne plus ultra* banner strung between the two vertical pillars became the dollar sign of the United States, symbol par excellence of the Western materialism that is running rampant as the Age of Pisces closes and the Age of Aquarius begins. Furthermore, like the Sphinx, the doorway through the Pillars points not only to a time but to a place, because across the ocean, on roughly the same latitude, we find Washington, D.C.! As mentioned earlier, Washington, D.C., is the 90° partner with Rome. The Masonic origins of Washington have been identified by David Ovason in his *Secret Architecture of Our Nation's Capital* (2000). The unrecognized galactic implications in this esoteric symbolism will be taken up in chapter 16.

One more aspect of the Pillars needs to be addressed—their astronomical symbolism. The Age of Aquarius, as we have discussed, is an encoded way in Western astrology of referring to events occurring 90° away, at the Galactic Center. Near the Galactic Center, the dark rift is the cosmic portal comparable with Coomaraswamy's "Sundoor at World's End." This active doorway opens and shuts as the Clashing Cliffs do their trick, and the white arms of the Milky Way that frame the dark rift suggest the Symplegades—steep walls that border the abyss. Coomaraswamy writes that the basic symbolism of the Symplegades is that of a union of contraries or opposing polarities. The two branches of the Milky Way on either side of the dark rift are thus the Symplegades on the galactic level, dividing the north and south galactic hemispheres. Each of these hemispheres has its own set of spin properties, defining opposed sets of phenomena related to the principle of angular momentum and the Coriolis effect. The opening and shutting occurs as a result of the seasonal quarters aligning with the dark rift and Galactic Center—alignments occurring four times during each precessional cycle.

If the Sphinx and the Pillars serve as pointers to the times and places of the alpha and omega of our historical cycle, we can only wonder at how such information, giving meaning to historical processes extending over many millennia, could have been encoded into coincidences of topology and geography. One wonders if the Gaian matrix, the mind of Earth, is intelligent in ways that we can hardly imagine. Whatever the answers are to "how" such an explicit pointer as the Pillars of Hercules could have "happened," we are left with its message staring us right in the face. And so we have a good reason for visiting Washington's District of Columbia.

SIXTEEN

The United States
of the Virgin

Most people might find it hard to believe that the capital of the United States contains many esoteric mysteries. Nevertheless, as David Ovason reveals in his book *The Secret Architecture of Our Nation's Capital*, Washington, D.C., is an expression of the Hermetic wisdom of the ancient Egyptian Brotherhood of Isis.

The Founding Fathers of the United States were members of the Masons, a secretive fraternity offering degrees of initiation into the perennial wisdom, derived from teachings going back to the Hermetic schools of Greece and Egypt. In order to understand the agenda and ideals of the Founding Fathers as they prepared to create a new nation, we need some background in the tradition of Freemasonry.

The religion of Egypt revered Isis, the supreme mother of the gods whose true nature was veiled to mortals. The front of her temple in the ancient city of Sais contained the inscription: "I, Isis, am all that has been, that is or shall be; no mortal man has ever unveiled me." As mother of all stars, suns, and gods, she was the center and source of life. Though she was hidden from mortal eyes, she acted as if from behind the scenes, seeming to be always present. One cannot help thinking about the similar qualities of the Galactic Center, hidden behind the veil of interstellar dark clouds, but emanating constant suprasensory energy and influence. In the Osiris mythology, Isis helps to restore Osiris to life, indicating her function as life-giver. In my opinion, the ankh symbol is revealing of her astronomical reference (see fig. 16.1).

The shape of the ankh combines the cross with a vulvalike opening. Here we have the two basic features near the Galactic Center—the cross of Milky Way and ecliptic (denoting "center") and the oval-shaped cleft of the dark rift in the Milky Way (the cosmic birthplace). A form of the ankh also came to symbolize the planet Venus, which has all the qualities of Isis but on a lower level of manifestation. Also, it appears as if the symbolism of Isis was transferred to the zodiacal sign of Virgo at some point in history. Virgo, Sirius (the Galactic Anticenter indicator), and the Galactic Center are geometrically related in the sky, and Isis has found a home in each location.

Ovason discovered that Virgo-Isis symbolism is encoded into the statues, architecture, and overall alignment of Washington, D.C. Any resident or visitor might begin to notice the frequent occurrence of astrological symbols in the nation's most important public buildings, including the Library of Congress and the Statuary Hall of the Capitol. The Federal Reserve Building and the Library of Congress contain several complete zodiacs. Virgo also seems highlighted by planetary conjunctions that occurred when buildings were dedicated. For example, when the Library of Congress was dedicated on August 28, 1890, the sun and Saturn were both in Virgo. Also, the horoscope for Philadelphia's first Continental Congress, at 10:00 A.M., September 5, 1774, has four planets in Virgo, a situation astrologers would call beneficial.

Figure 16.1. Isis holding the ankh

Ovason identifies many other correspondences with Virgo. For instance, the first marker stone of the city was laid by a group of men (mostly Masons) at Jones Point near Alexandria, Virginia, at 3:30 P.M. on April 15, 1791. At this time Jupiter was rising in the constellation Virgo. The cornerstone was dedicated and sealed in a Masonic ceremony that anointed the stone with corn, wine, and oil. These symbols, especially

Figure 16.2. George Washington laying the cornerstone

corn, play an important role in the identification of Virgo as the mother goddess of life.

A year and a half later, on October 13, 1792, the Georgetown order of Masons laid another marker stone, for the foundation of the White House. On this day, the moon was in Virgo. Ovason observes, "The chances of the correspondence being mere coincidence are so remote that we must assume that whoever was directing the planning of Washington, D.C., not only had a considerable knowledge of astrology, but had a vested interest in emphasizing the role of the sign Virgo."[1]

It is clear that the Founding Fathers were not exactly who we imagined them to be, especially when we consider the evidence of their allegiance to Hermetic principles. For example, George Washington was the Grand Master Mason in the Alexandria Lodge when he became the first president of the United States.

The dedication of the capitol building occurred on September 18, 1793, with Master Mason George Washington presiding. The Sun and Mercury were in the constellation Virgo, and it was year 5793 in the Masonic calendar. (Year 2000 in the Gregorian calendar was year 6000 in the Masonic calendar.) The dedication ceremony is depicted on the bronze doors of the Senate; one door shows George Washington wearing a white Masonic apron and using a trowel to lay the cornerstone. The apron is now on view at the George Washington Masonic Memorial in Alexandria—it depicts American and French flags, a gavel, and a pyramid or triangle surrounded by stars. Since the French and American revolutions paralleled each other and the French were allies, France influenced the ideological development of the United States and often contributed important monuments. For example, France gave the United States the Statue of Liberty, which is a variant of the Virgo-Isis archetype. She represents freedom, but she also represents life. The flame she holds replaces the ear of corn or wheat held by Virgo (see fig. 16.4).

A final example (though we've barely touched upon all the material explored by Ovason), is the laying of the cornerstone of the Washington Monument, which occurred on July 4, 1848, while the Moon was in Virgo. Strangely, construction on the monument was delayed for more than thirty years. When it was officially restarted on the morning of August 7, 1880, the star Spica (in Virgo) was rising over the eastern horizon. (Spica, according to Ovason, is the ear of corn.) The dedication ceremony for the completed Washington Monument did not take place on February 22, 1885 (Washington's actual birthday), but a day earlier. Jupiter was in Virgo.

Beyond the intentional selection of dedication dates, alignments play a significant role in the capital's Virgoan message. The original laying out of the street grid was intended to highlight a specific day. The sun sets directly down Pennsylvania Avenue on August 12 (the first day of the Long Count calendar and the zenith-passage date at Izapa). Right after sunset, if the skies are clear, three stars become visible in a straight line from the capitol building to the White House. These stars are Regulus, Arcturus, and Spica, and they form a right-angled triangle that frames the constellation Virgo. Now, this may seem like a fortuitous coincidence except for the fact that Ovason went on to identify twenty-three complete zodiacs in Washington, many on official public buildings, and over a thousand individual planetary and zodiacal symbols. Furthermore, the encoded message repeatedly refers to Virgo, the virgin who holds the key to life. As Clio, she is the Muse of History who orchestrates the fates of men as if from behind the scenes. Nowhere is there a better statement of this—as well as something else—than in *The Car of History* (fig. 16.3).

In 1819, a sculpture made by the Florentine artist Carlo Franzoni called *The Car of History* was placed in Statuary Hall. It became a central piece of

Figure 16.3. *The Car of History*
(from Ovason, *The Secret Architecture of our Nation's Capitol*)

evidence in Ovason's thesis, and depicts Clio, the Muse of History, seated
in a chariot resting on three zodiacal signs: Sagittarius, Capricorn, and
Aquarius. In this way, *The Car of History* highlights the quarter of the
zodiac occupied by the Galactic Center. In fact, Clio is clearly a version of
the Mary-Isis motif, and she is placed right over the arrow point of the
Sagittarian archer, the sidereal location of the Galactic Center. Unfortunately, no galactic references were explored by Ovason, although this appears
to be the deeper level of the symbolism: Virgo as Isis refers to the Galactic Center. The image of a deity standing on a zodiacal globe is related to
the figure of Aion, the god of time and mover of the heavens, as well as
Mithras, whose duty was the precessional shifting of the zodiacal frame.[2]

It cannot be doubted that deep currents of esoteric doctrine were being transplanted to American soil during the colonial period, and the intention was to honor Virgo, the virgin mother of all creation. This motif would ultimately take us back to the Egyptian Isis cult, with Isis symbolizing the great mother of the gods, the Galactic Center. In addition, the connection of Masonry with ancient Egyptian sacred geometry begins to place the profound model we have sketched into an identifiable historical flow.

But how does this relate to the galactic alignment? Well, we have to remember the fact that Western astrology used the equinox as the marker for precession. As with the cyclic cross at Hendaye, the equinox-galaxy *cross* is just another way of representing the solstice-galaxy *alignment*, 90° away. The two forms of expression are actually equivalent. The symbol of Aquarius, for example—of the renewing waters of life flooding over the earth—is derived from the image of energy flowing into the local planetary system as a result of the solstice alignment with the Galactic Center, 90° away. Astronomically speaking, late Virgo in the unadjusted tropical zodiac (in use in the late 1700s) was 90° away from late Sagittarius. The situation is confused, however, by the need to locate the true sidereal position of Spica, while using an unadjusted astrological zodiac that does not reflect the actual constellations.

I suspect that a reevaluation of the dedication dates and astrological charts examined by Ovason might reveal more explicit associations with Sagittarius. It might also be significant that the Sagittarian archer on *The Car of History* points his arrow toward Capricorn, which is the opposite of the situation in the sky. This allows the Virgin to stand on the point of the arrow, the Galactic Center, near the cusp of Capricorn. In the unadjusted zodiac used by the Founding Fathers (and most Western astrologers today), the Galactic Center is located at 28° Sagittarius. (Its true sidereal position, of course, is 6° Sagittarius.) Nevertheless, the unspoken connection in the minds of the Founding Fathers could have been generalized as a 90° relationship between Spica at 23° Virgo and the Galactic Center at 28° Sagittarius, despite the mixing of frameworks. The observable situation in the sky was more compelling, though equally generalized: When the sun set down Pennsylvania Avenue on August 12 and the triangle of stars that framed Virgo became visible just after sunset, the nuclear bulge of the Galactic Center—the veiled Isis—could be observed arching through the southern skies. Perhaps more relevant are the facts that Spica and the Galactic Anticenter are almost exactly 90° away and the Galactic Anitcenter is on the same meridian as Sirius (associated with Isis).

David Ovason's book is a revelation, though we should take his findings a step further toward a galactic grand finale. Whether or not this be judged advisable, the stellar linkup of Washington, D.C., is undeniable, though what may have motivated it remains mysterious. Ovason concludes, "In 1790, someone conceived of linking this city with the stars and that tradition continued for 200 years. . . . It died out about 1950. I could never find out who did this, but someone, somewhere, maintained this incredible esoteric view of the zodiac."[3]

After the Revolutionary War, Masonry spread westward with the pioneers and evolved under the guidance of Grand Master Albert Pike, who traveled the American West in the mid-1800s and after whom Pike's Peak in Colorado was named. He exemplified the latter-day phase of Masonry in the United States, when Masonry played an active role in building American towns but forgot its deep connection with Egyptian wisdom. Still, with the spread west across America, Masons went everywhere and laid out towns with their surveyor's art, not unlike the ancient dodmen of the British Isles. Geographical and topological placements were always at work, augmenting the architectural design of government and private buildings. Their dedications and cornerstone-laying ceremonies are documented in small-town archives throughout middle and western America, and Freemasons were often called upon to consecrate time capsules, as with the time capsule in Boulder, Colorado, to be opened in A.D. 2076. Old buildings dedicated by Masons in little towns throughout the West are often adorned with Hermetic symbols traceable to ancient Egypt! With this in mind, Washington, D.C., simply fits a larger pattern as an expression of an underground stream of wisdom, and it shouldn't surprise us to find Hermetic symbols and alignments there, not unlike the carefully concealed messages in Gothic cathedrals.[4]

The mysteries of Isis were central to the ancient Egyptian initiatory religion, the highest revelation of which we might imagine having been the knowledge that Isis, a place in the sky, generates, centers, and regenerates the world in measurable time cycles. The secret society of Isis went underground as history moved forward into new eras of greater materialism and ignorance of the ancient wisdom. Yet the core symbol—Isis as Cosmic Mother—survived by becoming the Virgin Mary. Cults in

Figure 16.4. Virgo-Isis

medieval Europe honored her transforming power in the guise of the
Black Madonna, and mainstream Christianity reserved a special place for
her as the Mother of God. Throughout history, Hermetic teachings preserved core information about Isis without overtly revealing her identity,
which was strictly prohibited. In fact, the obscurantist tendency of esotericism is noticed in how the Isis symbology was transformed to the
zodiacal sign of Virgo. There's no way to really tell when this happened,
but it might have been during the age when the equinox corresponded
with the Pleiades, around 2200 B.C. The vernal equinox became the
marker for the shifting ages of the zodiac, but as we mentioned before,
the important reference in these zodiacal alignments were often to the

solstice position, 90° away. This seems to be the case with the identification of Isis with Virgo; although as the Galactic Center she stands in Sagittarius, it was safer to place her 90° away in Virgo so as to protect her wisdom from unworthy soma rapers. In a similar way, the dawning of the Age of Aquarius is only significant because it indicates the solstice alignment with the Milky Way, 90° away.

Even if we ignore the probable role played by the Galactic Center in the use of Virgo symbolism in Washington, D.C., we can at least accept that the Mother Goddess is placed high in this Masonic cosmography. But this esteem is not limited to Masonry. Christian congregations throughout the United States often assemble in churches called "Our Lady of the Immaculate Conception" and the Virgin Mary plays an important role in Christian doctrine. In fact, she plays such an important role that the title of this chapter, "The United States of the Virgin," is completely justified: At the Council of Baltimore in May 1845, the American Catholic bishops declared Mary Immaculate the patroness of the United States.

Mary's role is ubiquitous throughout Latin America. Church facades in Mexico, Central America, and South America usually depict a hierarchy of spiritual beings, including Jesus, saints, and angels. Often, the highest niche of the facade houses the Virgin Mary, known in esoteric traditions as Sophia or Isis—the ever-merciful bestower of grace, wisdom, and renewal. The underground Hermetic stream underlies the exoteric dogmas of Christianity and is rooted in the same ancient wisdom from which springs Freemasonry. It is not surprising that the underground wisdom came to the Americas with European colonists, and found strange confirmation in Native cosmologies, though such correlations remain largely unexplored.

Washington, D.C., appears to be the western terminus in our model of the geography of precession. Beginning in Vedic India, we traveled halfway around the world, but stayed at the same latitude. For a true opposition in geography-based epochs, we need to travel into the southern hemisphere. There, directly south of Washington, D.C, we find Peru and the high Andes, which we have mentioned together with Tibet as the likely seed points for the ascending and descending eras of precession. It is strange to think that these locations, opposing each other on the globe, are the highest plateaus on Earth, where human beings are closest to the celestial realm.

SEVENTEEN

Circles of Water:
The Galaxy in South America

L ima and Cuzco were centers of colonial Christianity in South America, and many Gothic-style churches can still be found in those towns. Most of the church facades were designed according to the traditional religious iconography of fifteenth- and sixteenth-century Spain. These styles in turn were influenced by late-Gothic symbolism as we find it in Spain and France. What is usually referred to as "Hermetic" has played a larger role in history than most historians will admit. The dynastic alliances that funded New World colonization were rooted in Hermetic movements stemming from the Templar reclamation of Jerusalem in the twelfth century. It was fashionable and politically desirable for rulers to claim descent from Aurilac and Anjou, because those families claimed to be heir to the bloodline of the House of David, to which Jesus belonged. Thus, secular kingship and rule could be validated by a demonstrated or declared relationship to the sovereign Lord of the World himself. Conscious recognition of these ideas was largely submerged by the late 1400s, though ruling dynasties still claimed God-given rights to rule and sought alliances with other powerful dynasties through marriage.

Such was the case with Ferdinand and Isabella, whose marriage united the houses of Castile and León in Spain. Their role in history was to fund Columbus and the early stages of New World conquest. They, and other European financiers over several centuries, also funded the construction of Christian cathedrals. Colonial religious architecture, as mentioned earlier, structures a cosmological hierarchy of deities and angels up to the Most High, who presides over all lower levels of manifestation. The "waters" of life and transcendent spiritual vision then flow downward, blessing all beings. Contrary to what we might expect, however, in colonial South

Figure 17.1. Spanish colonial church, Lima
(from Wethey, *Colonial Architecture and Sculpture in Peru*)

America the Most High is almost always the Virgin Mother of God. The Egyptian Isis is the ultimate source of this motif, and her association with the Galactic Center has already been discussed.

It is quite possible that the Vedic civilization precedes the Egyptian Isis cult, and in this context we can return briefly to the insights of Ananda Coomaraswamy. In his essay "On the Loathly Bride," Coomaraswamy shows how the Mother of God is always depicted as a flower who rises from a lotus as an earth goddess. She precedes all other manifestations and underlies all earthly expressions of power, including kingship. Secular or royal power is female or, more commonly in the West, is granted by a prospective king's contact with a female being, usually of a divine nature. This formula reflects the Gnostic Christian view that the prior miracle giving rise to the Savior himself was the miracle of the Immaculate Conception of Mary. God the Father still lurks behind Mary, but we don't find him much in colonial-era Christian iconography.

Colonial architecture certainly provides interesting support for the Isis origin of the Virgin in Washington, D.C. A galactic knowledge encoded into esoteric traditions thus seems to have moved westward, crossing the Atlantic and taking root on new soil. It didn't bring anything new to the Americas, however. Mayan, Aztec, Incan, and virtually all native civilizations in the Americas already had an appreciation for the Milky Way. And the Maya, for certain, mythologized the Milky Way as a Great Mother. More to the point, the Maya were probably the most cosmologically advanced civilization in the Americas, and they recognized the Galactic Center as the womb of the Great Mother—the source and origin of the Sun and all life. When the invasion occurred, indigenous Americans saw in the Virgin Mary atop the Spanish churches a reflection of their own deepest beliefs about the Cosmic Mother. And rightly so, for both ideologies stem from a metaphysical understanding of the role played by the Galactic Center in human spirituality—although both worlds were oblivious to the galactic roots of their beliefs during the colonial period. Suffice it to say that colonial religious architecture in Mexico and Central and South America honors the Virgin Mary as the deity that is Most High, above the world of duality and death; she is the Mother of God and is an expression of Isis, the Galactic Center Mother Goddess of ancient Egypt.

Peru was home to a thriving Incan empire when the Spaniards arrived. In Incan cosmology we find clear evidence that the Milky Way was of great interest, and the Galactic Center was occupied by a life-giving-mother motif. *At the Crossroads of the Earth and the Sky* by Gary Urton remains the best source for the galactic sky lore of the contemporary Quechua Indians of highland Peru. When I say "galactic" I simply mean *ideas and beliefs involving the Milky Way, our galaxy.* Urton did his fieldwork in the village of Misminay, not far from Cuzco. The beliefs of the

Quechua undoubtedly reflect general beliefs among the ancient Inca, and the Milky Way plays a central role. In fact, the life-giving Vilcanota River that runs through the town of Misminay symbolizes the Milky Way and is oriented to the Milky Way overhead at agriculturally important times of the year.

In South America, the region of the Milky Way containing the Galactic Center is very high overhead. This fact, combined with pristine viewing conditions in the high altiplano of Peru, makes the nuclear bulge in Sagittarius-Scorpio dramatic and impossible to ignore. The Milky Way is so distinct that, in addition to the great cleft running north of Sagittarius that interested the Maya, many dark-cloud features along the Milky Way were identified by the Inca (see fig. 17.2). These dark-cloud "constellations" include the Fox, Toad, Tinamou, Snake, and Mother Llama and her suckling baby. The latter two represent the life-nurturing quality that we see in the Virgin Mary motif. Perhaps it is no coincidence that the Mother Llama and her baby are located on the Galactic Center. The Fox is close by, and in his book *The Secret of the Incas* William Sullivan argued that the Fox is involved in Incan precessional mythology.[1]

The Scorpio constellation is very important for the Quechua, and was thought of as a plow or a storehouse. The opposite side of the Milky Way, near the Pleiades, is also significant; both the tail of Scorpio and the Pleiades are thought of as storehouses (of sustenance). One or both of

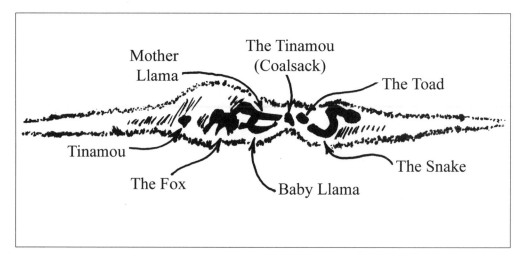

Figure 17.2. Dark-cloud constellations in Quechua star lore
(adapted from Urton, *At the Crossroads of the Earth and the Sky*)

these areas seem to have been thought of as the top of the cosmic mountain. Perhaps they were conceived as poles of a "storehouse" axis; if so, this Scorpio-Pleiades polarity indicates a conscious recognition of the Galactic Center–Galactic Anticenter axis. The sun passes through the Scorpio side around the December solstice, and life-giving rain is generated by this passage. The rainy and dry seasons are triggered by the Sun's passage through the Milky Way, and this knowledge is encoded into the "intentional flooding of Cuzco" tradition as well as the design of the mysterious ancient site of Tiahuanaco, to the south. As we shall see, both of these traditions involve the life cycle of rain and are triggered by the alignment of the Sun with the Milky Way on the solstices. Although many aspects of Incan tradition could be explored, I will focus on these two traditions in this chapter.

According to the Spanish chronicler Molina, just after the December solstice the people of Cuzco threw food, coca, gold, spices, clothing and other things into the water behind a dam above the city. After sunset they opened the floodgates and the water poured through the streets of the city, scouring everything in its path and sweeping away all the burned offerings that were left curbside. Below the city, where the Tullumayu and Huatanay Rivers meet, runners were waiting. They helped the offerings channel into the Vilcamayu River and then began a riverside race of some thirty miles to a point near Ollantaytambo where the river drops steeply into a canyon, ultimately to merge with the Amazon and the "northern sea" (the Atlantic Ocean).

The ceremonial event took place during a time of the year when the Milky Way angled southeast-northwest overhead after sunset. Along the sides of the Vilcamayu River people held lanterns to light the runners' way. The Milky Way itself, ablaze with points of light, reflected the dramatic spectacle on Earth. Urton wrote that the procession along the Vilcamayu was equivalent to a journey along the Milky Way—the implied ultimate goal being the "northern sea," meaning heaven.[2] In this tradition the entire Sacred Valley of the Vilcamayu River reflects the Milky Way, and the ceremony facilitates what Urton calls "the cosmic circulation of water."[3] The release of the renewing waters of life was keyed to the Sun's alignment with the Milky Way.

The pre-Incan city of Tiahuanaco, south of Cuzco, is designed in such a way as to encode a religious system of renewal involving the "circulation of water." The intention was agricultural, and was tied to irrigation systems that fed fields for miles around. However, the process was essentially inspired by cosmological insights involving the galaxy. As with the Cuzco tradition described above, the Tiahuanaco system was aligned with the solstices, and the Milky Way was the great river of life believed to supply rain at certain times of the year. The ceremonial precinct of Tiahuanaco was surrounded by a moat, to give the impression of the site as a floating island. The central feature of the core precinct is a man-made mountain of seven levels rising some fifty feet high, called Akapana. The adjacent Semi-subterranean Temple and the Kalasaya lie along an east-west axis— the Sun's rising and setting horizons on the equinoxes. A sunken courtyard was found atop the Akapana temple. Its purpose was to catch rainwater, and a system of drains within the pyramid channeled the water along the edges of each level and back, flowing horizontally underneath to be ingeniously drawn out again at the top level of the temple.[4]

As William Sullivan summarizes, "Like any true cosmic mountain, the Akapana recycled as well the waters of life, whose headwaters arose at the top of the cosmic mountain, at June solstice in the precincts of the Milky Way."[5] I need to emphasize that the solstice-galaxy alignments underlie the sacred function of both Tiahuanaco and the Flooding of Cuzco ceremony. We can compare this fact with the early Greek doctrine of the ascent and descent of souls through the galactic gateways on the solstices—a circulation of life essence. I mentioned earlier how the solstice sun's alignment with the galaxy might apply for upward of 1,500 years (because the Milky Way is wide and the alignment can be generalized). This range embraces the Incan empire as well as the latest phase of occupation at Tiahuanaco (ca. A.D. 600).

Tiahuanaco holds many mysteries, and there is no space to do justice to them here. I can only mention that the calendrical inscriptions on the Gate of the Sun deserve close scrutiny in light of precession.[6] Strangely, the structure of the glyphs on the Gate of the Sun is similar to the facade structure of colonial churches—little niches of deities all facing center, topped with a prominent "most high" figure. It's tempting to equate the Gate of the Sun with Coomaraswamy's Sundoor at World's End; its purpose appears to have been metaphysically equivalent.

Arthur Posnansky's *Tihuanacu: The Cradle of American Man* has rattled academics for decades, and contains many points of great interest. His

Figure 17.3. Gate of the Sun, Tiahuanaco

dating of Tiahuanaco to 12,000 B.C. may ultimately be incorrect—his astronomical argument doesn't support such precise calculation.[7] Nevertheless, although modern archaeologists are prone to date Tiahuanaco to circa A.D. 600 (which may simply be a later phase), certain mysteries persist. Underwater ruins in nearby Lake Titicaca have been found, which itself is an anomalous inland sea containing vestiges of saltwater marine life. No one has been able to explain how such a lake could exist at 11,000 feet above sea level, nor why many cyclopean walls of stone in the area appear slanted, like a sheet of ancient concretized seabed pushed sideways by continental uplifting. Such questions have been explored extensively,[8] but we must let these mysteries rest and move forward to identify something new about the Peruvian altiplano.

The dark rift that plays such an important role in Mayan precessional cosmology is so large a feature viewed from South America that it was thought of as simply a great canyon dividing the Milky Way into two white branches. It's interesting to remember here that the Milky Way was associated with water, and Cuzco is situated between two large river branches, the Tullumayu and Huatanay, that join southeast of town and flow down the Sacred Valley, eventually reaching the Amazon. The sacred geography of Cuzco is mirrored in miniature at Misminay. In other words, the framework of the Milky Way alignments at Misminay reflects the larger context of the entire Sacred Valley of the Vilcamayu-Urubamba River, in which the Urubamba itself is the Milky Way. In fact, the entire chain of the Andes conforms to this orientation, which may indicate something important.

If Peru is viewed from above, the entire high plateau appears to be roughly rectangular, a fact that led writer Jim Allen to argue that Peru was the site of Atlantis.[9] Measurements given by Plato conform to the dimensions of the upper plateau, and Allen found a strange circular mountain in Peru that fits other criteria given by Plato. His work may be on target, but the "lost city" may ultimately be astronomical in nature. As just mentioned, Cuzco lies between two rivers that form the symbolic Milky Way in Incan thought. The unusual geological bifurcation of rivers that surrounds Cuzco most closely conforms to the part of the Milky Way that is bifurcated by the dark rift north of Sagittarius. In this sense, if we map the sky onto Peru, Cuzco is in the dark rift. The entire rectangular upper plateau could be seen to reflect the large dark rift whose southern terminus touches the ecliptic and nuclear bulge of the Galactic Center. If Cuzco itself is not the Galactic Center on earth, we might look a little south of Cuzco, where we find Lake Titicaca and Tiahuanaco. The Incan emergence or Creation myth occurs at a cave near Titicaca, and as with all Creation myths, this is no doubt an encoded reference to celestial events.

Only Peru and Tibet contain large sections of continuous high plateau. Travelers have often noted that the Andean and Tibetan cultures resemble each other in many ways. Geologically, they are the places on Earth that are in closest contact with the sky. The chain of the Andes, the Sierra Madres, and the Rockies run roughly northwest-southeast through the Americas. In fact, we can track the high points northward from the Peruvian Andes through Central America, Mexico, the western United States, Alaska, along the North Pole, and down through Central Asia, the Himalayas, western Australia, and underneath Antarctica to emerge at the southern tip of Tierra del Fuego—the southern Andes. Without a topographical globe in hand it's hard to picture this, but no one can deny that a circular chain of mountains runs crosswise around the globe, at roughly a 60° angle to the equator. If we imagine this mega-chain to be the terrestrial counterpart to the Milky Way, then two locations present

Figure 17.4. Cuzco, crossroads of the galactic globe

themselves as candidates for being the Galactic Center on Earth: Tibet and Peru. This is the biggest mapping of sky onto Earth that we could imagine. This is "as above, so below" in a big way.

Cuzco and Tiahuanaco thus occupy a unique place on the globe. We can further elaborate this fact by fusing it with the idea of a "geography of precession" discussed in chapter 15. The Age of Leo in Tibet/India represents the era in which the December solstice sun aligned with the Galactic Anticenter, where the Milky Way runs through Gemini. Thus, the Age of Aquarius in the Americas represents the era in which the December solstice sun aligns with the Galactic Center. Two extremes of Earth geography, both crowned by the highest mountain ranges on Earth, are combined with the two extremes of precession—the alpha and omega of time. This model encodes a kind of "unified theory" of space-time, with human history being some kind of essence that gets generated by the process that directs the civilizing impulse.

We might want to be more specific with the placement of the Galactic Center in South American topography. The altiplano of Peru certainly provides an excellent counterpart to the dark rift, and if Atlantis was truly galactic in nature, perhaps Tiahuanaco with its moat and seven-tiered temple fits the bill. Tiahuanaco is at 16° south latitude, and at a certain latitude in South America the Galactic Center can pass through the zenith—the exact center of the sky overhead. If we look, however, for what's happening on the Mayan calendar end-date, December 21, 2012, we find that the solstice sun–Galactic Center combo pass through the zenith together at the Tropic of Capricorn, 23°26' south. In addition, at the moment of the Galactic Center's passage with the solstice sun through the zenith, Sirius is at nadir. This means that twelve hours later Sirius, because it is on the meridian of the Galactic Anticenter, will pass through the zenith—quite an astounding double display of cosmic convergence.

We could examine many other South American mysteries, but the point has been made: galactic lore is everywhere in Incan and pre-Incan traditions, and the Galactic Center as well as solstice-galaxy alignments are implicated quite clearly. Nevertheless, we are drawn back to the Cuzco region, for its Incan traditions are so intimately tied to the cycles of the Milky Way. We should recall that the cross at Hendaye in France points to Peru as the place of refuge from the catastrophe timed by the impending solstice-galaxy alignment. Cuzco was divided into precincts, much like Aztec and Mayan cities, such that four zones were created, corresponding roughly to the four cardinal directions. The great tradition of sacred topography reemerges here, which we examined first in ancient Britain, where the Isle of Man was revealed to symbolize the Galactic Center on earth. And here we are, halfway around the world, in Cuzco, arguing for the same thing. This appears contradictory, but every culture wanted to map or "download" the cosmic center into the local environment. It is a testimony to the perceptive brilliance of so many ancient cultures that they all decided upon the Galactic Center as the true celestial center, and mapped out their terrain accordingly to reflect such an understanding. Perhaps the ultimate irony of these discoveries is that Western civilization has only recently caught up to this level of knowledge.

With these ley-line considerations in mind we should revisit Izapa, which was an early locus for the development of Mayan civilization. Since the Long Count calendar that gives us 2012 originated with the Izapan civilization, its alignments and monuments should reveal a primary interest in the Galactic Center. And they do. Furthermore, new discoveries at Izapa and its nearby sacred volcano, Tacana, reveal a large grid of geographical alignments that point to the Galactic Center as well as major Mayan cities. It thus appears that, as in the Mayan Creation myth, the earth was mapped out by "stretching the measuring cord" over the landscape. Incredibly, in this ley-line grid, Tulum, Copan, and Palenque are centered on Tacana volcano, which truly must be the navel of the Mesoamerican cosmos.

EIGHTEEN

Izapan Galactic Cosmology and the Ley-Line Grid

I n order to understand the importance of the ley-line grid centered on Tacana volcano, we need to review the Izapan alignments to Tacana as well as those to the Galactic Center. The message of Izapa's monuments can only be understood in light of their orientation to horizon astronomy. Three primary monument groups lie in different areas of the site, and each represents one of three cosmic centers—polar, zenith, or galactic. Groups A (polar), B (zenith), and F (galactic) encode something profound and unrecognized about the Izapan awareness of astronomy.

Izapa's monuments contain recognizable scenes from Mayan Creation mythology—adventures of the Hero Twins and their father, and their triumph over the vain and false ruler of the previous World Age, Seven Macaw. These themes were later incorporated into the Quiché *Popol Vuh*. (Although the *Popol Vuh* is sometimes called a postconquest document, its stories and deities are first portrayed on the monuments of Izapa, circa 100 B.C.) For example, Stela 25 from Group A contains a recognizable *Popol Vuh* episode in which Hunahpu's arm is torn off by Seven Macaw. Since Seven Macaw is associated with the polar region, I have suggested that the "fall" of Seven Macaw involved the demise of an old cosmological system centered upon the polar region. The shamanistic concern with knowing where the center of the sky is located is central to understanding this "cosmological shift." The shift, after Seven Macaw was done away with, was to an opposite orientation.

Not only does Stela 25 depict an episode from the *Popol Vuh* Creation myth, it also embodies a dialectic between two parts of the sky—the Big Dipper polar region and the "head" of the Milky Way monster near Sagittarius. Group A is oriented some 21° east of true north, which is the sight line to the peak of Tacana volcano. Also significant, the perpendicular to

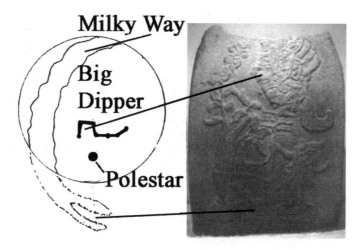

Figure 18.1. Stela 25 and the polar center–Galactic Center opposition

this main axis is sighted on the December solstice horizon. These are the astronomical horizons of the polar-galactic dialectic. The dialectic sets the head of the Stela 25 caiman in opposition to Seven Macaw. This "caiman head" symbolizes the location of an important "center of the sky"—it is the location of the center of our Milky Way galaxy. Generally, this monument, as well as many others from Izapa (for example, Stela 11) indicate an interest in the Milky Way, the dark rift in the Milky Way (the caiman's mouth is the dark rift), and the Big Dipper.

The symbolism of the monuments in Groups A and B is very interesting, but for now let's move to the monuments of Group F. My basic idea is that the message of the monuments cannot be fully understood unless we take into account the site's orientation, local topography, and horizon astronomy. These factors will be particularly significant for understanding how Group F's monuments encode the solstice-galaxy alignment of era 2012.

Group F is on the north side of the site, and its ballcourt is an important feature. In fact, most of Group F's monuments are located in the ballcourt section. We will need to zoom in to the ballcourt very closely to see how the lengthwise axis of the ballcourt is oriented to the December solstice horizon. These monuments were found in situ in the 1960s by a team from Brigham Young University. The throne group at position B faces the December solstice horizon. In addition, the entire lengthwise axis of the ballcourt is oriented toward that horizon.

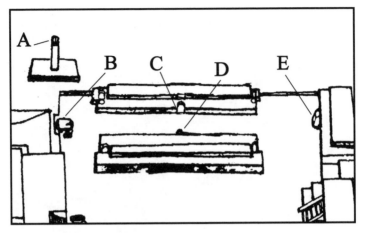

Figure 18.2. Group F: galactic alignment monuments in the
Izapan ballcourt. *A,* Sitting figure on pillar facing north;
B, Throne 2, snake-mouth ballcourt marker, ball, and goal-
ring stones; *C,* Stela 67, period-ending solar lord in Milky
Way canoe; *D,* M.M. 25, eroded paddler god or sky-lifter
sculpture; *E,* Stela 60, victorious ball player stands over a
defeated Seven Macaw (Big Dipper).

Monument A portrays a crouching figure on top of the pillar. Despite
its broken condition, it is clear that the figure faces Tacana to the north.
The monuments at position B include Throne 2, a ring and ball, and a
serpent head with open mouth that originally served as a ballcourt marker
stone. If one sat on Throne 2 at the west end of the ballcourt, one would
look out over the stela at position E toward the December solstice horizon.

Although eroded, it is clear that Stela 60 at position E depicts a victorious ballplayer, possibly one of the Hero Twins, standing over a
defeated Seven Macaw bird deity. This indicates to the viewer two things:
the former god, now defeated, and the new god, newly "born" or newly
"risen." This scene relates to the Creation myth wherein the Hero Twins
must defeat the vain, false ruler of the previous World Age, Seven Macaw,
before their father, One Hunahpu, can be reborn. An examination of early
Mesoamerican calendrics demonstrates that One Hunahpu was originally
associated with the December solstice sun.[1] This scenario confirms that
separate argument. And, of course, it needn't be emphasized—because we
can see it in figure 18.3—that the December solstice sun rises over the
stela depicting the defeated Seven Macaw. The stela says "The polar god
is dead, the solar god is born." The solar god's rebirth, however, is inex-

tricably involved in its future alignment with the Milky Way, as we shall see.

One feature not illustrated in figure 18.3, for clarity, is the Milky Way. The solstice horizon would actually look like figure 18.4. Here we see the Milky Way converging with the position of the dawning December solstice sun in a process caused by the precession of the equinoxes. This is a very significant fact: The horizon that we are examining is where a precession-caused convergence between the Milky Way and the December solstice sun

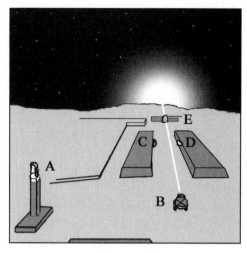

Figure 18.3. December solstice sunrise from the ballcourt throne

has been occurring for thousands of years, and the solstice solar god and the Milky Way align in the years around A.D. 2012. Would the designers of the Group F ballcourt have been interested in the horizon along which this convergence occurs? As skywatchers and calendar priests, without a doubt.

But let's look now at the monument found at location C, which is midway along the ballcourt, halfway between Stela 60 and the Throne 2 monuments.

On the north side of the ballcourt, at position C, a monument depicts a solar lord sitting in the middle of a canoe with his arms outstretched. The canoe probably represents both the ballcourt and the Milky Way, toward which the ballcourt is oriented. The outstretched arms indicate a period-ending "measuring of time" event. Since the contextual orientation of the ballcourt is to the December

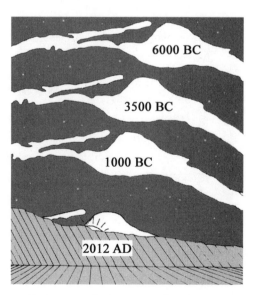

Figure 18.4. Convergence of solstice sun and Milky Way

Figure 18.5. Stela 67, solstice sun in the Milky Way canoe

solstice, which itself is a period ending, we might presume that the solar lord is the December solstice lord. (This is a conclusion supported by the "First Father/One Hunahpu = December solstice sun" evidence mentioned earlier.) This stela thus seems to portray the December solstice sun sitting in the middle of the Milky Way "canoe." It is extremely interesting that the part of the Milky Way that rises over the solstice horizon to the southeast is the nuclear bulge of the Milky Way—the part of the Milky Way that contains the Galactic Center. (The nuclear bulge can be seen with naked-eye observation by anyone who looks at the Milky Way on a dark night.)

It is an astronomical fact that 2,200 years ago the Milky Way, with its nuclear bulge, was 30° above the dawning December solstice sun. Furthermore, in our era, the two have now converged and the December solstice sun now "sits in the middle" of the Milky Way. It is a period-ending event, as indicated on Stela 67, because the 13-*baktun* cycle of the Long Count ends in A.D. 2012. My main thesis is that the creators of the Long Count calendar intended the 2012 date to indicate this alignment of the December solstice sun with the Milky Way's center. In the Creation myth, this astronomical convergence was encoded as the rebirth of One Hunahpu from the womb of the Great Mother. Since the earliest Long Count monuments are dated to Izapa's heyday (first century B.C.), it is clear that the Long Count and the Creation myth arose at the same time and in the same place: Izapa.

At position D there is an eroded sculpture, opposite the stela we just described. It has been compared to a "danzante" sculpture found nearby at Tuxtla Chico, which in turn is iconographically related to the San Martín "sky-lifter" deity of the Olmec, who holds a bar that represents the Milky Way. Linda Schele interpreted the lifting of the Milky Way as a creation event; at the very least it seems to indicate that the sky can move or shift. The image suggests a deity who shifts the galactic frame of the sky.

The most compelling monuments in the Group F ballcourt revolve around position B, all of which speak to my hypothesis that the people who designed Group F were aware of the future convergence of Milky Way and solstice sun, occurring over the southeastern horizon. The main feature here is the throne, which gives birth to a human head from between two splayed legs—a motif called the hocker position, indicating birthing. (This throne group actually faces Stela 60 on the opposite end of the ballcourt; in figure 18.6 I have rotated it for viewing purposes.) In *Maya Cosmogenesis 2012* there is a lengthy discussion about throne-sitting shamans as lords, birthers, ballplayers, and conjurers. Here I'll simply focus on the most obvious symbolism of the throne monuments. The birth canal between the legs of the throne figure is analogous to the dark rift in the Milky Way. This "black cleft" feature is called by the modern Quiché Maya the *xibalba be*, the "Road to the Underworld." As translator Dennis Tedlock has shown, the *xibalba be* plays an important role in the *Popol Vuh*, being the Black Road that at one point speaks to the Hero Twins. Generally, as an underworld portal, it is related to the complex of motifs assigned to the jaguar's mouth, caves, cenotes, a woman's birth canal, temple doorways, and so on. A significant inflection of this mythic complex is the "dark rift as birth canal," for it is through the birth canal of the Milky Way that the solstice sun will be reborn in the years around 2012.

The head emerging from between the legs is the sun, and the splayed legs frame the birth canal that is the dark rift in the Milky Way. Below this head is a ball and ring, which refer to the symbolism of the ball game. In the Mayan ball game, the game ball is the December solstice sun and the goal-ring is the dark-rift in the Milky Way. Finally, the upside-down serpent head on the left side of the diagram is a ballcourt marker. These

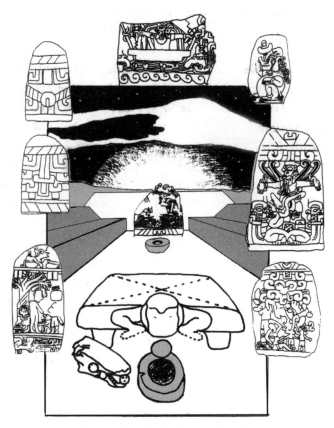

Figure 18.6. Galactic cosmology in
the Izapan ballcourt

markers usually had a solar lord in their mouths; this one appears to be broken off. The sun in the serpent mouth is equivalent to the two other symbols, all of which indicate, in three different ways, the convergence occurring over the distant horizon. The Sun being born, the Sun being swallowed, and the ball game—these three ways of thinking about the alignment are not in conflict. Instead, they reveal to us the way that the creators of the Long Count thought about the era-2012 alignment. There is no "prophecy" here. It says that there is a possibility of renewal, a possibility of death, and the ball game indicates that we are active participants in how the game (of the current historical cycle) ends. Much has and will be written about 2012. This date is a Mayan artifact, but, as we have seen, what it refers to (the solstice-galaxy alignment) was recognized by many ancient civilizations. Nevertheless, it is obvious that to understand the meaning of 2012, we must look at the culture that invented the Long Count that gives us that date.[2] Izapa's Group F ballcourt is ground zero of this knowledge, and there is plenty there to help us understand what we, today, are fated to live through. The encoded message of the ballcourt is a testimony to the brilliance of the ancient Izapan skywatchers.

Much more could be added to this brief summary. What I have attempted to do is interpret the message of these monuments based upon the horizon astronomy toward which they are oriented and which they were intended to encode. One thing is interesting to consider: Given the integrative continuity of its monuments, sculptures, calendrics, and alignments, is it possible that Group F *does not* have anything to do with the precessional convergence of Milky Way and solstice sun? That's the galactic side of the equation, the cosmic orientation adopted by the Izapans after they forsook the false polar god to the north. And there is testimony at Izapa about this abandoned, ancient, polar god. Group A contains monuments that depict the rise and fall of the Seven Macaw bird deity (the Big Dipper) over Tacana volcano to the north. All of these monuments are oriented to Tacana, such that priests making offerings on the altars in front of each monument would (on a clear day) have a view of Tacana. Without a doubt, the Izapans considered Tacana to be their primary sacred mountain, and Seven Macaw can still be seen there, as a reminder, rising and falling.

Today, daykeepers among the Quiché Maya in highland Guatemala make offerings at shrines in the hills surrounding their villages. The shrines are associated with the primary directions, and are visited on certain days in the 260-day calendar. Shrines higher in elevation are visited on day signs having a higher number, from 1 to 13. The four highest (and most distant) peaks surrounding the town are reserved for the shrines of the four year-bearers—sacred day signs that initiate the New Year. The monument groups at Izapa clearly have a calendric function, and Tacana must have been conceived as the residence of one of the highest year-bearers. We can imagine that pilgrimages to Tacana were undertaken regularly by Izapan calendar priests. Strangely, even today a tradition exists in which hikers from Guatemala and Mexico converge at the peak of Tacana twice every year—on Good Friday and around the December solstice. The Mam Indians still leave offerings at a little hearth shrine atop Tacana. Tellingly, the border between Mexico and Guatemala cuts right

Figure 18.7. Galactic Center rising, viewed from the peak of Tacana

across the peak of Tacana, making it a geopolitical Symplegades dividing Central and North America. To compound the strange survival of Mayan rituals on Tacana, a Mexican friend of mine who has climbed Tacana reports that an iron cross is at the top. Photographs reveal that this iron cross is oriented to the southeast, to another high volcanic peak, Tajumulco, the highest peak in Central America. The orientation of the cross to Tajumulco also happens to be the precise orientation to the December solstice sunrise, as viewed from the top of Tacana. Of course, the Galactic Center rises along the exact same place on the horizon, and the nearby Milky Way and ecliptic compose the "cosmic cross."

This situation is unprecedented. Some 2,100 years ago, when the Izapan skywatchers and calendar priests climbed Tacana around the December solstice, they could have sat up there all night, enduring the frigid winds near the abode of the gods at 14,000 feet, waiting to observe the heart of creation and the cosmic cross rise over Tajumulco, followed quickly by the dawning sun. Today, we would need to climb Tacana in late January or early February to witness the same spectacle. Perhaps climbers have gazed across the highlands to see the tail of Scorpio rising, or Sagittarius perhaps, known to the Quiché Maya as the Thieves' Cross.

The importance of Tacana in the ritual mind-set of the ancient Izapans shouldn't be underestimated. It was the primary topographical reference point for the Izapans, and a close look at a good map of the region reveals some surprises. As mentioned, from atop Tacana one notices the peak of Tajumulco to the southeast, aligned with the December solstice sunrise. This sunrise position of course was all-important for the Izapan alignment cosmology. Tacana's peak is almost precisely at 15° north latitude. Directly to the east, along this latitude, a highpoint rises in the terrain, indicating sunrise on the equinoxes. To complete the picture, to the northeast another peak near Ixchiguan precisely indicates the direction of the summer-solstice sunrise. The horizon east of Tacana provides a seasonal calendar, which indicates that Tacana occupies a special place in the sacred geography of the region; it is no wonder that the Izapans thought of it as an *axis mundi* of their world. But there's more.

The equinox direction from Tacana of course lies directly east. It is well known that Copan, the great southern city of the Maya, also lies on this latitude. In the myth, at the dawn of time, First Father, like some cosmic geometer, stretched the cord to map out the earth. It is believed that Izapan calendric traditions may have been transferred to Copan; they share a latitude that divides the year into zenith-passage intervals of 260 and 105 days. Next, imagine standing atop Tacana, watching Scorpio and the Galactic Center rising over the December solstice horizon to the southeast. Since we are aware of the Scorpio-Pleiades polarity in Mesoamerican thought, we might turn around and think we could point to the Pleiades in the opposite direction. The sky doesn't exactly move in such a way, but if we were mapping the sky onto the earth, such a perspective could very well be maintained. Is it a coincidence then if we draw a line from the Galactic Center rising over Tajumulco through the Tacana peak and northwestward, that the line points right to Teotihuacan, built by the People of the Pleiades? A main southeast-northwest axis is thus defined, based on the Galactic Center–Pleiades polarity, providing the primary axis for a ley-line grid that extends over most of Mesoamerica.

Notice in figure 18.8 that the main axis conforms to the backbone of

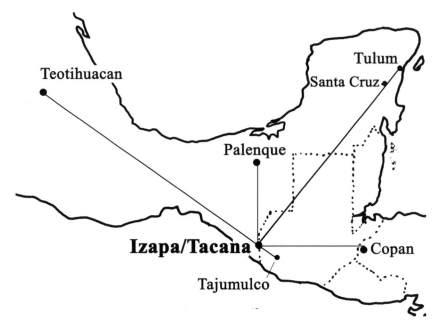

Figure 18.8. Ley-line grid emanating from Tacana volcano

the Sierra Madres that I suggested earlier could be thought of as the Milky Way mapped onto the earth. The Galactic Center direction points toward South America. Observe in the map how Copan lies directly east of Tacana/Izapa. Also, another great Mayan city, Palenque, lies directly north of Tacana/Izapa. As if this weren't enough, a perpendicular line from the main axis points to Tulum and a little Cruzob Mayan town called Santa Cruz, where the prophetic talking cross directed the Mayan Caste War in the 1850s. The latitude of this town is significant, because it is the latitude at which the zenith-Pleiades cosmology culminates over Chichen Itza in the twenty-first century—the return-of-Quetzalcoatl scenario discussed in chapter 2.

What can all this mean? In the great geomantic tradition of sacred topography, Tacana is clearly a winner. It seems to identify Tacana and Izapa as centering loci for the manifestation of Mesoamerican civilization. Perhaps it was the visionary contact with the Galactic Center by Izapan shamans atop Tacana that "downloaded" the organizational patterning of civilization. Perhaps it is the realization of our deep connection to our galactic heart that orients us consciously toward a higher perspective, stimulating our spiritual unfolding in the process. As with the Pillars of Hercules, one can never be sure if these compelling and undeniable patterns in the landscape are consciously worked out by human beings, or if we are somewhat blindly obeying a guiding force of the Gaian matrix in which we are embedded. Civilization itself might be thought of as the manifestation of things unseen, the embodiment of a suprasensory dimension that provides a template for how things on Earth develop. And the archetypal dimension of myth may provide access to the source of patterning. In the words of Joseph Campbell, "Myth is the secret opening through which the inexhaustible energies of the cosmos pour into human cultural manifestations."[3] Noticing the patterning of a higher order on Earth is more than half the battle. The end result is perhaps not an understanding born of "a conclusive answer," but an openness to the ineffable mystery at the heart of humanity. This openness allows for a clear vision of our relationship to the galactic heart, the womb of the Great Mother, or, as the Greek philosophers called it, the Hypercosmic Sun.

NINETEEN

The Portal of
Spiritual Conception

T here are few places in the world that contain, within a few square miles, as many esoteric mysteries involving sacred architecture as Antigua, Guatemala. For example, the church facade in figure 19.1 could be mistaken for a Gothic cathedral in France, yet it is on the eastern outskirts of Antigua. As many art historians and researchers now concur, the Gothic Renaissance was a rare flowering of esoteric, Hermetic knowledge in the Old World, beginning in the twelfth century. Unfortunately, other forces in European history stemmed the esoteric flowering and drove it into a marginalized underground of alchemists, kabbalists, and astrologers. When the New World was opened up for colonization, the esoteric underground was most prominent in France and Spain—precisely those countries that were closest to the western expansion. Subsequently, the underground stream, though oppressed in Europe, jumped the Atlantic Ocean with idealistic, utopia-seeking colonists, where it found strange confirmation in the universal insights of Native American cosmology and religion.

And yet the merging of indigenous and Christian symbology, called syncretism, is now an accepted fact of the conquest. More accurately, we should understand this as a veiling of indigenous knowledge, preserved below a veneer of Christian pageantry. We see it in Holy Week parades, in the Tzutujil deity Maximon, and in festivals timed by both the Christian and the Mayan calendars.[1] A neglected area of study, valuable in identifying profound esoteric concepts of time, metaphysics, and human spirituality, is the study of sacred architecture and religious iconography as found on church facades, sculpture, and doorway transoms. How profound and deep this information can be was thrust upon me on a recent trip to Guatemala, where I encountered a most interesting sculptured

Figure 19.1. The church of Santa Cruz, Antigua, Guatemala

facade, an enigmatic statement containing insights into spiritual vision, transcendence, and the end of time.

Antigua, originally known as Santiago de los Caballeros (Saint James of the Gentlemen, or Horsemen), was the capital of Central America during the seventeenth and eighteenth centuries. For over two hundred years it was the most important Spanish colonial center between Mexico City and Peru. In the eighteenth century, however, three huge earthquakes, especially the one in 1773, left its convents, churches, and monasteries in ruins. Today some of these have been restored, while the crumbling facades of the rest create a mystique of bygone glory and crumbling extravagance. The ornate motif-filled facade of La Merced is perhaps the best known; but there are also Iglesia Carmen, San Francisco, San Augustin, San Bartolo, and many others.

Figure 19.2. Approaching the sacred portal

Iglesia de San Francisco, for example, is a spectacular old convent that sprawls over a huge area. Some Franciscan murals are preserved within, and its front facade contains images of priests, angels, and saints, as well as the Castile-León coat of arms. One of the crumbling fortresslike structures on the east end of town is La Concepcion, Antigua's very first and largest convent, dedicated by name to the Virgin of the Immaculate Conception, the Mother Goddess who grants spiritual rebirth and presides over the spiritual education of souls. As such, she is beyond past, present, and future, beyond the dualities of phenomenal existence. The surviving *portada*, or entranceway, to La Concepcion (see fig. 19.2) contains a carved facade the meaning of which could only have been known to a master alchemist or some Hermetic Renaissance genius living in the New World. The old entryway is a short distance down the block from any indication of the ruins of La Concepcion. The original nunnery was built in the mid-1600s with a grant from Francisco Marroquin and still sprawls in ruins over the entire block in back of the newer street-front buildings. But the main doorway and its facade are still intact.

The walls on either side of the *portada* were built at a much later date, for as one approaches it one can see a dedication date above the doorway. It reads: "Esta Portada ce acabo en 23 de Feb de 1694" ("This doorway was dedicated on February 23, 1694"). Little did its architects and designers know that within eighty years of this date, three major earthquakes would devastate Santiago, the last one forcing the relocation of the capital to present-day Guatemala City, forty-five kilometers away.

There are two books—one by Sidney David Markman called *Colonial Architecture of Antigua Guatemala* (1966) and one by Verle Annis of similar title—that contain photographic records of Antigua's ruins. Being only descriptive, neither explores the religious symbolism or esoteric ideas that are portrayed on the buildings. Other features on the *portada* incite awe and curiosity: a sun and moon, a little naked boy who hoists the Virgin above him, Santiago (Saint James) riding his horse on the far right, and a strange crest with corn-devouring vultures or eagles on the far left.

In my interpretation of the *portada* I will draw from the sacred science of universal symbolism as outlined in the work of René Guénon and others. It may seem unlikely that the designer of the *portada* intended all of the meanings I will discuss. However, in my reading of the *portada*, I will tune in to the traditional symbolism it encodes, whether or not its designers consciously intended such a reading. Art historians are responsible for more than value appraisal as they apply their knowledge of stylistic variations and likely dates and locations for a piece's origin. In his essay entitled "The Rape of a Nagi," Coomaraswamy discusses traditional symbolism and his transcendental approach to interpreting art.[2] According to such an approach, universal (or traditional) symbolism can usually be identified in religious architecture, and such symbolism carries with it a meaning that transcends the conscious knowledge of any artisan. For this reason we can say that the Virgin Mary, for example, wherever she appears, ultimately represents the Galactic Center.

In the photograph of the *portada*, we immediately notice that the sun and moon, on the left and the right, resemble the same motifs on the cross at Hendaye. In fact, what will emerge here is a strange parallel, at least in the individual elements of the facade, to the symbols on the cross at Hendaye. Beyond these individual elements, the overall message of the *portada* also refers to the "end" (or transcendence) of time, but, we might say, from a primarily metaphysical viewpoint.

Figure 19.3 is a close-up of the symbolic motifs in this amazing late-seventeenth-century carving. What can we say about this image? What was it intended to mean? Is it purely Franciscan or European in its symbolism? How much Mayan symbolism might be found here? First of all, this sculptural statement is unlike anything else in Antigua. There are many uniquely creative and anomalous figures found in Antiguan architecture, but this one actually says something complex and metaphysically significant. As we might suspect, it has something to do with spiritual experience, the opening of the spirit to a divine, higher being. And it says something about time, apocalypse, and a world-transcending, miraculous event.

The full image is separated into a two-part statement. There is a higher level (where the Virgin and her attendants are located) and a lower level (where the lotus boy, two niche figures, the sun and moon, the quartered crest, and Saint James are located). The lower level is the realm of manifest existence, exemplified by the dual dynamics of all mortal existence. It is the realm of life and death, good and bad, the earth school that

Figure 19.3. The carved facade above the portal

is ruled by dualisms. The two niche figures appear to be teachers or priests. They seem to be the same priests depicted with the Virgin on the higher level. There, their hands are clasped together in prayerful worship at the feet of the goddess divinity. They are learning; they are hearing the Divine Word—in fact, their ears are overlarge, indicating an opened wisdom sense of hearing. The experience is one of religious ecstasy that takes place while communing with the Divine Mother.

On the lower level, the realm of sun and moon, the figures are simply teachers, trying to enlighten the world with the insights of their higher experiences. Here, one has only the right hand outstretched, suggesting that in the realm of opposites, one must take one of two dualist positions in relation to the unity that was experienced on the higher level. Joseph Campbell pointed out the Mosaic versus Hermetic approaches to religion, reflected in the Western versus Eastern approaches. The former approach is outward and literal, while the latter approach is esoteric and concerned with essences. We can also characterize this as literal versus metaphorical, or denotation versus connotation. In the image, these two approaches to religious experience are symbolized by the two niche figures on the lower level, reiterated by the solar and lunar sides of the sculpture. The union of these two worldly forces occurs in the figure of the androgynous lotus-loined boy who hoists the Virgin's realm of higher consciousness above the limited realm of duality.

The New World, created by a merging of the opposites, is represented by this Herculean babe, who hoists the transcendent above the realm of opposites. The lotus imagery is completely appropriate. What is shown is the slow unfolding of the spirit, the lotus, out of the mud of unconsciousness, to bloom quickly in the light of a newly found (or newly revealed) higher light. The babe can also be thought of as the Christ child.

In the higher space the two figures are sitting at the feet of the Virgin, who (like Clio, the Muse of History) holds the scrolls of all learning (or the karmic fate of mortals). The Virgin stands on three heads, for she is the triple goddess above time, presiding over the past, present, and future. They are like the three Norns at the base of the Nordic Tree of Life. They are barely discernable in the photograph, but they look like cherubs.

Markman's book on Antigua contains a list of architects and masons who were active during the several centuries of Antigua's building program. The person who seems to me most likely to have been responsible for this design is one Augustin Nuñez. In 1687 he was granted the title *maestro mayor de arquitectura* by the *ayuntamiento*, the commission set up to approve qualified designers and builders for the city's illustrious convents and churches. In 1689, he was approved as *maestro mayor de las artes de escultura y ensamblatura*, suggesting he was a rare practitioner of three disciplines: architectural design, sculpture, and *ensamblatura*, which was a form of assembled sculpture that made a complex religious statement. Markman also reports that, according to Antigua's archives, in 1689 Augustin Nuñez was awarded the contract to build the retable, including the sculptures, for the church of La Concepcion. That pretty much settles *who* did it, but *who was* Augustin Nuñez? Like many intellectuals and highborn artisans of colonial Antigua, he may have been born in Spain and then came to New Spain as a young adult. He may have spent years in Guatemala, practicing his craft, then returned to Spain. Markman notes that many architects came from Seville. Given the esoteric symbolism of the La Concepcion *portada* and most other churches in Antigua, these masons and architects must have been well acquainted with the esoteric discourses of late-seventeenth-century Spain and France. Nuñez is not heard from again until 1706, when it is documented that he delivered two retables for the church of the Compañia de Jesus in Antigua. I'm not aware if these still exist.

To understand the message of the *portada*, we need to look at the two figures on the far left and right of the sculpture. On the right, we find Saint James, riding forward on his horse in a kind of blazing cloud of dust (fig. 19.4). Antigua was originally called Santiago de los Cabelleros—Saint James of the Noblemen, or Horsemen (because only noblemen rode horses). In Spain, Saint James is associated in folk consciousness with the Milky Way. "Saint James's Way" is the pilgrimage route leading to Santiago de Compostela, a place of initiation and healing in northwestern Spain. Coincidentally, the pilgrimage route of Saint James runs fairly close to Hendaye, where the cyclic cross contains a Sun and Moon very similar to the ones shown here.

Historically, Saint James was one of the first four apostles of Jesus. Son of Zebedee and Salome and the brother of John the Evangelist, he appears to have been born at Jaffa, close to Nazareth. James became one of Jesus' favorite disciples, and belonged to his group of intimates. He assisted in the Tabor of the Transfiguration, accompanied Jesus in the Garden of Gethsemane, and witnessed the resurrection of the daughter of

Figure 19.4. Close-up of Saint James on his way

Jairo. The zealous and sometimes vehement son of Zebedee received occasional reprimands from Christ, who gave him the nickname "Son of Thunder."

After the crucifixion, in A.D. 42 he was beheaded in Palestine for preaching the gospel of Jesus. The legend tells that his disciples stole James's corpse, or at least his severed head, and sailed away, landing seven days later at the mouth of the river Ulla in Galicia (Spain). After a series of problems and miraculous happenings, the apostle's head was buried in the place that would later become the town of Compostela. Centuries later the neglected tomb of Saint James was rediscovered, and after the voice of the martyr was miraculously heard—his head reawakening as it were—the apostle James became the focus of the pilgrimage we know today. But the pilgrimage to the western tip of Galicia near Compostela is part of a very ancient tradition.

Compostela, or more anciently, "Land's End," was the final destination of pilgrims who sought the ultimate initiation. They traversed the ancient way (symbolically, the Milky Way) westward to the edge of Europe, where they saw the sun glowing red and dying into the vast ocean beyond the known borders of the world. They had reached the place of initiation, where divinity could be touched and renewal was possible. The death of the Sun—and its ultimate renewal—must have been a yearly pilgrimage that probably took place at the winter solstice. The ancient pilgrimage tradition was overlaid with Christian symbolism in the form of Saint James and his relics. The severed head is the dying sun-face, sinking into the ocean of renewal at World's End, which has a temporal meaning not only in the yearly cycle, but in the vast cycle of the ages.

Saint James's Way—the Milky Way—is the way of pilgrims, leading to an initiatory experience at the center of one's being where time ceases.[3] World's End represents the end of the age, the end of time. In the initiatory usage, one seeks to enter the realm beyond time and space, to touch the transcendental eternity, if only for a moment, for the renewing nectar that one feels in that instant of pure bliss reaffirms ones own deep connection with higher being. This same message is encoded into the *portada* of La Concepcion.

Pilgrimage destinations were always places where divinity could be accessed, central source points of the godhead on earth. In that Saint James's Way is the Milky Way—a naming convention adopted by New World Indians after the invasion (for example, the Chortí and the Quechua)—the image suggests the road to renewal. Saint James is also much like a Templar, a worldly warrior for the lady, the goddess of the grail wisdom. On the *portada*, his sword points over to the Virgin, and he shows the way to her. He is on the lunar side of the sculpture, and represents the cyclical nature of lunar or goddess energies. Renewal is ultimately unavoidable, and we must charge forward on the divine path to arrive at higher wisdom.

Turning to the strange crest on the left and solar side of the *portada*, we see a family crest, the coat of arms of the Castile-León alliance of Ferdinand and Isabella (fig. 19.5). It is found in variant forms on other buildings around Antigua (the University of San Carlos and San Pedro church, for example). The royal house that it stands for was one that, like many European dynasties (such as the houses of Anjou and Bourbon), grew out

Figure 19.5 Close-up of the coat of arms

of the twelfth-century Gothic crusades to the Holy Land to establish a New Jerusalem based on descent from the House of David. Esoteric enough, but apart from this level of meaning, upon closer inspection there is a great deal more going on in the crest. The standard "meaning" of the coat of arms is that the castles and lions represent the alliance between the families of Castile and León, but another interpretation can be made of its meaning based upon its relationship to other motifs and the universal language of traditional symbolism. Moreover, there are additions to the basic form of the coat of arms that make this version unique. On either side we see a vulture eating corn. The devouring of corn suggests the rapacious feeding on the flesh and blood of humanity that occurs at the end of the age, in the darkest epoch, for according to Mayan myth, human beings are made from corn. The four-part form of the crest, as with the four A-shaped glyphs on the Hendaye cross, indicates the four ages of precession. The World Ages in Greek myth are Golden, Silver, Bronze, and Iron, and they corresponded to the Hindu precessional *yugas*. In this cross we see two wild animals (lions) and two towers that seem to be places of safety from the wild, devouring animal nature outside. (The mundane, historical, reference to the Castile-León alliance is irrelevant here.) One is tempted to interpret this as a statement that the church provides civilized refuge from the lower nature of life-devouring animalism—indeed, below the quadripartite frame we see a pig, symbol of the lower nature. Above the frame, an abstract flowering culminates in a divine crown, cross, and infinity symbol—symbols of the upward aspirations to higher being.

The entire crest can be seen as a three-part statement in which (1) the pig is a symbol of lower nature; (2) the quartered frame portrays the human struggle within the field of time, between external devouring (or dissipation) of life energies and the conservative turning inward of life energies, with the goal being a higher vision; (3) the flowering at the top represents the anagogical unfolding of consciousness into a transcendental apotheosis of crowning glory, the infinity beyond the dualistic limitations of earthly existence.

The four quarters are the central feature of the crest and indicate a time element, the four seasons perhaps, which nevertheless consist of two themes: animal devouring (death seeking) and spiritual refuge (life preserving). This suggests not only the four seasons of the yearly cycle but also the four ages of precession, both of which can be divided into descending and ascending halves. The descending phase culminates in the ultimate solar dissipation of life energies (thus the devouring theme). This is quite appropriate, since the crest is on the extreme solar side of the entire sculpture. Within the crest, the ascending phase of precession is symbolized by the two towers or temples, which preserve the life force inside the sacred chamber, making possible the involution of life energy and the evolution of humanity toward spiritual insight. Overall, the devouring lions and vultures, as well as the crest's solar-side placement, suggest the ultimate apocalyptic culmination of the current dominator-style (solar) trend of civilization.

The crest balances Saint James on the lunar side, who leads the way to renewal and initiation in the cyclic process of time. The two sides are Mosaic and Hermetic, linear and cyclic, exoteric and esoteric, solar and lunar. The unification of the dualities creates an androgynous little being who hoists the transcendental wisdom above the world of conflict and illusory death. There, the Virgin gives *darshan* to the priest-attendants who have opened their minds to the Divine Word; they also perform the function of way-pointers and teachers in the mundane world of duality by each taking one of two possible positions (Mosaic or Hermetic) that speak to the dual manifestation of wisdom in the phenomenal world.

The idea represented here is one of taking spiritual refuge from the apocalyptic meltdown to be expected as we approach World's End—the ultimate endgame of the descending phase. The extreme solar manifestation is a self-devouring end-of-age apocalypse. The extreme lunar expression is Santiago as the Virgin's consort on a pilgrimage to her heart—for rebirth and the insemination or conception of the higher spirit within. Thus, the use of both the coat of arms and Saint James on the *portada* of La Concepcion indicates a profound Hermetic understanding of World Ages, astronomy, and spiritual process.

If we recall the symbolism of the Pillars of Hercules, we find a precise parallel in this portal that leads beyond the realm of worldly dualities. We noted that the Pillars were an "end of world" symbol, pointing to America and the dawning Age of Aquarius, which heralds the solstice-galaxy alignment. In fact, it was the Pillars that pointed us to Washington, D.C., and led us to Peru, Izapa, and now, to the doorway of the Mother of God. We've seen that Saint James and the quadripartite cross symbolize the lunar and solar dualities. And the crest itself is a dual symbol, depicting the ascending and descending phases of history—the temporal Symplegades, if you will. We also shouldn't forget that the crest is still, most obviously, the Castile-León coat of arms. In this regard, should we be surprised that a variant of the Castile-León coat of arms (see fig. 19.6) contains the Pillars of Hercules?[4]

In this version, the *ne plus ultra* banner wraps around the pillars and passes behind the coat of arms. Here, however, the banner reads simply *plus ultra*, "greater beyond here," rather than "nothing greater beyond here." The reason for this is because after the discovery of the Americas, the old adage was no longer correct. In addition, by stating that "it's greater over there," and blocking the way with their logo, the Castile-León alliance declared their sovereignty over the New World. It was basically a propaganda strategy of saying "we got what you want." They had stolen the soma and were now controlling access to it.

Moving into the central niche of the *portada*, we see the male and female cosmic forces united in an androgynous boy with a lotus in his belly, symbolizing the flowering of the lower nature of sex and sustenance

Figure 19.6. The Castile-León coat of arms in the Pillars

seeking. This is a typical sublimation motif related to the *kundalini* doctrine of Tibetan mysticism; when the two bodily currents are united in the *muladhara* chakra, the evolutionary energy is triggered and rises upward along the inner spine to awaken the higher centers of consciousness. This process is much like the lotus flower blooming out of a muddy pond. And this upward awakening opens the initiate, the newly awakened, to the higher realms beyond identity as male or female, for the spirit is beyond duality. And so the innocent little androgynous being, symbol of the newborn spirit, is the foundation of one's relationship to the Divine Wisdom.

We must not forget the entire context of this *portada* sculpture, for it frames the entrance into the convent of La Concepcion, the Virgin of the Immaculate Conception. The *portada* thus tells a story about how the striving human being can achieve a relationship to the Divine Sophia by reversing the outward dispersion of energies to fuel an upward-moving connection to higher being. In addition, it emphasizes the importance of spiritual transcendence and recommends an initiatory path (Saint James's Way) that one can take.

If not a literal statement of exactly when the apocalyptic process reaches maximum expression, at least the portal of conception encodes the spiritual process of death and renewal and points the way beyond the end-of-age devouring of life energies that seems inevitable in any historical process. The Immaculate Conception is the insemination of wisdom into our receptive souls, a birth of our vision into a higher plane, beyond the animal propagation of species that feeds death on lower levels of manifestation. This immaculate conception can occur only in the realm above the past, present, and future, above the temporal plane of life and death, when our ears are opened to the Divine Word inside the temple of refuge, inside the heart of the endless round of becoming.

In summary, the message of the *portada* of La Concepcion encodes

* Lunar and solar duality
* Saint James, the Milky Way, World's End, pilgrimage, renewal, initiation
* Royal patronage with a Hermetic background in the Gothic Renaissance, conveyor of the underground stream as it sprang up in New World sacred architecture
* Temporal ascending and descending processes of history in the context of four World Ages
* The lotus boy symbolizing the sublimation of duality forces in *kundalini* awakening as a foundation for the higher experience of Divine Wisdom
* The Virgin of the Immaculate Conception as guardian of spiritual awakening and renewal, higher wisdom, and the overseer of souls existing in a dimension beyond past, present, and future; transcendence of time and the sensory "world"
* Tree of Life image with three Norns at the base
* Priests as initiates into Divine Wisdom operating on two levels— worldly and spiritual
* The Portal of Spiritual Conception, that is, the way to spiritual awakening and rebirth of the spirit

Inside La Concepcion, very little remains to suggest that the Mother of God was once celebrated there. However, in one huge vaulted hallway the

Figure 19.7. Isis at La Concepcion

domed ceiling preserves an image. According to traditional symbolism, the four walls of a church's domed chamber culminate at the apex, symbol of the center of the cosmos, the eye of God, the heart of wisdom, the north gate of Heaven, the Hypercosmic Sun, the seventh chakra that releases the soma of vision . . . the Galactic Center. Or, we might say, the abode of Isis.

PART FIVE

Science and the End
of an Illusion

TWENTY

Reiserian Cosmecology: Galactic Alignments and Evolution

I t is a curious fact that the Galactic Center is just about 26,000 light-years from Earth. The number of years it would take light, or energy, or a superwave burst of energy traveling at the speed of light equals the cycle of precession. But why should this be? This coincidence seemed to be a vector for understanding something important about galactic astronomy.

My research suggests that the alignment alone could explain most of the ancient World Age notions, including the apocalypse doctrines. The empirical mechanism by which the alignment might cause transformation, or change, is irrelevant in terms of my primary focus to reconstruct the galactic dimensions of ancient cosmology. Paul LaViolette's superwave theory, however, presents just such an empirical mechanism, without using the galactic alignment.[1] The fact that precession and the distance to the Galactic Center are linked suggests, as LaViolette explained, some kind of entrainment between superwave bursts and the precessional cycle. He suggests that when the earth's North Pole is tilted away from the Galactic Center, a superwave burst arriving at that time would propel the earth to wobble on its axis. (This is the explanation for why the arrival of his hypothetical superwave corresponds to an era of solstice-galaxy alignment.) Repeated bursts at regular long-range intervals then entrain the earth's wobble to the superwave periodicity. It is unclear, however, why the superwave-burst intervals should correspond with the distance in light-years between us and the Galactic Center.

The sense is that something emanating from the Galactic Center is responsible for precession. Alignment or superwave? The truth of the matter may lie somewhere in between. Then again, drawing from the work of Oliver Reiser, the perspectives sketched in this chapter just may

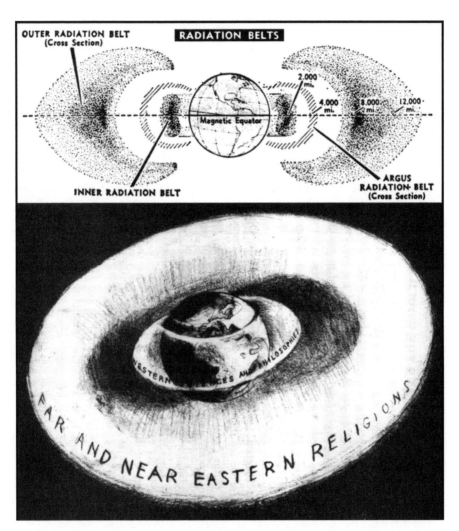

Figure 20.1. Reiser's insight into the existence of the Van Allen radiation belts

solve our dilemma without recourse to a "cause-and-effect" explanation.

As a reminder, my work is not really to identify a mechanism that could empirically explain why a solstice-galaxy alignment might have transformative effects for life on Earth. My work has been to decode how the solstice-galaxy alignment forms the centerpiece of ancient Mayan, Egyptian, and Vedic cosmology. By now the reader must know that I believe the alignment somehow underlies the unprecedented global transformation of modern times. Whether or not there is a scientific basis for the efficacy of the alignment is an important question.

First of all, to argue for such a causative relationship seems foolish, because we in fact *exist within* the energetic field of the Milky Way galaxy. The changing orientation of our local Earth-Sun system to this field is what is occurring with precession. We might suppose that any kind of change of this nature would, quite naturally, affect life on earth. And the "effect" would be instantaneous because we are already within the field. Yes, perhaps this occurs in very subtle energetic ways, perhaps even in terms of the field orientations of electrodynamic particles within the cells of our bodies, and within the molecules and atoms inside of those cells. Here we touch upon Terence McKenna's understanding of the problem, as he wrote in the introduction to *Maya Cosmogenesis 2012*:

> First of all, is there some scientific basis for the idea that when the winter solstice sunrise "stands" on the Galactic Center that any unusual physical effects might be expected? Today science answers in the negative. But science, unlike religion, is ever-growing and revisiting and revising its own past simplifications. Do the spiral structure of the galaxy and the spiral structures of the molecules that create and maintain all life exist in a relationship of resonance? This should be investigated. "As above, so below" taught the alchemists of our own esoteric traditions. Did the Maya make more than a metaphor out of the perception that man is the mirror of the macrocosm? [Are] human fate and the larger drama of the galaxy somehow linked? Coupling mechanisms may be difficult to prove, but elucidation of subtle coupling mechanisms is what the new science of dynamics is designed to do.[2]

McKenna's comment is based on the nonlocality theorem, deriving from experiments that showed a strange thing: widely separated atoms that were once unified will reflect each other's behavior, instantaneously.

Being inside the field of the galaxy, cause-and-effect transmission of influence is not necessary for relationships of behavior to exist, and I am not even referring to the nonlocality principle. To make this point more clear, let us recall the classic science experiment in which iron filings are placed on a pane of glass, and a magnet is moved underneath the glass, making the iron filings stand on end. As the magnet is moved and rotated, the filings entrain with the electromagnetic lines of force surrounding the magnet. This is just to demonstrate that any responsive object within a larger electromagnetic field will *instantly* reorient itself to the changing angular position of the source of the field. The source and target are already connected.

Now, it should be obvious that the earth itself is a field generator and contains a large iron core. Could the earth really somehow be responding to its constantly changing orientation to the larger galactic plane, and *its* field? That an electromagnetic entrainment between the earth, the plane of our solar system, and the galactic plane might be taking place is suggested by the following statistical improbability. The Milky Way and the ecliptic cross at a 61° angle. The ecliptic zodiac passes through the Milky Way very close to where the Galactic Center is located. The zodiac is the plane of the earth's orbit around the Sun—it is the plane of our solar system. No known law exists to explain why the earth's orbital plane should be locked to the coordinates of the Galactic Center, unless some kind of magnetic entrainment principle is responsible. Statistically, it is very unlikely that this would be an accident; however, what seems probable here is that the Galactic Center is a giant field generator, to the degree that the rotational plane of our solar system naturally entrains itself to it.

Based upon these simple observations, we can say that the earth's field is related to, and responds to, the field of the galaxy in which it exists. Secondarily, we can also emphasize that the earth's angular orientation to this field is changing with precession. In addition, the relationship between the earth's rotational plane (the celestial equator) and our solar system's orbital plane (as indicated by sidereal positions of the equinoxes and solstices) is yet another factor that must be considered. In the end, we have the ever-changing relationships between the planes of Earth, Sun (or solar system), and galaxy. Precession is the timing factor behind these ever-shifting planes, and again we may ask, why 26,000 years? The traditional explanation involves gravitational forces of the planets and the Moon yanking the earth into a wobble. But this theory has never been proved. Then, of course, there is LaViolette's theory; he may be right, but the scientific need for direct causative influence strikes me as not the only option, and in fact there is a more elegant and simpler explanation that will fulfill the requirements of Occam's razor.

While I was browsing through an equation-riddled tome called *Subatomic Wave-Particle Electrodynamics,* a section called "Gyromagnetic Proton Precession and Field Strength" caught my attention. Proton *precession?* The section described a little-known electrodynamic principle that operates on protons. Within a larger, encompassing electromagnetic field, a proton exhibits a precessional wobble, very much like the earth's wobble on its axis. I read that *the speed of the proton's wobble is directly related to the strength of the encompassing field, as well as the proton's distance from the source of the field!* Here was a principle identified in nuclear particle physics that described precession on the microcosmic level. In fact, there was nothing I could see that would prohibit this principle from applying to the relationship between the earth (as the "proton") and the Galactic Center (as the source of the field). What intrigued me most was the way it provided a connection between the precession rate of the proton (or the earth) and the distance from the source of the encompassing field (the Galactic Center). Could this explain the fact that the distance in light-years between the earth and the Galactic Center is equivalent to the rate of precession? Precession would therefore appear to be keyed—directly and immediately, not through the agency of superwaves—to the electromagnetic field-generating dynamics of the Galactic Center.

I then came across the work of Oliver Reiser, whose philosophical system perceived the Galactic Center as a formative influence on the evolution of consciousness:

> What is here being proposed is that we explore at greater length the possibilities inherent in the analogy between the human brain and the spiral galaxy, thus transforming the galactic disc into the cosmic lens by endowing it with the generative capacity that the brain of man possesses. This, if valid, would mean that both galaxy and brain can serve as time-spanning (intelligent) guidance systems for their respective sensoria.[3]

Reiser is a greatly underappreciated twentieth-century thinker. As professor in the philosophy department at the University of Pittsburgh for fifty years, he fleshed out abstract ideas for Einstein, developed a theory of cosmic humanism (originally called galactic humanism), and counted Rabindrinath Tagore, Sri Aurobindo, and John Bennett among his correspondents. Eulogized in 1974 as a "cosmic synergist," a "twentieth-century Pascal," and "a guide who put no boundaries on his followers," Reiser was a deep and profound thinker and his theories ranged over many disciplines.[4] He truly was a cosmic philosopher well ahead of his—and our—time, so his interest in the Galactic Center should direct our attention.

He wrote a series of monumental and almost completely ignored books, including *The World Sensorium, Cosmic Humanism and World Unity*, and *The Intent of Creation*. His book *Cosmic Humanism* (1966) is considered the definitive summation of his core ideas. Reiser believed that human evolution was tied to the movements of the larger galaxy, and he had an interlocking set of arguments and scientific evidence to back up his claims. His main interest was in the relationship between geomagnetic field forces and human evolution. He coined the term *Psi Bank* and predicted new scientific discoveries years before they occurred. His Psi Bank concept was more scientific than Teilhard de Chardin's related notion of the noosphere and describes a field of energy above the earth that influences human consciousness. In his 1937 article called "Cosmecology: A Theory of Evolution," Reiser exposed the blind spots in Darwin's theory of evolution, noting that "little progress was made in connection with the problem of the origin of biological mutations until the important work of Muller on the effect of X-rays in producing those changes."[5] As evidenced in the geological record, evolution has advanced in spurts rather than by means of the gradual changes one would expect with the theory of natural selection; this data was fitted into Darwinian theory by coining the term *punctuated evolution.* Modern-day cataclysmologists point to random acts such as asteroid strikes to explain punctuated evolution, and this does indeed seem to be the case in several scenarios—for example, the asteroid strike 60 million years ago that wiped out the dinosaurs. However, although these events were undeniable "facts of life," Reiser didn't believe that the universe could evolve planetary systems and conscious beings through such random acts.

Concluding that evolution was primarily stimulated by periodic increases in cosmic rays, he searched for a cosmic source of enhanced mutational rays that was regular and periodic. His first thought was that the geological scale of evolution should be related to a large astronomical cycle, and the orbit of our solar system around the Galactic Center—roughly 300 million years—seemed to fit the bill. But he identified two problems in this supposition, one of which was that "there does not appear to be any reason why a periodic 300,000,000-year 'day' should make any difference in the sending and receiving of an extra heavy dose of cosmic rays."[6]

This consideration shifted his focus to looking at another mechanism that would lower the protective radiation belts around the earth and thereby allow a greater cascade of mutational rays to the surface. The ionosphere is an electromagnetically charged blanket that effectively shields the earth from the potentially deadly ocean of cosmic rays that surround it. If the earth's magnetic field were temporarily nulled—perhaps during a magnetic pole flip—then for days or weeks a huge amount of mutational rays would reach the living beings on the earth's surface. In *This Holyest Erthe*, Reiser notes that the earth's field is currently decreasing in strength, and the next reversal could be upon us soon. But what might trigger such a magnetic-field reversal? It was years before Reiser's original essay was republished and commented on by Robert J. Uffen, who acknowledged that Reiser's 1937 article anticipated the discovery of the Van Allen radiation belts as well the discovery of reverse-magnetized rocks (indicating magnetic pole reversals in the past). Reiser's rebuttal to Uffen notes that his main point was ignored—that changing field dynamics are linked to his theory of biological evolution. Writing in the mid-1960s he reiterates his primary "hunch" that "the coil of life [DNA] which supplies the architectural pattern for the fabrication of all organisms has something to do with the earth's rotation and its magnetic polarities, and . . . cosmic ray showers which originate . . . in our own spiral galaxy."[7]

Over many decades Reiser tried to identify the basic mechanism that changed the earth's magnetic orientation to the larger galactic plane of field forces to complete his cosmecology theory of biological evolution. Unfortunately, he seemed to be unaware of the concept of galactic alignment, which may indeed provide the missing puzzle piece for an empirical model of how periodic solstice-galaxy alignments trigger or stimulate evolution.

Of course, this entire approach only considers physiological evolution and not the faster-paced evolution that occurs on the level of cultures—not to mention the even faster pace of an individual consciousness throughout a lifetime. Perhaps consciousness is more sensitive than genes to the fields under consideration. In this view, biological change is a trickle-down effect following a transformation of consciousness.[8] Using Reiser's arguments and studies, and inserting the solstice-galaxy alignment as the missing key, we get the following model: *Precession changes our angular orientation to the larger magnetic field of the galaxy in which we are embedded. During regularly occurring eras in the precessional cycle, as indicated by the solstice-galaxy alignments (probably the equinox-galaxy alignments, too), the earth's protective magnetic field becomes unstable and oscillates. With-out a complete field reversal being required, this oscillation allows greater amounts of mutational rays to strike the surface of the earth. While this may result in mutations and a greater chance for "evolution," of greater significance is the possible transformative effect on human consciousness during alignment eras, when human beings are exposed to higher doses of high-frequency radiation.*

Reiser intimated as much, though without direct reference to the alignment concept. In his posthumous *Cosmic Humanism and World Unity*, Reiser wrote:

> In my own "Cosmecology" article of 1937, there are suggestions about the possible biological effects of the motion of the earth and the solar system relative to the spiral nebula which is our galaxy. More recently other theories along these lines have been proposed. Among such is the theory that the inclination of the plane of the ecliptic . . . may be the cause of the earth's magnetism. This theory, based on the effects of the precession of the earth every 28,000 years, has recently been advocated by Dr. W. V. R. Malkus. If this hypothesis turns out to be correct, or only partially valid, the precession of the equinoxes is not only related to a galactic background, but may also serve as [one] of the causal factors in geomagnetism, the earth's periodic field reversals, drifting continents, and therefore the course of biological evolution. This would indeed be a synthesis on the grand scale, truly a cosmic "strategy of evolution."[9]

We now know that the ozone hole is growing, and the average tempera-tures across the United States are expected to rise five to eight degrees by the end of this century. Fulcanelli's prophecy was that the Northern Hemisphere would be scorched by fire. Punctuated evolution is always bad news to 90 percent of the living beings that are around when it hap-pens. Perhaps the increased "heat" or radiation that is expected for us will indeed damage or even kill many, but a small percentage may end up enhanced with new faculties and abilities. Reiser's published legacy is extensive, and I suspect that an empirical model for a galactic-alignment basis for human evolution could be developed from his pioneering work.

While researching Reiser in 1998, I looked up Wilhelm Reich's 1953 *Cosmic Superimposition*. This intriguing book contains a model by which two orgone-energy streams combine to create spiral vortex phenomena. Reich identifies the two streams with the plane of our galaxy (the Milky Way) and the celestial equator (Earth's plane of rotation). The plane of our solar system (the ecliptic) is ignored, but Reich identifies certain latitudes on the earth's surface, related to the crossing angle of the two streams he identified, that pinpoint where aurora borealis phenomena and hurricane trajectories occur. This simply suggests that gravitational, electromagnetic, and angular momentum on a galactic level play little-understood roles in Earth phenomena and should all be taken into account in any further examination of this topic.

David Wilcock has understood these considerations and has gone a long way toward establishing a multidimensional physics of soul evolution. His theory involves the energy dynamics of the galaxy, reevaluates and revises the long-cherished (and faulty) postulates of astrophysics, and draws from recent scientific discoveries that would normally take decades to be integrated into a more advanced paradigm. Wilcock, in books and research available on his Web site, rallies together unusual evidence that is always "whitewashed" out of the data, and presents a fascinating new understanding of the nature of time and space and the evolution of consciousness on planetary systems undergoing energetic enhancements caused by our solar system's movement through different sectors of the galaxy. In his work, the galactic alignments are acknowledged but are only one facet of the larger galactic cycles he examines.[10]

I also want to mention in this context the reevaluation of the Milankovich theory of ice ages. The idea that the advance and retreat of polar ice is related to precession was put forth over a hundred years ago by the Scottish thinker James Croll. Milankovich reanimated the ice age–precession theory in the 1920s, but only recently has science reconfirmed Croll's convictions with overwhelming new evidence, vindicating his work. Now, taking this all a step further by embracing the galactic-alignment phenomenon, Dr. William Gaspar has rekindled and expanded the implications of the Croll-Milankovich model in his recent book, *The Celestial Clock*.[1]

In Reiser's *The Intent of Creation*, published posthumously in 1978, a diagram confirmed what I had stumbled across with regard to the preces-

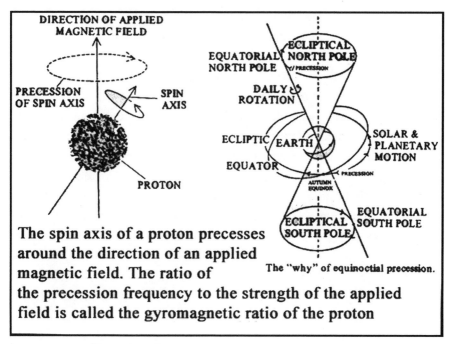

The spin axis of a proton precesses around the direction of an applied magnetic field. The ratio of the precession frequency to the strength of the applied field is called the gyromagnetic ratio of the proton

Figure 20.2. Precession: microcosmic and macrocosmic

sion of protons (see fig. 20.2). Reiser writes: "It does seem that the precession of the equinoxes and the precession of the proton particles in atoms—both manifest as 'wobbles' in their respective levels of organization—point to one trans-level pattern: there must be 'worlds within worlds' from the microcosm through the mesocosm to the macrocosm, all parts of a cosmos that is alive from top to bottom and back again."[12] Although these words are very intriguing, they do not openly address or explain the concept of galactic alignment. We would need to admit into the model a third level—perhaps the electron that orbits the proton would be the true counterpart to the earth. The precession of protons doesn't address the many nested levels of atomic systems, and how their interlocking cycles, and precessional "wobbles," might relate *to each other*, or how the larger domains would "appear" from any particular level— much in the way that we have a unique vantage from the earth such that we observe the solstice sun eclipsing the Galactic Center twice every precessional cycle. So, how far can we take this analogy? Does a leptonian citizen living on a lepton observe its parent electron eclipsing the great proton center twice every .0000026 nanoseconds?

With regard to identifying an empirical mechanism behind the alignment's "effect" on we earthlings, here is what can be said:

1. The need for a "causal influence" may be irrelevant, because the "change" or "effect" occurs within the field of the galaxy. Angular orientation to gyroscopic fields of force, however, is the best candidate so far. In any case, we need to look closely at the parameters of the alignment, other factors in the alignment such as the closest approach of the solstice sun to the Galactic Center, and a possible timing range for a supposed "shift" (see chapter 21).
2. The impact may be more on our spiritual and energetic beings, in a metaphysical sense, than on a physically measurable domain of evolutionary biology. In this context our active participation is critical (see chapter 23).
3. Sociological expectation is just as transformative at these critical nexus points as anything empirically "affecting" us.

While the first point may be disturbing to the empiricist, that conclusion seems to be where the discussion inevitably leads. I am not prepared to devote a great deal of time to constructing an empirical model of alignment-dynamics and evolution—although Reiser's work, when carefully studied, provides everything one would need, even though galactic alignment is not mentioned by name. The real area of interest to me is not in whether or not transformation will take place in the near future; the questions are about *when* and *where*, and how human beings are likely to respond.

We looked at "where" in part 4, but now precise timing parameters of the alignment become a concern, as well as its deeper metaphysical meaning and the purely sociological effects of a looming "end-date" in our near future. Let's take a look at these other options.

TWENTY-ONE

Timing Parameters of the Alignment: 1998, 2012, 2220, 2240

I f the galactic alignment is meaningful in terms of effects, then we
need to look closely at the various factors and parameters involved.
My work in Mayan calendrics and cosmology has been to show that
the Maya intended 2012 to target the precession-caused alignment of the
solstice sun with the Milky Way. With this very general way of stating the
alignment, a range of many centuries is implied. The precise way of
describing the alignment is in astronomical terms: It is the alignment of
the solstice meridian with the galactic equator (fig. 21.1).

Assuming astronomical coordinates and spatial definitions are precise,

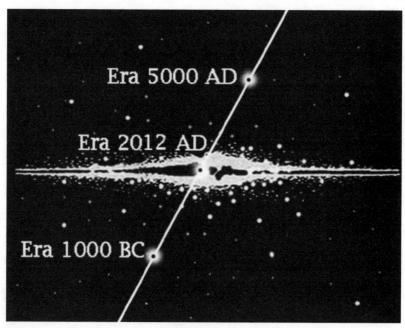

Figure 21.1. The alignment of the solstice meridian with the galactic equator

we could go with the calculation by European astronomer Jean Meeus. In his 1997 book *Mathematical Astronomy Morsels,* Meeus calculated the alignment as occurring in May of 1998. English astrologers organized by David Baker at Kingsley Hall in London celebrated the alignment on May 10, 1998. I preferred to recognize May 29 as the shift day, because that was 1 Ahau in the *tzolkin* calendar. The U.S. Naval Observatory calculated October 27, 1998, as the date. In December 1998 I suggested that the impending solstice would be the first day of the first year of the next 26,000-year precessional cycle.

These dates are based upon a scientific precision that is perhaps unwarranted. In thinking this through carefully, I feel that the parameters and features involved in this question allow for at least plus or minus one year for the event. More generally, any calculation could easily be "off" by some five to ten years, for several reasons. The precise calculation of the solstice-galaxy alignment is predicated upon identifying the precise location of the solstice meridian *and* the galactic equator. Of these two abstract locations, the galactic equator is subject to variation depending on whether one chooses to identify with gravitational, visual, or electromagnetic criteria. If the currently accepted astrophysical location for either the solstice meridian or the galactic equator is inaccurate by as little as one-sixtieth of a degree (one minute of arc), the calculation of the precession-caused alignment of the solstice meridian with the galactic equator would be subject to a plus/minus variable of five months. And how big is one-sixtieth of a degree? Well, the full moon is about one-half a degree or thirty minutes of arc in diameter. So, imagine slicing the full moon into thirty parts—one of those parts is one-sixtieth of a degree. It would seem reasonable that variations in the currently accepted locations of either the solstice meridian or the galactic equator could be *at least* this much. We might therefore be conservatively looking at 1998, plus or minus three years. Another important consideration involves acknowledging that we are not dealing here with abstract lines and meridians, but with astrophysical bodies (such as the Sun) that have size, shape, and gravitational centers.

For a realistic assessment we need to remember that gravitational and electromagnetic effects are in play, and the Sun itself is one-half a degree wide. If the precession-caused shift of the Sun to the "other side" of the Milky Way is what will trigger an inversion of phenomena, in some sense, for human beings, then we can draw from an analogy to understand this shift.

The Milky Way's equator is analogous to the earth's equator. The earth's equator divides the earth into northern and southern hemispheres. As is well known, opposed spiraling phenomena occur in each hemisphere. For example, tornadoes and hurricanes spin counterclockwise in the Northern Hemisphere, while south of the equator they spin clockwise. Likewise, water too will spin down the drain one way or the other depending on which side of the equator you are on. This phenomenon is based in a principle called *the conservation of angular momentum.* Now, which way does the water spin if it drains exactly on the equator? Or more to the point, how far would one need to move into one or the other hemisphere to get a definitive result? This range would correspond to the temporal range allowable for the "alignment zone." The analogy, of course, is to the Milky Way's equator as the dividing line for these Coriolis effects on a galactic level. And the Sun would be the body that needs to be, definitively and effectively for the "shift" to begin, on one side or the other.

Being one-half a degree wide, the body of the Sun will take thirty-six years to move through the galactic equator (precession shifts one degree every seventy-two years). So here we have a reasonable range of, say, plus or minus eighteen years. Given 1998 as the date, the range is thus 1980 to 2016. However, since we need the body of the Sun to clear the galactic equator, we must take into account that the galactic equator and the solstice meridian cross at a 61° angle, making the zone of contact slightly longer. Figure 21.2 illustrates

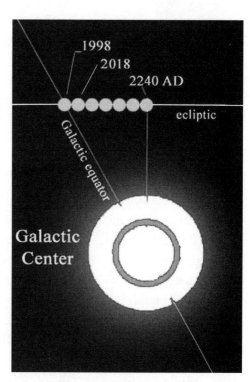

Figure 21.2. Timing parameters of the galactic alignment

these ranges and parameters. As the figure shows, there are two different alignments that must be considered: the solstice sun's crossing through the galactic equator, and the solstice sun's closest approach to the Galactic Center. Because of the 61° angle of the cosmic cross, the solstice sun will actually be slightly closer to the Galactic Center more than two centuries after 1998. (This is a fact discussed in all of my books on the alignment.) But how much closer? And when, exactly? Luckily, we have calculations from Patrick Wallace, an astronomer at Rutherford Appleton Laboratory.

> The winter-solstice Sun is closest to the Galactic equator in A.D. 1998. This presumably corresponds to the Meeus / USNO calculation. The distance from the Sun to the Galactic centre at that time is 6.4396 degrees (measured in apparent place). The winter-solstice Sun has cleared the Galactic equator by A.D. 2021. The winter-solstice Sun is closest to the Galactic centre in 2219, with a couple of years either side also candidates for this epoch because of nutation. The distance to the Galactic centre at the A.D. 2219 solstice is 5.6367 degrees, 0.8029 degrees closer than in 1998. The winter-solstice Sun and Galactic centre share the same apparent-place meridian in A.D. 2225.[1]

Notice that in A.D. 2219 the solstice sun will be 0.8029 degrees closer to the Galactic Center than in 1998. This is equal to 1.6 solar diameters, which I assume is measured from the center point of each celestial body. We might consider this to be significant, but perhaps it's negligible, considering that the center of the galaxy cannot be nailed down to a point, because it has diffuse (and different) gravitational, ultraviolet, and magnetic centers. Nevertheless, clearly a distinction should be made between era 2012 and, let us say, era 2220. In 1995, I suggested that the true solstice-galaxy alignment would occur sometime around 1997–1999, rather than 2012. I based this rough calculation on the data in the ACS Publications ephemerides. I also suggested that we should look to 1998–1999 as the true alignment era, even though I knew the closest approach to the Galactic Center would not be for another 220 years. The reason for this is based in the "crossing the equator" analogy described above, wherein definitive field-effect reversals of spin properties of matter might be expected after that crossing is complete. That said, nobody knows for

sure, and certainly not I. So we might want to be open enough to entertain a 260-year transformation window that would embrace the "two"
alignments. Maybe this span frames the "double catastrophe" alluded to
by Fulcanelli.

A recurrent subtext in this discussion has to do with the difference
between 1998—the ideal "precise" year of alignment—and the 2012 end-
date of the Mayan 13-*baktun* calendar. Yes, perhaps the ancient Maya
were off by some fourteen years in their calculation of the precise alignment, but does this nullify my theory that 2012 was intended to target the
alignment? Of course not. A 14-year discrepancy in a 2,100-year forward
calculation in precession is less than negligible: 14 years of precession
amounts to about twelve minutes of arc, or one-fifth of a degree. We
know what they were intending, and now we can look more closely at the
details of the alignment that they calculated so many centuries ago.

In figure 21.2 the last date is A.D. 2240. Although this is almost
twenty years after the "closest approach to Galactic Center" calculated by
Patrick Wallace, I think it is a very important eschatological date, a year
important to a very ancient tradition: Since A.D. 2000 was 5760 in the
Jewish calendar, the year 2240 will be year 6000.

Gershom Scholem wrote extensively about Jewish mysticism, Kabbalah, messianic movements, and cosmology. The body of exegetical writings on Jewish doctrines stretches back to the Old Testament. Hebrew
religion is, in fact, over 5,000 years old if their calendar is any indication
of their historical beginnings. Jewish mysticism of the kabbalistic variety
dates to more recent times, to the thirteenth-century Zohar, although it
too is deeply rooted in ancient tradition.

Year 6000 in the Jewish calendar is of interest to us because it corresponds—within eighteen years of astronomical precision—to the closest
approach of the solstice sun to the Galactic Center. And year 6000 is no
arbitrary turning point in the Jewish calendar. The doctrine of the *shemit-
tot* (cosmic cycles) is based on a fixed periodicity in the emanation and
reabsorption of creation. Astrological ideas drawn from Greek and
Islamic sources resulted in the conception, as stated by Rav Katina, that
the world would last for 6,000 years, and be destroyed in the seventh millennium by being reabsorbed into the cosmic source.

The kabbalistic writings from Gerona embraced this conception, as it
conformed to the six days of creation followed by the Sabbath. Each cosmic

Figure 21.3. The kabbalistic Tree of Life

cycle, or day of creation, was seen to correspond with one of the *sephiroth* on the kabbalistic Tree of Life. As Scholem summarizes, "In the seventh millennium, which is the *shemittah* period, the Sabbath-day of the cycle, the sefirotic forces cease to function and the world returns to chaos. Subsequently, the world is renewed by the power of the following sefirah and is active for a new cycle."[2] At the end of the seventh *shemittah* (50,000 years), all of the lower worlds and the seven supporting *sephiroth* themselves are reabsorbed into the Binah—the highest center of the kabbalistic Tree. At that time a Great Jubilee is celebrated. In fact, minijubilees are celebrated every seven and every fifty years. According to William Whiston, the next fifty-year jubilee will occur in A.D. 2028. Jay Weidner, an expert in kabbalistic cosmology, tells me that the Binah *sephiroth* corresponds to the Galactic Center, and is also considered to be the Great Mother of Worlds.

With its seven levels, this doctrine is clearly related to the Hindu-Vedic chakra model. The point to emphasize here is that year 6000 (A.D. 2240) signals the beginning of the seventh millennium in Judaic eschatology, the reabsorption *shemittah*. That 2240 is also very close to the solstice sun's closest conjunction with the Galactic Center might give us pause—but it should actually make us fall flat on our faces. How are we to explain this? Coincidence? Can so many strange coincidences that seem to dance around the galactic alignment be dismissed so easily?

In summary, two major alignment eras and several subdates are suggested by a full consideration of the parameters involved in the galactic alignment:

★ The solstice meridian's alignment with galactic equator: 1998 +/- three years

★ The solstice sun's first contact and final clearance of the galactic equator: 1975–2021

★ The 2012 end-date of the Mayan 13-*baktun* cycle

★ The solstice sun's closest approach to the Galactic Center: 2220 +/- three years. Year 2220 is also 2012 plus two Venus Round cycles of 104 years each (four Calendar Rounds).

★ Year 6000 in the Jewish calendar, the dawn of the seventh *shemittah:* A.D. 2240

In Yucatan, 13 *katuns*, or 256 years, was the prophecy cycle. We might thus consider a 13-*katun* alignment/transformation range between 1984 and 2240. This would also embrace the centuries-long era during which the Sun and the Pleiades join in the zenith over the Pyramid of Kukulcan at Chichen Itza. Within this range, however, several distinct zones can be identified. I still feel that the galactic equator crossing is the most significant. Augmented by considering the actual size and shape of the Sun, this equator crossing, so symbolic of "crossing the threshold," will apparently be complete by 2021. And the 2012 date itself cannot be overlooked, for it has its own special power based on the Mayan 13-*baktun* cycle calculation, which by now many millions of people are aware of.

We have been interested in the timing of possible effects for human beings on earth, but have overlooked one important consideration: You can lead a horse to water, but you can't make it drink; that is, humanity's participatory expectation or collective belief is as much a determinant on transformation as anything else we have looked at. In fact, without the human element of participation, a *desire* for transformation, nothing will happen. In this sense, 2012 may be our best hope as a trigger point for creating a new world. I've pointed out that whether or not one believes in the urgent imperative of the alignment and its empirical effects, one thing is for sure: 2012, as a long-anticipated calendrical shift, will be a rally cry for indigenous people throughout the Americas—perhaps the world—to rise up and reclaim their self-determination and power. However this occurs and whatever it entails for the ruling sectors, it must be about a fair redistribution of wealth.

Within this framework, what might get destroyed and what might be renewed? How does the global transformation occur? What emerges, as it usually will at some point or another, is the perplexing and vexing question: Is this about *cosmogenesis* or *catastrophe?* This is a difficult and complex question: Eternal death for the planet, or new life?

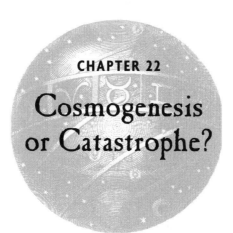

CHAPTER 22

Cosmogenesis or Catastrophe?

A common misconception, reinforced in the mass media, is that the ancient Maya believed the world will literally end in 2012. Writers claim that earthquakes, pole shifts, asteroids, or aliens are described in Mayan mythology. The prophecies of Nostradamus and Edgar Cayce are invoked to back up these beliefs, but such a sensationalist stance belittles the true complexity of the subject and distracts us from taking seriously the astronomical reference encoded into the 2012 date. But if we do base our understanding of 2012 on the solstice-galaxy alignment, many will then assume that whatever is going to occur is "fated" in the stars. However, an astronomically defined event does not necessarily result in deterministic consequences, although a framework is created in which a general understanding about the process can be reached. For example, one would not "predict" that the Sun will rise tomorrow morning; one would calculate and project forward and then expect the Sun to rise. One does not know exactly what will take place tomorrow morning, but daybreak is a given that will frame all events. Likewise, the Maya calculated galactic midnight to occur in 2012, when maximum night shifts into the dawning of day, and within that framework a death and rebirth can be expected, but the specifics of what occurs remain to be seen. The underlying assumption in modern doomsday prophecies—that a specific, literal, and historically predictable event is fated to occur—suggests we are all helpless automatons who contribute nothing to how our future will look. But Edgar Cayce himself believed, in regard to predictions of coastal flooding, that "it's not so much where you live, it's how you live."

The "end of the world" will eventually occur for each of us, perhaps in a cosmic catastrophe, or merely in the inevitable end of each of our individual lives. Our expectations and fears about 2012 are closely related to our feelings about death. In other words, 2012 is a handy screen on which to project our beliefs about death. And do we really know what lies beyond the threshold of death? How do we know that death is not the portal to another life? Applying this to the 2012 end-date, what would it mean if the end of the world were truly scheduled at that time? Is 2012 about a cosmogenesis (a universal rebirth) or a global catastrophe? As I've made clear in previous books, I adhere as faithfully as possible to the message of the earliest creation monuments at Izapa to support the Mayan notion that 2012 is more about rebirth than about death—but human participation and free will are factors. In the Mesoamerican legend of the Suns, or previous World Ages, humanity always gets transformed into something else, not annihilated. Drawing from the Mayan, Egyptian, and Vedic understanding of the precessional alignment that we are currently experiencing, it is clear that we are entering the 13,000-year ascension phase of the Great Year of precession. In this sense, it is time for our deepening immersion in materialism and death-worshiping behaviors to end. This question is ultimately contingent upon how we—as individuals and as a civilization—feel about life. Though we as individuals may claim healthy attitudes toward life and nature, our parent paradigm has been busy bulldozing jungles and enslaving—or destroying—life in all its myriad forms. Western civilization has a death wish that may make a disaster of 2012, not because it's in the cards, but by way of "self-fulfilling prophecy."[1]

Mainstream prophets who predict the future sometimes project their intuitions about their own fate onto the larger situation in the world. In this regard, a study of modern prophets and their eschatological utterances is revealing. Many of these visionaries make passionate—and very specific—predictions about the end of the world. For all of them, the end was near, and they were convinced this was true. When the predicted date rolled around, a great majority of these prophets experienced accidents, or died suddenly. Now, what does this say about self-determination, free will, and their "prophetic ability?" There are basically two possibilities here, which may be applied to the 2012 conundrum. First, one's passionate conviction that something will happen constellates events in the universe so that when the appointed time arrives the expectations are, in some sense, vindicated. Second, we may ascribe to the notion that the disaster is out there, fated, and one's vision that something will occur is a prophetic glimpse. The prophecy is fulfilled, perhaps not exactly as expected, but something happens. This relies on determinism and negates free will.

I favor the subjective causation of external events. How we think about 2012 may very much determine what will happen. We create our reality. This is not to ignore certain facts—that we are polluting the earth carelessly and are running out of resources, and we have ozone holes and overpopulation. Based on these facts, the future certainly cannot possibly look much like the present, so this might be a case of the end of the world *as we know it.* The issue here is whether we can direct the process of transformation, which is simply the flow of time no matter where we find ourselves, so that the future does not become a projection of our deepest fears, but a manifestation of our highest aspirations.

It may be unpopular to say it, but it's true: what 2012 was intended to target is not about 2012, it is about a process-oriented shift. It's really about an open door, a once-in-a-precessional-cycle zone of opportunity to align ourselves with the galactic source of life. There are forces already set in motion propelling us through a crucible of transformation unlike anything experienced in millennia. The process is occurring on the scale of decades, even centuries—but it is occurring on a global level! The sober and humbling fact is that we are being called to create, nurture, and help unfold something that will not flower until long after we, as individuals, have died. The larger life-wave of humanity is at stake. The Algonquin teaching to look ahead seven generations before decisions are made should be our guiding maxim.

Birth-growth-death-renewal—this process follows a universal law that appears "predictable," but if it is part of the natural cycles of change, then what do we have to worry about? We will worry to the extent that we are incapable of letting go. Cycle endings are attended by the destruction of everything belonging to the previous cycle, and like the legendary Phoenix, the new world will be born out of the ashes of the old. The metaphor is about birth and death. Not everyone believes in rebirth (reincarnation), but no one can deny the inevitability of death. Unfortunately, few spend much time reflecting on death—the Great Transformer. Meditations on mortality can lead to profound insights and realizations about our humanity, and the denial of death—which is what Western civilization is about—drives us more quickly and less elegantly to it.

If one believes that the world is going to end completely—in 2012, 2020, 2240, or any other year—then a meditation on mortality is the only constructive thing we could do. What is the alternative? Last-minute jettisons of cryogenically preserved millionaires into outer space? A frenzy of uncontrolled carnage, raping, and grabbing for earthly pleasures, fearful of their impending loss? What if the ancient spiritual traditions are correct, that Earth serves as a way station of souls on a journey of incarnation through many dimensions? Earth may be one frequency of experience in the soul's journey to self-realization, where a specific spectrum of desires is lived out and spiritual lessons are learned. If the Earth suffocates or explodes and every living being on it is exterminated, wouldn't earth-souls transmigrate to another Earth-like world elsewhere in the galaxy? Perhaps. But what if there are no Earth-like worlds to go to? Maybe the half-bloomed earth-souls would be suspended in interdimensional ice until somewhere a world evolved to receive them. And if the Earth does explode, the ultimate lesson that one can't ignore is: *It didn't have to happen!* We would need to understand that we limited our immortality, drove ourselves deeper into materialism and unconsciousness, that we and nothing else—no external fated agency of gods or prophets—pulled the lever.

If we can truly embrace this responsibility—which is really the gift of free will—then we might be able to transcend the collective unconscious death wish and appreciate the importance of larger cosmic cycles in which we are embedded—for the era-2012 alignment initiates the ascension phase of the precessional day. We—that is, humanity—have been falling deeper into unconsciousness for 13,000 years. But the alignment of the solstice meridian with the galactic plane (1975–2021) is the shift zone, after which consciousness begins a reversal, a disembodiment of spirit as we en-lighten through each successive year and each successive incarnation, the universe now fully supporting our spiritual endeavors and our yearning for the highest freedom. Our role, as the alignment generation, seems to be to not blow it, to believe in our highest potential, buried though it may be under millennia of ignorance and materialism.

So, catastrophe for everything that is built upon a foundation of materialism, lies, and unconscious death wishing does not appear to be a bad thing, and this means primarily the prevailing Western paradigm. This also suggests that indigenous cultures that have made it to the threshold of the end-date are favored exemplars of survivability. They may be the true midwives of our rebirth into the next World Age, a birth attended like all births with the destruction of the old, spiritually restricting value system.

The tearing asunder that accompanies birth is akin to what happens when more energy breaks into a system; the effect is terrible, destructive, but ultimately opens up larger channels for new energy to flow in. The earth, as the location of a specific spectrum of consciousness-in-evolution, has been said to correspond with the fifth level of the Tibetan chakra system, the linguistic or *vishuddha* chakra. Human beings are currently beings of language but are striving to evolve into beings of pure mentation. We need to widen our mental framework to channel in the higher faculties that will allow this to happen. The alignment augments this metaphor perfectly, so that we can transcend the debate of "catastrophe or cosmogenesis" and instead envision the "catastrophe *of* cosmogenesis" as an energy increase flowing through Earth as it and our Sun align with the Galactic Center. Our inner beings, and our inner energy centers, are vibrating in sympathy with the goings on in the larger galaxy, where a chakra system of galactic proportions is rumbling louder and louder while *kundalini*, the evolutionary energy of the Serpent Goddess, uncoils.

TWENTY-THREE

The Galactic Chakra System

In *Journey to the Mayan Underworld* (1989), I explored an interesting connection between Hindu and Mayan cosmology. The five World Ages in Mesoamerican time philosophy correspond to the five energy levels in the Hindu/Tibetan chakra system. They are united in that both systems draw from the idea of the five elements: earth, water, fire, air, ether (or space). These "stages" of change move from dense matter (earth) through increasingly subtle energy states, corresponding to the spiritualization of consciousness as the human race evolves. The fifth stage is ether, or space, meaning that pure spirit has been reached.

The left side of figure 23.1 contains a diagram of the chakra system, a model of the energy anatomy of the human body that comes down to us from ancient Tibetan doctrines. There are actually seven centers of force, or chakras, but the top two operate together, as do the lower two. Thus, there are five distinct centers. In addition, the seven chakras and five centers can be further generalized into three levels: The root and navel centers belong to the underworld of primal forces; the heart center is the zone of the earth school, the evolving and learning heart of humanity; the throat and crown centers belong to the higher faculties of speech, thought, and spiritual vision.

The central vertical channel running from the root center to the crown center is known as the *sushumna* nerve current, and corresponds to the spinal cord. The *ida* and *pingala* currents lie to the left and right of the *sushumna,* and correspond to the male and female (solar and lunar) currents that function in various ways in our bodies. When these two currents are brought together in silent meditation in the root chakra, the two energies converge and stimulate the dormant energy residing in the root chakra that is known as *kundalini.* Coiled up in the root chakra until it is awak-

THE FIVE CENTERS, THREE LEVELS, SEVEN CHAKRAS, AND THE FIVE ELEMENTS	ORGANS CONTROLLED BY THE FIVE CENTERS	CORRESPONDING MAYAN "SUNS" OR WORLD AGES
	5. Pineal gland. A small conical body deep in the brain; its tissue is similar to optical tissue and regulates serotonin. **4. Throat plexus.** Relates to speech and respiration. **3. Heart.** Integrative center of love; controls blood circulation. **2. Solar plexus.** The sympathetic nervous system; controls organs of assimilation and digestion. **1. Sacral plexus.** Controls organs of elimination and reproduction; seat of latent *kundalini* force.	**Movement.** The present Sun, which unites the previous four. The struggles of our era are symbolized by the Ollin glyph. This age was destroyed by earthquakes. **Water.** The fourth Sun was destroyed by torrential rains; humanity became fish in order to survive. **Rain.** A rain of lava and fire destroyed this epoch. People transformed into birds to survive. **Wind.** The crocodile-headed god, Ehecatl, rules this age. When the human race was destroyed by hurricanes, people became monkeys. **Jaguar.** This age was ruled by the primal forces of the jaguar. In this age the giants were eaten by jaguars.

Figure 23.1. Spiritual energy centers, human physiology, and Mayan World Ages.
Left, (1) root center; (2) navel center; (3) heart center; (4) throat center;
(5) crown center; *(A)* Underworld; *(B)* Earth; *(C)* Upper World.
From *Journey to the Mayan Underworld* (1989).

ened during an individual's spiritual transformation, the *kundalini,* or serpent power, rises through the five centers and seven chakras, awakening and cleansing each. When it reaches the crown or pineal center, a union of Śiva and Shakti, the male and female energies, occurs, and the individual transcends the limitations of dualism, becoming a fully awakened being. There the spirit bathes in the nectar of soma, imbibing the wisdom of a revitalizing higher vision.

The chakras, although consisting of subtle energy knots, do nevertheless correspond roughly with physical organs. The middle column sketches these correspondences. Often, ailments effecting a particular organ can be alleviated by exercises that will stimulate and send breath energy into the appropriate chakra center, thereby awakening the area to function properly. In the last column, the five World Ages are listed, showing how the Mesoamerican conceptions of time correspond to the ancient doctrine of the elemental chakras.

The subject under consideration here has everything to do with spiritual growth and human awakening, both individual and collective. This awakening can be likened to a process of sublimation, wherein the raw energy of the root center is rarefied, stimulating the next-higher chakra into activity, and so on up the spinal ladder. The central axis is a symbol of the World Axis as it exists in the individual human being. Our spines are microcosmic counterparts to the cosmic axis that runs from the center (or root) of the cosmos through Earth and out into the vast expanse of infinite space. It would not be inappropriate to think of the Galactic Center as the root of the cosmic tree. We can visualize the spiral of our galaxy viewed from above, and map it onto the chakra model (see fig. 23.2). In this way we can imagine a galactic chakra system stretching from the Galactic Center through distinct energy bands, including Earth, extending out past the Pleiades into extragalactic space.

If we were standing somewhere on Earth, say, on top of Tacana volcano, we could look to the southeast and see the Galactic Center rising.

Figure 23.2. Galactic chakra system in the human microcosm
(image on left from Darlene)

We would be gazing into the center of the galaxy, the hearth of creation and source of everything in our world. If in our mind's eye we turned around and gazed at the opposite side of the galaxy, we would be looking past the Pleiades, past Orion, toward the Galactic Anticenter—the path that takes us out of our galaxy. Now, if we acknowledge the galactic level of organization, placing Earth, Moon, planets, Sun, and solar system in their proper order, we can understand how the true cosmic axis—the evolutionary galactic axis—can be visualized. It is exactly pictured in figure 23.2. Earth would be at the fifth chakra level, evolving between the fifth and sixth chakras, between linguistic ability and the faculty of pure mentation, or Uranian conceptualization.

Let's briefly recap my reconstruction of Mayan cosmology. In *Maya Cosmogenesis 2012*, I identified a precession-caused alignment to the Galactic Center. I also decoded a precession-caused alignment to the Pleiades as they ascend into the zenith with the Sun. I called the two cosmologies the galactic cosmology and the zenith (or Pleiades) cosmology. They are cosmological systems created by Mesoamerican skywatchers who were fixated on two opposite sides of the sky. But why these locations? The answer is quite simple. The Pleiades lie in the direction of the Galactic Anticenter; so too do Orion and Gemini, but the Pleiades have always been associated with higher consciousness. Because the Pleiades are opposed to the Galactic Center, the Mesoamerican cosmology I elaborated is really about a Galactic Center–Galactic Anticenter alignment, one that is astronomically timed by precession to culminate between 1975 and 2240. The Pyramid of Kukulcan, which encodes the Pleiades cosmology, is a marker pointing to an opening portal to the Galactic Anticenter. So too, Izapa is the place where the galactic cosmology was formulated, and its monuments are aligned, like geodetic markers, to the source of the evolutionary energy.

A couple of considerations are important here. We might prefer to see the Galactic Center as the crown in this model, and several writers make this assumption, even though the Galactic Center is clearly a root and source place. Why should the center be the crown? Is it our destination, or our evolutionary origin point? The difficult truth is that both conceptions are true. Śiva (crown) and Shakti (root) are ultimately one and come from the same place in a mystical and transcendental sense. One of Coomaraswamy's essays was on the inverted tree. The kabbalistic Tree of Life is said to be an inverted tree, and Binah, the highest *sephirah*, is really the root of the system. And if we place our crowns at the Galactic Center, we might feel like we were rooted by our heads in an infinity beyond time and space, beyond our local galaxy, which is quite true. We are rooted in infinity, we dangle by our toes (or our heads) from it. Whichever conception one prefers perhaps has to do with whether one favors top-down or bottom-up management. I favor associating the Galactic Center with the root center—the source of deep insight, renewal, and evolutionary energy.

In exploring architectural domes and how they model the body, Coomaraswamy associates the center of a chapel's dome with the crown suture of the human skull, where the pineal gland is located—the seat of higher consciousness. This association can be found in much religious architecture, but it should not be fashioned into an absolute, for "reversible dialectics" can come into play. As with the nodal symbolism we explored in part 2 for example, the tail or the head of the lunar dragon can be mapped onto Sagittarius or Gemini, though the tail in Sagittarius seems favored. Here we are dealing with dialectical symbols that transcend dualisms, indicating that we must be well balanced, and if we can hold the opposed meanings without losing sight of the middle, we'll be on our way.

The galactic chakra system helps us understand the process of transformation that is going on in the world today. It can be understood with the terminology of a *kundalini* awakening. Reports of these experiences are numerous, but they are often a mixture of ecstatic, beatific states and confused, painful feelings. As reported by Indian sage Gopi Krishna, the process—which is triggered by a sudden awakening but usually extends over many years—is akin to giving birth. Indeed, the awakened *kundalini* will wreak havoc on an unprepared physiology, but the end result, if the seeker survives the ordeal, is a complete transformation of consciousness. Perhaps one who has lived through this awakening can explain it best:

> The illumination grew brighter, the roaring louder, I experienced a rocking sensation and then felt myself slipping out of my body, entirely enveloped in a halo of light. It is impossible to describe the experience accurately. I felt the point of consciousness that was myself growing wider, surrounded by waves of light. It grew wider and wider, spreading outward while the body, normally the immediate object of its perception, appeared to have receded into the distance until I became entirely unconscious of it. I was now all consciousness, without any outline, without any idea of a corporeal appendage, without any feeling or sensation coming from the senses, immersed in a sea of light simultane-

ously conscious and aware of every point, spread out, as it were, in all directions without any barrier or material obstruction. I was no longer myself, or to be more accurate, no longer as I knew myself to be, a small point of awareness confined in a body, but instead was a vast circle of consciousness in which the body was but a point, bathed in light and in a state of exaltation and happiness impossible to describe.[1]

As Gopi Krishna attests, the person he once was is gone, having been destroyed, or transfigured beyond recognition into a new being operating on a higher plane, transformed down to the level of his cellular structure.

Another twentieth-century Indian saint, Muktananda, underwent an intense *sadhana* during which he experienced a full *kundalini* awakening. He reported his incredible journey in his *Play of Consciousness*:

> The great Shakti Kundalini dwells in the central nadi, sushumna, and when awakened by the Guru's grace, is carried by the five pranas throughout the body, passing through the 72,000 nadis. This Shakti flows into the seven elements, into the particles of blood and other bodily fluids, and makes the body pure, well proportioned, clean, and beautiful, giving it luster and radiance. As I have already said, this pranashakti does countless tasks. Sometimes, in a seeker who is steadfast and full of devotion to his Guru, it pulsates with its grand, joyous vibrations in extraordinary ways. At that time he dances, sings, and weeps. Sometimes he will shout, or the different parts of his body will start to move. He may hop like a frog, spin, twist, run in circles, roll on the ground, slap his face, roll his head round and round, adopt different yogic postures and mudras, shake, sweat, do the jalandhara, uddiyana, or mula bhanda; his tongue may be drawn in or up against the palate in the kechari mudra, his eyeballs rolling upwards. He may make different sounds; he may roar like a lion or make other animal noises, or he may loudly chant OM and other mantras. All these kriyas occur spontaneously during meditation.[2]

From this frightening description of a seeker undergoing the purification activities of *kundalini*, one wonders how many people committed to our mental hospitals have experienced an activation of this evolutionary process, and are now doomed to medication hell because of our culture's ignorance of this process. Muktananda continues:

> Sometimes a kind of intoxication surges through the seeker. His head feels heavy and he remains in the sleeplike state of tandra. In this state he often sees visions. He sees Siddhas and lights, he wanders through other worlds—heaven, hell, Pitruloka (the world of the ancestors), and Siddhaloka (the world of enlightened saints)—and he even sees his own Guru. A divine and unparalleled joy rises up in waves from within, currents of happiness flow through all the nadis, and in his state of intoxication, the seeker begins to sway to and fro. The whole creation, even the most ordinary things, seem to him so beautiful and full of love that he feels as if he has been reborn in a new world, as if celestial beauty, delight, and pleasure have incarnated in the mortal world. Realizing how joyous and sweet life is, the sadhaka becomes overwhelmed with ecstasy. Love springs forth from his heart and compassion surges for all creatures.[3]

These individual experiences, which we can compare to the collective awakening that awaits humanity in the coming decades, are fraught with difficulty and pain, but ultimately result in a higher stability and a new vantage point of great wisdom.

The as yet unspoken message in this survey is that the galactic alignment opens a channel for the galactic *kundalini shakti* to flow through the earth, cleanse it (us), and excite it (us) into a higher level of being. The alignment will wax, maximize, then wane, possibly leaving many of us high and dry. The astronomical dynamic of the alignment indicates that the door will not be open forever. Yes, a realistic look at the parameters of the alignment perhaps gives us a few more centuries, but the peak of the alignment is occurring now, so can we really afford to sit around and not participate with all of our hearts, not contribute to the collective unfolding that invites us to realize our purpose as conscious beings? The point to emphasize is that *the door will close!* The rare zone of maximized opportunity will pass. As with the active door of the Symplegades motif that snips off the stern ornament of the *Argo*, we might barely get through in the nick of time.

TWENTY-FOUR

The End of an Illusion

We are approaching the end of our current cycle of historical manifestation. The Mayan end-date of 2012, despite the variables involved in the alignment phenomenon it was intended to target, has become *the* date in popular consciousness for "the end." But, the end of what? At the terminal point of the darkest age of materialism and illusion, what is it that will be ending? The answer can only be—materialism and illusion. Perhaps then we should welcome this transformation as a much-needed shift away from everything that deludes and binds us more deeply into realms of despair and decadence. We are so far gone that we no longer even acknowledge the current situation as being lamentable, but actively buy into and feed all that kills us.

The certainty of the impending "end" of modern civilization is not a new revelation. René Guénon, still hugely ignored in the West, nailed it to the wall over fifty years ago. Despite being criticized as nihilistic, his message is optimistic for those who can transcend their historical, ego-rooted, identities and be in service to a higher good.

> Those who will be successful in overcoming all these obstacles [of modern spiritual decadence] and in triumphing over the hostility of an environment opposed to all spirituality will doubtless be few in number; but, once again, it is not numbers that count here, for this is a realm where the laws are quite other than those of matter. There is therefore no occasion for despondency; and even where there is no hope of achieving any visible result before the collapse of the modern world through a catastrophe, that would still not be a valid reason to refrain from embarking upon a work extending in scope far beyond the present time. Those who may feel tempted to give way to discouragement should remind themselves that nothing accomplished within this order can ever be lost, that

confusion, error and darkness can enjoy no more than a specious and purely ephemeral triumph, that every kind of partial and transitory disequilibrium must perforce contribute towards the great equilibrium of the whole, and that nothing can ultimately prevail against the power of truth; for their motto they should take the one adopted in former times by certain initiatory organizations in the West: Vincit omnia Veritas.[1]

Vincit omnia veritas: Truth conquers all. Let go of illusion. Stop feeding fear.

These are times of death and renewal, big questions, hard truths, and universal processes powerfully coming into play within a human culture that has lost its ability to appreciate its connection to such universal processes. What is now ending thus seems to be a paradigm that has already lost all sense of orientation, all sense of true being. Everything of value that might be lost in a global cataclysm has already been lost in the steep attrition of Kali Yuga. The materialist delusion has run its course. There is no better way to end than with the prophetic words of Guénon himself, written over half a century ago. The ultimate terminal moment of the current historical cycle only appears to be the "end of the world"

> to those who see nothing beyond the limits of this particular cycle. A very excusable error of perspective it is true, but one that has nonetheless some regrettable consequences in the excessive and unjustified terrors to which it gives rise in people who are not sufficiently detached from terrestrial existence; and naturally they are the very people who form this erroneous conception most easily, just because of the narrowness of their point of view. . . . The end now under consideration is undeniably of considerably greater importance than any other, for it is the end of a whole Manvantara, and so of the temporal existence of what may rightly be called a humanity, but this, it must be said once more, in no way implies that it is the end of the terrestrial world itself, because, through the "reinstatement" that takes place at the final instant, this end will itself immediately become the beginning of another Manvantara. . . . If one does not stop short of the most profound order of reality, it can be said in all truth that the "end of a world" never is and never can be anything but the end of an illusion.[2]

Notes

Chapter One

1. In R. A. Schwaller de Lubicz, *The Temple of Man*, trans. Deborah Lawlor and Robert Lawlor (Rochester, Vt.: Inner Traditions, 1999), xix.
2. Michael Coe, *Breaking the Maya Code* (London: Thames & Hudson, 1999), 112.
3. See David Freidel, Linda Schele, and Joy Parker, *Maya Cosmos: Three Thousand Years on the Shaman's Path* (New York: William Morrow & Co., 1993).
4. Dennis Tedlock, *Breath on the Mirror: Mythic Voices and Visions of the Living Maya* (San Francisco: HarperSanFrancisco, 1994), 233–34. My book *7 Wind: A Quiché Maya Calendar for 1993* (Boulder, Colo.: Four Ahau Press, 1993) provides background into contemporary Quiché Maya calendar ceremonies and can be viewed in full at my Web site: Alignment2012.com.
5. Jean Meeus, *Mathematical Astronomy Morsels* (Richmond, Va.: Willmann-Bell 1997).

Chapter Two

1. V. Garth Norman, "Astronomical Orientations of Izapa Sculptures," master's thesis, Brigham Young University, 1980.
2. Bernardino de Sahagún, *Florentine Codex, General History of the Things of New Spain*, Bk. 7, trans. Arthur J. O. Anderson and Charles E. Dibble (Santa Fe, N.M.: School of American Research, Archaeological Institute of America, 1953).
3. In their article "The Observation of the Sun at the Time of Passage through the Zenith in Mesoamerica," Anthony Aveni and Horst Hartung wrote, "a fundamental coördinate axis in the Mesoamerican celestial reference frame consisted of four lines connecting the world to the four cardinal points, a fifth axis being directed toward the zenith." *Archaeoastronomy* 3 (1981).
4. See José Diaz-Bolio, *Why the Rattlesnake in Mesoamerican Civilization?* (Merida, Mexico: Area Maya, 1988) and *The Geometry of the Maya and Their Rattlesnake Art* (Merida, Mexico: Area Maya, 1987).

5. Appendix 3 in John Major Jenkins, *Maya Cosmogenesis 2012* (Santa Fe, N.M.: Bear & Co., 1998) explores the varying date-ranges of zenith-passage phenomena.

6. Readers interested in empirical background should see the works of Oliver Reiser, *Cosmic Humanism* (Cambridge, Mass.: Schenkman Publishing Company, 1966) and *The Intent of Creation* (Lakemont, Ga.: CSA Press, 1978); David Bohm's work discussed in David R. Griffin, ed., *Physics and the Ultimate Significance of Time* (Albany: State University of New York Press, 1986); Wilhelm Reich, *Cosmic Superimposition: Ether, God, and Devil* (New York: Farrar, Straus & Giroux, 1973); and Theodor Landscheidt, *Cosmic Cybernetics: The Foundations of a Modern Astrology*, trans. Linda Kratzch (Aalen, Germany: Ebertin Verlag, 1973).

Chapter Three

1. Linda Schele and Peter Mathews, *The Code of Kings: The Language of Seven Maya Temples and Tombs* (New York: Simon & Schuster, 1998), chap. 6.

2. Miguel Angel Vergara. *Chichen Itza: Astronomical Light and Shadow Phenomena of the Great Pyramid* (Nolo, Yucatan, Mexico: Centro de Investigacion Maya Haltun-Ha and K'u-Kuul-Kaan Academy), www.1spirit.com/kukuulkaan.

3. Michael Coe, "Native Astronomy in Mesoamerica," in *Archaeoastronomy in Pre-Columbian America*, ed. Anthony F. Aveni (Austin: University of Texas Press, 1975), 23–24.

4. Schele and Mathews, *Code of Kings*, 141.

5. David Kelley, *Deciphering the Maya Script* (Austin: University of Texas Press, 1976), 36. See also Jenkins, *Maya Cosmogenesis 2012*, 52–53, 285.

6. Joseph Campbell, *The Inner Reaches of Outer Space* (New York: Harper & Row, 1986), 34–40, 87; Frank Waters, *Mountain Dialogues* (Athens, Ohio: Sage/Swallow Books, 1981), 136–48; Gordon Brotherston, *Book of the Fourth World* (Cambridge: Cambridge University Press, 1992), 298–302.

Chapter Four

1. Gerald Hawkins, *Stonehenge Decoded* (New York: Dell Publishing, 1966), 64; Peter Tompkins, *The Magic of Obelisks* (New York: Harper & Row, 1981), 372–80.

2. John Michell, *At the Centre of the World: Polar Symbolism Discovered in Celtic, Norse, and Other Ritualized Landscapes* (London: Thames & Hudson, 1994), 105.

Chapter Five

1. The term *cross* to name the "alignment" was used by Nick Anthony Fiorenza at the International Forum on New Science in Fort Collins, Colorado, in September 1995.
2. Jay Weidner and Vincent Bridges, *A Monument to the End of Time: Alchemy, Fulcanelli, and the Great Cross* (Mount Gilead, N.C.: Aethyrea Books, 1999).
3. Although this identity is unlikely. See André VandenBroeck's memoir of Schwaller de Lubicz, *Al-Kemi: A Memoir—Hermetic, Occult, Political, and Private Aspects of R. A. Schwaller de Lubicz* (Rochester, Vt.: Inner Traditions International, 1987).
4. Weidner and Bridges, *A Monument to the End of Time*, 131. A photograph of the ceiling mural is in Giuseppe Sesti, *The Glorious Constellations*, trans. Karin H. Ford (New York: Henry N. Abrams, 1991), 122–23.
5. Mark Kurlansky, *The Basque History of the World* (New York: Penguin Books, 1999). Ignatius Loyola was a famous Basque.
6. Fulcanelli, *Le mystere des cathedrales*, trans. Mary Sworder (London: Neville-Spearman, 1971), 166.
7. This interpretation comes from a general consensus among modern students of Egyptian gnosis. See essays at: www.sacredmysteries.com.
8. Equinox eclipses occur in 1997, 2006, and 2015.
9. Paul LaViolette. *Earth Under Fire: Humanity's Survival of the Apocalypse* (Schenectady, N.Y.: Starlane Publications, 1997).
10. Personal communication; see also www.Alignment2012.com/Isis.html.
11. Weidner and Bridges, *A Monument to the End of Time*, 239.
12. Fulcanelli, *Dwellings of the Philosophers*, 515–22.
13. Weidner and Bridges, *A Monument to the End of Time*, 221.

Chapter Six

1. The lunar nodes and their 18.51-year zodiacal circuit are introduced here as an important timing mechanism for precession, and the analogy exists with precession because the nodes and the vernal point are both celestial "points" or "objects" that move backward. In Western astronomy, precession was tracked with the vernal equinox point. In Giorgio de Santillana and Hertha von Dechend's *Hamlet's Mill* (Boston: Gambit, 1969), the sixty-year trigons of Jupiter-Saturn conjunctions were shown to be one way that the larger cycle of precession was tracked. So too, we could argue that the 18.51-year nodal cycle is a key to precession. In my *Tzolkin* (Garberville, Calif.: Borderland Sciences Research Foundation, 1994) I showed how the 13-sign zodiac works with the 260-day *tzolkin* and the eclipse cycle: Every two

*tzolkin*s (520 days), three eclipses will theoretically occur, and the position of the eclipses will shift 27.7° (one sign in a 13-sign zodiac). Expanding further, the full nodal cycle thus equals 13 x 520 = 6,760 days. Two of these nodal periods (13,520 days) are significant, because a person celebrates his or her second nodal return and fifty-second "*tzolkin*" birthday exactly six days after his or her thirty-seventh "solar" birthday. At that moment the person will be 13,520 days old. Astrologically, the second nodal return heralds the opportunity to reconnect with one's sacred path.

2. Coomaraswamy explored the cosmology of knotted-tail fish beings in his *Yaksas: Essays in the Water Cosmology* (New York: Oxford University Press, 1993).

3. Willy Hartner, "The Pseudoplanetary Nodes of the Moon's Orbit in Hindu and Islamic Iconographies," *Ars Islamica* 5, part 1 (1938): 150.

4. It should be noted that these positions are in the sidereal or Vedic zodiac; the unadjusted Western zodiac is now some 23° out of synchronization with the true sidereal locations.

5. The *Bundahishn* (52.12.5), quoted in D. N. MacKenzie's "Zoroastrian Astrology in the *Bundahishn*," *Bulletin of the School of Oriental and African Studies* 27 (1964): 515.

6. Ibid. (60.3.22), 521–22.

7. Roger Beck, in "Interpreting the Ponza Zodiac, II," *Journal of Mithraic Studies* 2, no. 2 (1977), offers this interpretation, without reference to the Galactic Center.

8. See Weidner's piece on Kubrick at: www.sacredmysteries.com. Also the events of September 11, 2001, seem to supply the "unique ingress" referred to.

Chapter Seven

1. Jean Richer, *Sacred Geography of the Ancient Greeks: Astrological Symbolism in Art, Architecture, and Landscape*, trans. Christine Rhone (Albany: State University of New York Press, 1994), xxii.

2. René Guénon, "The Exit from the Cave," in *Fundamental Symbols: The Universal Language of Sacred Science* (Cambridge: Quinta Essentia, 1995), 158.

3. Reprinted as "The Wild Boar and the Bear" in Guénon, *Fundamental Symbols*.

4. The exact same shift is encoded into the monumental message at Izapa as the fall of Seven Macaw episode. Izapa's mythology appears some 1,500 years later in the Quiché sacred book called the *Popol Vuh*.

5. Macrobius, quoted in Santillana and Dechend, *Hamlet's Mill*, 242.

6. Ibid., 242–44.

7. Richer, *Sacred Geography of the Ancient Greeks*, 112.

8. Ibid., 20, n. 33.

9. Ibid., 20.
10. Ibid., 66.
11. Ibid., 19.
12. Alexandre Volguine, *L'Ésotérisme de l'astrologie* (Paris: Dangles, 1953), quoted in Richer, *Sacred Geography of the Ancient Greeks*, 19. This touches upon the astronomical symbolism of the biblical Revelation of Saint John, clearly related to precession and the galactic gateways, which must be left for another study.
13. Richer, *Sacred Geography of the Ancient Greeks*, 113.
14. Ibid., 66.
15. Plato, *The Republic of Plato*, trans. by Francis MacDonald Cornford (Oxford: Oxford University Press, 1941), 351–52.
16. Florence and Kenneth Wood, *Homer's Secret Iliad: The Epic of the Night Skies Decoded* (London: John Murray, 1999), 5.
17. Ibid., 11.
18. David Frawley, *The Astrology of the Seers* (Delhi: Narendra Prakash Jain for Motilal Banarsidass Publishers, 1990), and *Gods, Sages, and Kings: Vedic Secrets of Ancient Civilization* (Salt Lake City: Passage Press, 1991).
19. Jenkins, *Maya Cosmogenesis 2012*, 249–63. When I visited Guatemala in February 2001, I met with Mayanist Marion Popenoe Hatch at her house in Antigua. As director of the archaeological project at Abaj Takalik, she sees an awareness of this precessional shifting in the orientation of certain rows of carved stones at that preclassical site and thus confirms the relevance of my Izapan interpretation.
20. Richer, *Sacred Geography of the Ancient Greeks*, 125.
21. Ibid., 128.
22. Ibid., 130.

Chapter Eight

1. Although misleading, Cumont's book, *The Mysteries of Mithra* (trans. Thomas J. McCormack [New York: Dover Publications, 1956]), is still widely available in bookstores.
2. David Ulansey, *The Origins of the Mithraic Mysteries: Cosmology and Salvation in the Ancient World* (New York: Oxford University Press, 1989), 51.
3. See essays in John R. Hinnells, ed., *Mithraic Studies*, 2 vols. (Manchester, U.K.: Manchester University Press, 1975) and in *The Journal of Mithraic Studies*. More recently, see John R. Hinnells, ed., *Studies in Mithraism* (Rome: Erma di Brettschneider, 1994), and David Ulansey's Web site: www.well.com/user/davidu/.

4. See Marion Popenoe Hatch, "An Hypothesis on Olmec Astronomy, with Special Reference to the La Venta Site," Papers on Olmec and Maya Archaeology, no. 13 (Berkeley: University of California, 1971), and Jenkins, *Maya Cosmogenesis 2012*, 33-35. By 1200 B.C. the Olmecs at La Venta had oriented (and reoriented) their main pyramid with the precession-shifting stars of the Big Dipper. Olmec-Izapa connections are established, and the astronomical interests of the Izapans, circa 200 B.C., are clear. It would not be surprising if early Olmec astronomers passed star positions down through the centuries, and the rate of precession became better known until the Long Count calendar, which first appeared in the first century B.C., encoded the knowledge as a future alignment of solstice and galaxy to occur on 13.0.0.0.0 (December 21, A.D. 2012).
5. Ulansey, *The Origins of the Mithraic Mysteries*, 67–76.
6. Roger Beck, "Interpreting the Ponza Zodiac, I" in *Journal of Mithraic Studies* 1, no. 1 (1976). See also his book *Planetary Gods and Planetary Orders in the Mysteries of Mithras* (New York: E. J. Brill, 1988).
7. David Ulansey, "Mithras and the Hypercosmic Sun," in Hinnells, *Studies in Mithraism;* also posted on Ulansey's Web site: www.well.com/user/davidu/. The existence of two suns in the Platonic tradition (one visible and one hypercosmic) is derived from the Chaldaean Oracles, a collection of enigmatic writings from the second century A.D. The Hypercosmic Sun is accessed through the galactic gateway between Sagittarius and Scorpio, strongly suggesting that the Galactic Center is behind this ancient cosmoconception.
8. Beck, "Interpreting the Ponza Zodiac, II."
9. Ernest Renan, *Marc–Aurèle et la fin du monde antique*, 579, quoted and translated by Ulansey in *The Origins of the Mithraic Mysteries*, 4.

Chapter Nine

1. Quoted in R. A. Schwaller de Lubicz, *Sacred Science: The King of Pharaonic Theocracy*, trans. André VandenBroeck and Goldian VandenBroeck (Rochester, Vt.: Inner Traditions International, 1982), 286.
2. R. A. Schwaller de Lubicz, *The Temple of Man*, 832. Two considerations arise here. First, since de Lubicz was writing several decades ago, Mayan writing has been largely deciphered and the ideas of their "old tradition" should now enter a general discussion in the mainstream of the history of humanity's intellectual accomplishments. But it has been slow in doing so. So, second, the question arises as to when Mayan sacred science is going to be allowed into the general discussion of the history of science and astronomy, or even take a place of respect in the gnosis of esoteric metaphysics. Mesoamerican tradition is largely left out of these studies because it is difficult to catego-

rize—it is neither, strictly speaking, Oriental nor Occidental.

3. Ean Begg, *The Cult of the Black Virgin* (London: Arkana, 1985).

4. See www.sacredmysteries.com.

5. Plutarch, "Isis and Osiris," in *Moralia*, trans. Frank Cole Babbitt, quoted in Schwaller de Lubicz, *Sacred Science*, 89. The astronomical location of the Osirian episode reminds one of the inscription accompanying the Mayan ruler of Palenque, Pacal, on his after-death journey, to the effect that "he entered the road"—i.e., he entered the *xibalba be*, the "road to the underworld" (the dark rift in the Milky Way).

6. Orion is not exactly on the ecliptic, therefore its meridian extremes oscillate over a 40,000-year period. The Galactic Center and the Galactic Anticenter are closer to the ecliptic, therefore their meridian extremes are very close to 26,000 years and, moreover, correspond to the solstice-galaxy alignment eras. See chapter 14 for more on this. See Lynn Picknett and Clive Prince, *The Stargate Conspiracy: The Truth About Extraterrestrial Life and the Mysteries of Ancient Egypt* (New York: Berkley Books, 1999), for a critique of the new Egyptologists.

7. See Vincent Bridges, "Abydos, the Osireion, and Egyptian Sacred Science," 2000, at: www.aethyrea.com/egypt/abydos.

8. Ibid.

Chapter Ten

1. Swami Sri Yukteswar, *The Holy Science* (1949. Los Angeles: Self-Realization Fellowship, 1990), 7.

2. Frawley, *The Astrology of the Seers*, 48.

3. Yukteswar, *The Holy Science*, 8.

4. Ibid.

5. Frawley, *Astrology of the Seers*, 56.

6. Ibid., 63.

7. Ibid., 48.

8. Patrizia Norelli-Bachelet, *The Gnostic Circle: A Synthesis in the Harmonies of the Cosmos* (New York: Samuel Weiser, 1975), 160.

9. Ibid., 276.

10. I hope that this observation will lay to rest the absurd New Age notion that our solar system orbits the Pleiades. In many sources we are told that a great secret is contained in the knowledge that we orbit the Pleiades in a period of 26,000 years. Well, right away we should suspect that precession is somehow involved. As with the information related by Yukteswar and Norelli-Bachelet, the Pleiadian orbit is intended to refer to the Sun's apparent motion around the zodiac in relation to the fixed sidereal position of the

Pleiades (I discussed this in my 1995 book, *The Center of Mayan Time* [Boulder, Colo.: Four Ahau Press]).

11. Norelli-Bachelet, *The Gnostic Circle,* 160–61.

12. Patrizia Norelli-Bachelet, *The New Way: A Study in the Rise and Establishment of a Gnostic Society,* 2 vols. (Kodaikanal, India: Aeon Books, 1981).

13. Valentia Straiton, *The Celestial Ship of the North* (New York: Albert & Charles Boni, 1927), 168.

14. Edgar Conrow was apparently associated with a theosophical group in California, although his published writings are unknown.

15. Straiton, quoting Conrow in *The Celestial Ship of the North,* 167–68.

Chapter Eleven

1. See Kenneth Oldmeadow, *Traditionalism: Religion in the Light of the Perennial Philosophy* (Colombo, Sri Lanka: Sri Lanka Institute of Traditional Studies, 2000); William W. Quinn Jr., *The Only Tradition* (Albany: State University of New York Press, 1997); Roger Lipsey, *Coomaraswamy 3: His Life and Work* (Princeton, N.J.: Princeton University Press, 1977); Paul Chacornac, *A Simple Life* (Ghent, N.Y.: Sophia Perennis et Universalis, in press); and essays by Martin Lings, Marco Pallis, and Whitall Perry (see bibliography).

2. Martin Lings, "René Guénon," *Sophia: The Journal of Traditional Studies* 1, no. 1 (1995).

3. Chacornac, *A Simple Life,* 37.

4. Whitall N. Perry, "Coomaraswamy: The Man, Myth, and History," *Studies in Comparative Religion* 11, no. 1 (1977): 160.

5. Marco Pallis, "A Fateful Meeting of Minds: A. K. Coomaraswamy and René Guénon," *Studies in Comparative Religion* 12, nos. 3 and 4 (1978): 178.

6. Jean Biès, "A Face of Eternal Wisdom: An Interview with Frithjof Schuon," *Sophia: the Journal of Traditional Studies* 4, no. 1 (1998).

Chapter Twelve

1. In *Mayan Sacred Science* (Boulder, Colo: Four Ahau Press, 1994, 2000), I identified these as root-principles in ancient Mayan calendrics and time philosophy, related to the modern Tzutujil Maya paradigm of change called *jaloj kexoj.*

2. See Ananda Coomaraswamy, *Spiritual Authority and Temporal Power in the Indian Theory of Government* (New Delhi: Oxford University Press, 1993).

3. Seyyed Hossein Nasr, *The Need for a Sacred Science* (Albany: State University of New York Press, 1993), 25.

4. René Guénon, "The Wild Boar and the Bear," in *Fundamental Symbols: The Universal Language of Sacred Science* (Cambridge: Quinta Essentia, 1995).

5. Santillana and Dechend, *Hamlet's Mill*, 242. The quote from Macrobius is from his *Commentary on the Dream of Scipio* (trans. William H. Stahl [New York: Columbia University Press, 1952]), a work of Cicero's. The statement that Gemini and Sagittarius still rise heliacally on the solstices "even in our time" is only technically correct: only six degrees of each sign will be above the horizon as the sun rises, not enough to be actually visible before the sky brightens.

6. In 1998, as calculated by Jean Meeus in *Mathematical Astronomy Morsels*.

7. We see here an inversion of the Galactic Center as the root or *muladhara* chakra. For those who sought to encode esoteric truths, however, this kind of symbol can map both ways. For example, in kabbalistic symbolism the Tree of Life is an inverted tree; it doesn't grow upward from the earth but downward from the spiritual plane. In other words, it is "rooted" in the highest spiritual center and source.

Chapter Thirteen

1. Stephen Langdon, *Tammuz and Ishtar* (Oxford: Oxford University Press, 1914), 37–38.

2. R. Gordon Wasson, *Soma: Divine Mushroom of Immortality* (New York: Harcourt, Brace, Jovanovich, 1968), and *The Wondrous Mushroom: Mycolatry in Mesoamerica* (New York: McGraw-Hill, 1980).

3. Ananda Coomaraswamy, "On the Loathly Bride," in *Coomaraswamy 1, Selected Papers: Traditional Art and Symbolism*, ed. Roger Lipsey (Princeton, N.J.: Princeton University Press, 1977), 356, n. 10.

4. Uno Holmberg, *Finno-Ugric and Siberian Mythology*, The Mythology of All Races Series, ed. L. Gray (Boston: Marshall Jones, 1927), 350.

5. Eino Friberg, *The Kalevala: Epic of the Finnish People* (Helsinki: Otava Publishing, 1988), Runo 42:178–81.

6. Translated in Ananda Coomaraswamy, *The Door in the Sky: Coomaraswamy on Myth and Meaning* (Princeton, N.J.: Princeton University Press, 1997), 23.

Chapter Fourteen

1. The obliquity of the ecliptic also changes slowly, introducing a possible 2° margin of error in this latitude position. Providing precise calculations doesn't concern us here; it is recognizing that the process occurs at all, and how it is related to the solstice-galaxy alignment eras.

Chapter Fifteen

1. Arthur Bernard Cook, *Zeus: A Study in Ancient Religion*, vol. 3, pt. 2 (Cambridge: Cambridge University Press, 1940). According to the Greek writer

Strabo, quoted by Eustathones in "Dionysus," paraphrased by Cook: "Others . . . transferred both the Planktai and the Symplegades to the neighbourhood of Gadeira and identified them with the pillars of Hercules" (Cook, *Zeus*, 978; see also 983).
2. Guénon, "Concerning the Two Saint Johns," in *Fundamental Symbols*, 170–71.

Chapter Sixteen

1. David Ovason, *The Secret Architecture of Our Nation's Capital* (New York: HarperCollins, 2000), 62, 65.
2. Ulansey, *The Origins of the Mithraic Mysteries*. See also chapter 8.
3. In Julia Duin's review of Ovason's book, "Washington's Stellar Design No Coincidence, Author Says," *Washington Times*, September 5, 2000.
4. There are Masonic and Hermetic symbols on the American dollar, as summarized by Joseph Campbell in his book *The Inner Reaches of Outer Space*.

Chapter Seventeen

1. I commented at length on Sullivan's book in appendix 6 of *Maya Cosmogenesis 2012*.
2. Gary Urton, *At the Crossroads of the Earth and the Sky* (Austin: University of Texas Press, 1981), 201.
3. Ibid., 201–2.
4. William Sullivan, *The Secret of the Incas: Myth, Astronomy, and the War Against Time* (New York: Crown Publishers, 1996), 365.
5. Ibid.
6. See, for example, Bellamy's *Calendar of Tiahuanaco: A Disquisition on the Time Measuring System of the Oldest Civilization in the World* (London: Faber & Faber, 1956).
7. The calculation is based on the slowly changing *obliquity of the ecliptic*. This shift ranges over only 4° and is so slow that an error-range on the order of 3,000 years for any calculation would be necessary.
8. See, for example, David Hatcher Childress, *Lost Cities and Ancient Mysteries of South America* (Kempton, Ill.: Adventures Unlimited Press, 1986).
9. Jim Allen, *Atlantis: The Andes Solution* (London: Orion Publishing, 1999).

Chapter Eighteen

1. Jenkins, *The Center of Mayan Time*, and *Maya Cosmogenesis 2012*, 246.
2. Of course, the Maya did not use our Judeo-Christian dating system; in the Long Count calendar December 21, 2012, is written 13.0.0.0.0 (the end of the thirteenth *baktun*). In Anthony Aveni's revised edition of his book *Sky-*

watchers of Ancient Mexico (Austin: University of Texas press, 1980, 2000), he correctly supports the GMT correlation number 584283, but it is mistakenly given as December 8, 2012. Anyone with a Julian Day ephemeris can make the following simple calculation. December 21, 2012, is Julian Day 2,456,283. Subtract from this the number of days in 13 *baktuns* (1,872,000). The result is 584283, the Julian Day number of the Long Count's zero day back in 3114 B.C., thus confirming the end-date as December 21, 2012. As with Michael Coe's mistakenly reported end-date of December 24, 2011 (in the 1962 edition of his book *Mexico* [London: Thames & Hudson] and used by Frank Waters in *Mexico Mystique*), this faux pas will no doubt be considered authoritative and be endlessly repeated to the detriment of clarity on the correlation question.

3. Joseph Campbell, *The Hero with a Thousand Faces* (New York: Bollingen Foundation, 1949), 3.

Chapter Nineteen

1. *Art and Society in a Highland Maya Community: The Altarpiece of Santiago Atitlán* (Austin: University of Texas Press, 2001) by Allen J. Christenson examines the blending of Christian and Mayan religious iconography. The Tzutujil altarpiece that is the main subject of the investigation is structurally similar to the facades of Antigua's Spanish colonial churches, yet is covered with Mayan deities. Similarly, though without direct historical influence, the ninth-century mural in the Lower Temple of the Jaguars at Chichen Itza is comparable to Old World Gothic iconography, not just in structure, but in the religious meaning of the individual elements in the composition.

2. Ananda Coomaraswamy, "The Rape of a Nagi," in *Coomaraswamy 1, Selected Papers: Traditional Art and Symbolism* (Princeton, N.J.: Princeton University Press, 1977), 337–40. See also "Walter Andrae's *Die ionische Saule*" in the same volume.

3. The strange counterpart to Compostela in the west seems to be Jerusalem in the east. There is a saying: "All roads may lead to Rome, but they all end up in Compostela." Rome, of course, was the center of Christianity that replaced Jerusalem. These eastern and western pilgrimage destinations reflect the eastern and western gateways of the Mediterranean slightly farther south. The pilgrimage destinations are terrestrial "doorways," while the Pillars of Hercules and the Red Sea are oceanic. Again, latitudes come into play and they generally point to realms beyond (India and America; Leo and Aquarius).

4. This variant incorporates later alliances. The quartered zone shows the castle of Castile, the lion of León, the Pillars of Hercules (the House of Aragon),

and the chain of Navarra. At the bottom, a small pomegranate symbolizing Granada is included. The Pillars of Hercules were a symbol adopted by Charles V to declare his power on both sides of the Atlantic.

Chapter Twenty

1. Paul LaViolette, *Beyond the Big Bang: Ancient Myth and the Science of Continuous Creation* (Rochester, Vt.: Park Street Press, 1995), and *Earth Under Fire*. See also the video documentary of *Earth Under Fire* at LaViolette's Web site: www.etheric.com/LaVioletteBooks/email.html.
2. Terence McKenna, in Jenkins, *Maya Cosmogenesis 2012*, xxvii–xxviii.
3. Oliver L. Reiser, *Messages to and from the Galaxy*, quoted by Willard Van de Bogart at the web address in note 4, below.
4. Eulogy material by Robert Smith III, University of Alabama at Huntsville posted at: www.earthportals.com/Portal_Messenger/ reiser.html.
5. Oliver L. Reiser, *The Promise of Scientific Humanism* (New York: Oscar Piest, 1940), 305. Reiser's original cosmecology article appeared as "Cosmecology: A Theory of Evolution" in *Journal of Heredity* 28 (1937): 367–71.
6. Ibid., 308. The oscillation of our solar system above and below the plane of our galaxy is sometimes proposed as another source of increased bombardment, as a result of encountering debris as we pass through the galactic plane. I'm not sure if this scenario works, however, because whatever force warps the local space-time field to cause such oscillation must convey all other objects along the same trajectory. If the plane of the Milky Way is shaped like a standing-wave oscillation, then everything within it slides along the same track, and no eras of greater conflict with galactic debris actually occur. It's an illusion of perspective. The situation is similar to how space-time warping (near a strong gravitational field, for instance) causes light and all other objects to travel a curvy trajectory, but not from the perspective of anyone on the inside.
7. Reiser, *Cosmic Humanism* (1966), 442.
8. For a related discussion of astrobiology, see Max Knoll, "Transformations of Science in Our Age," in *Man and Time: Papers from the Eranos Yearbooks*, ed. Joseph Campbell (Princeton, N.J.: Princeton University Press, 1951), 264–307. A fascinating article, but unfortunately this author was apparently unaware of Reiser's work.
9. Oliver L. Reiser, *Cosmic Humanism and World Unity* (New York: Gordon & Breach, 1975), 113.
10. David Wilcock's studies can be accessed at www.Ascension2000.com. His online book *Convergence III* is comprehensive and should revolutionize—or even define—higher-dimensional physics.

11. Though rigorous in his analysis, Gaspar also transcends scientific preoccupations, and like Rush Allen on www.siloam.net, he explores deeper metaphysical terrain based on insights into comparative star lore and mythology.
12. Reiser, *The Intent of Creation*, 96.

Chapter Twenty-one

1. Personal e-mail, 1999.
2. Gershom Scholem, *Kabbalah* (New York: Meridian Books, 1974), 120.

Chapter Twenty-two

1. In her recent book *Catastrophobia* (Rochester, Vt.: Bear & Co., 2001), Barbara Hand Clow takes this up as her main thesis, drawing upon recent discoveries and her insights into ancient traditions.

Chapter Twenty-three

1. Gopi Krishna, *Kundalini: The Evolutionary Energy in Man* (Boston: Shambhala Publications, 1985), 13.
2. Muktananda, *Play of Consciousness* (South Fallsburg, N.Y.: SYDA Foundation, 1978), 32–33.
3. Ibid., 33.

Chapter Twenty-four

1. René Guénon, *The Crisis of the Modern World*, trans. Arthur Osborne (Ghent, N.Y.: Sophia Perennis et Universalis, 1996), 169–70. Translation from: www.geocities.com/CapitolHill/6824/eschat.htm.
2. René Guénon, *The Reign of Quantity and the Signs of the Times*, trans. Lord Northbourne (New York: Penguin Books, 1972), 330–31, 336.

Bibliography

Abū-Ma'shar. *De magnis conjunctionibus*. Venice, 1515.

Allen, Jim M. *Atlantis: The Andes Solution*. London: Orion Publishing, 1999.

Allen, Richard Hinckley. *Star Names: Their Lore and Meaning*. New York: Dover Publications, 1963.

Allen, Rush. "Adventures in Astroarchaeology" and "Timeline of Precession." At www.Siloam.net.

Annis, Verle Lincoln. *The Architecture of Antigua, Guatemala, 1543–1773*. Guatemala City: University of San Carlos, 1968.

Argüelles, José, *The Mayan Factor*. Santa Fe, N.M.: Bear & Co., 1987.

Aveni, Anthony. *Skywatchers of Ancient Mexico*. Austin: University of Texas Press, 1980, 2000.

Aveni, Anthony, and Horst Hartung. "The Observation of the Sun at the Time of Passage through the Zenith in Mesoamerica." *Archaeoastronomy* 3 (1981).

Aztlan, an e-mail discussion list for Mesoamerican studies. Subscribe at: www.ukans.edu/~hoopes/aztlan/

Bauval, Robert, and Adrian Gilbert. *The Orion Mystery: Unlocking the Secrets of the Pyramids*. New York: Crown Publishers, 1994.

Beck, Roger. "Interpreting the Ponza Zodiac, I." *Journal of Mithraic Studies* 1, no. 1 (1976).

———. "Interpreting the Ponza Zodiac, II." *Journal of Mithraic Studies* 2, no. 2 (1977).

———. *Planetary Gods and Planetary Orders in the Mysteries of Mithras*. New York: E. J. Brill, 1988.

———. "The Seat of Mithras at the Equinoxes: Porphyry, *De Antro Nympharum* 24." *Journal of Mithraic Studies* 1, no. 1 (1976).

Begg, Ean. *The Cult of the Black Virgin*. London: Arkana, 1985.

Bellamy, H. S. *The Calendar of Tiahuanaco: A Disquisition on the Time Measuring System of the Oldest Civilization in the World*. London: Faber & Faber, 1956.

Biés, Jean. "A Face of Eternal Wisdom: An Interview with Frithjof Schuon." *Sophia: The Journal of Traditional Studies* 4, no. 1 (1998).

al-Bīrūnī. *The Book of Instruction in the Elements of the Art of Astrology*. Translated by R. Ramsay Wright. London: Luzac & Co., 1934.

Boehme, Jacob. *Dreyfaches Leben*. 1682.

———. *Theosophische Wercke*. 1682.

Bogart, Willard Van De. "Dr. Oliver L. Reiser." At: www.earthportals.com/Portal_Messenger/reiser.html.

Bridges, Vincent. "Abydos, the Osireion, and Egyptian Sacred Science," 2000. At: www.aethyrea.com/egypt/abydos.html.

Brönsted, Peter Oluf. *Voyages dans la Grèce*. Paris: Firmin Didot, 1828.

Brotherston, Gordon. *Book of the Fourth World*. Cambridge: Cambridge University Press, 1992.

Burckhardt, Titus. *Sacred Art in East and West: Principles and Methods*. Translated by Lord Northbourne. Bedfont, Middlesex, England: Perennial Books, 1967.

Campbell, Joseph. *The Hero with a Thousand Faces*. New York: Bollingen Foundation, 1949.

———. *The Inner Reaches of Outer Space*. New York: Harper & Row, 1986.

Campbell, Leroy A. *Mithraic Iconography and Ideology*. Leiden, Netherlands: E. J. Brill, 1968.

Chacornac, Paul. *A Simple Life*. Ghent, N.Y.: Sophia Perennis et Universalis (in press).

Childress, David Hatcher. *Lost Cities and Ancient Mysteries of South America*. Kempton, Ill.: Adventures Unlimited Press, 1986.

Christenson, Allen J. *Art and Society in a Highland Maya Community: The Altarpiece of Santiago Atitlan*. Austin: University of Texas Press, 2001.

Cicero. *Nine Orations and the Dream of Scipio*. Translated by. Palmer Bovie. New York: New American Library, 1967.

Clow, Barbara Hand. *Catastrophobia: The Truth Behind Earth Changes in the Coming Age of Light*. Rochester, Vt.: Bear & Co., 2001.

Coe, Michael. *Breaking the Maya Code*. London: Thames & Hudson, 1992.

———. *The Maya*. London: Thames & Hudson, 1966.

———. *Mexico*. London: Thames & Hudson, 1962.

———. "Native Astronomy in Mesoamerica." In *Archaeoastronomy in Pre-Columbian America*, ed. Anthony F. Aveni. Austin: University of Texas Press, 1975.

Coe, Michael, et. al. *The Olmec World: Ritual and Rulership*. Princeton, N.J.: Princeton University in association with Harry N. Abrams, New York, 1995.

Cook, Arthur Bernard. *Zeus: A Study in Ancient Religion*. Vol. 3, part 2. Cambridge: Cambridge University Press, 1940.

Coomaraswamy, Ananda K. *The Dance of Śiva: Essays on Indian Art and Culture*. New York: Dover Publications, 1985.

———. *The Door in the Sky: Coomaraswamy on Myth and Meaning.* Princeton, N.J.: Princeton University Press, 1997.

———. "Early Iconography of Sagittarius." Essay, Princeton University archives, early 1940s.

———. *Hinduism and Buddhism.* New York: Philosophical Library, 1943.

———. *Mediaeval Sinhalese Art.* Broad Campden, England: Essex House Press, 1908.

———. "On the Loathly Bride." In *Coomaraswamy 1, Selected Papers: Traditional Art and Symbolism,* edited by Roger Lipsey. Princeton, N.J.: Princeton University Press, 1977.

———. *Spiritual Authority and Temporal Power in the Indian Theory of Government.* New Delhi: Oxford University Press, 1993.

———. *What is Civilization? And Other Essays.* Ipswich, England: Golgonooza Press, 1989.

———. *Yaksas: Essays in the Water Cosmology.* New York: Oxford University Press, 1993.

Corbin, Henry. *Cyclical Time and Ismaili Gnosis.* London: Kegan Paul International, 1983.

———. *Spiritual Body and Celestial Earth: From Mazdean Iran to Shi'ite Iran.* Translated by Nancy Pearson. Princeton, N.J.: Princeton University Press, 1977.

———. *Temple and Contemplation.* Translated by Philip Sherrard. London: Kegan Paul in association with Islamic Publications, 1986.

Cumont, Franz. *The Mysteries of Mithra.* Translated by Thomas J. McCormack. New York: Dover Publications, 1956.

Diaz-Bolio, José. *The Geometry of the Maya and Their Rattlesnake Art.* Merida, Mexico: Area Maya, 1987.

———. *Why the Rattlesnake in Mesoamerican Civilization?* Merida, Mexico: Area Maya, 1988.

Duin, Julia. "Washington's Stellar Design No Coincidence, Author Says." *Washington Times,* September 5, 2000.

Ervast, Pekka. *The Key to the Kalevala.* Translated by Tapio Joensuu. Nevada City, Calif.: Blue Dolphin Publishing, 1999.

Evola, Julius. *The Mystery of the Grail.* Translated by Guido Stucco. Rochester, Vt.: Inner Traditions International, 1997.

Feuerstein, Georg, Subhash Kak, and David Frawley. *In Search of the Cradle of Civilization.* Wheaton, Ill.: Quest Books, 1996.

Frawley, David. *The Astrology of the Seers.* Delhi: Narendra Prakash Jain for Motilal Banarsidass Publishers, 1990.

———. *Gods, Sages, and Kings: Vedic Secrets of Ancient Civilization.* Salt Lake City: Passage Press, 1991.

Freidel, David, Linda Schele, and Joy Parker. *Maya Cosmos: Three Thousand Years on the Shaman's Path.* New York: William Morrow & Co., 1993.

Friberg, Eino. *The Kalevala: Epic of the Finnish People.* Helsinki: Otava Publishing, 1988.

Fulcanelli. *The Dwellings of the Philosophers.* Translated by Brigitte Donvez and Lionel Perrin. Boulder, Colo.: Archive Press, 1999.

———. *Les demeures philosophales.* Paris: Jean-Jacques Pauvert, 1964.

———. *Le mystere des cathedrales.* 1926; 2nd ed., Paris: Jean-Jacques Pauvert, 1957. Translated by Mary Sworder as *Fulcanelli: Master Alchemist.* London: Neville-Spearman, 1971.

Gaspar, Dr. William A. *The Celestial Clock.* Clovis, N.M.: Adam and Eva Publishing, 1999.

Giamario, Daniel. "The May 1998 Galactic Alignment: A Shamanic Look at the Turning of the Ages." *Mountain Astrologer* 11, no. 2 (1998).

Gimbutas, Marija, *Goddesses and Gods of Old Europe.* London: Thames & Hudson, 1981.

Gould, Stephen Jay. *Questioning the Millennium: A Rationalist's Guide to a Precisely Arbitrary Countdown.* New York: Harmony Books, 1997.

Griffin, David R., ed. *Physics and the Ultimate Significance of Time: Bohm, Prigogine, and Process Philosophy.* Albany: State University of New York Press, 1986.

Guénon, René. "Atlantis and the Hyperborean Region." In *Formes traditionnelles et cycles cosmiques.* Paris: Éditions Gallimard, 1970. Translated by Paul Antal. Unpublished.

———. *The Crisis of the Modern World.* 1927. Translated by Arthur Osborne. Ghent, N.Y.: Sophia Perennis et Universalis, 1996.

———. *East and West.* 1924. Translated by William Massey (a.k.a. Martin Lings). London: Luzac Co. 1941. Reprint, Ghent, N.Y.: Sophia Perennis et Universalis, 1995.

———. *Formes traditionnelles et cycles cosmiques.* Paris: Éditions Gallimard, 1970.

———. *Fundamental Symbols: The Universal Language of Sacred Science.* Cambridge: Quinta Essentia, 1995.

———. *The Great Triad.* Cambridge: Quinta Essentia, 1991.

———. *Introduction to the Study of Hindu Doctrines.* 1921. London: Luzac Co., 1945.

———. *The Lord of the World (Le Roi du Monde).* 1927. North Yorkshire, England: Coombe Springs Press, 1983.

———. *Man and His Becoming According to the Vedanta.* 1925. Translated by Richard C. Nicholson. New York: Noonday Press, 1958.

————. *The Reign of Quantity and the Signs of the Times.* 1945. Translated by. Lord Northbourne. New York: Penguin Books, 1972.

————. "The Solstitial Gates." In *Fundamental Symbols: The Universal Language of Sacred Science.* Cambridge: Quinta Essentia, 1995.

————. *Symbolism of the Cross.* Ghent, N.Y.: Sophia Perennis et Universalis, 1996.

————. "The Wild Boar and the Bear." In *Fundamental Symbols: The Universal Language of Sacred Science.* Cambridge: Quinta Essentia, 1995.

Hancock, Graham, and Robert Bauval. *The Message of the Sphinx: A Quest for the Hidden Legacy of Mankind.* New York: Crown Publishers, 1996.

Hartner, Willy. "The Pseudoplanetary Nodes of the Moon's Orbit in Hindu and Islamic Iconographies." *Ars Islamica* 5, part 1 (1938).

Hatch, Marion Popenoe. "An Hypothesis on Olmec Astronomy, with Special Reference to the La Venta Site." *Papers on Olmec and Maya Archaeology*, no. 13. Berkeley: University of California, 1971.

Hawkins, Gerald. *Stonehenge Decoded.* New York: Dell Publishing, 1966.

Hinnells, John R., ed. *Mithraic Studies.* 2 vols. Manchester, U.K.: Manchester University Press, 1975.

————. *Studies in Mithraism.* Rome: Erma di Brettschneider, 1994.

Holmberg, Uno. *Finno-Ugric and Siberian Mythology.* The Mythology of All Races Series, ed. L. Gray. Boston: Marshall Jones, 1927.

Homer. *The Iliad.* Translated by Robert Fagles. London: Penguin Books, 1991.

————. *The Odyssey.* Translated by E. V. Rieu. Harmondsworth: Penguin Books, 1946.

Hurtak, J. J. *The Book of Knowledge: The Keys of Enoch.* Los Gatos, Calif.: Academy for Future Science, 1973.

Jenkins, John Major. *The Center of Mayan Time.* Boulder, Colo.: Four Ahau Press, 1995.

————. "The Finnish Sampo: The Stellar Frame and World Ages." *Scenezine: The Newspaper of the Chicago Peace and Music Festival*, August 1995.

————. "The How and Why of the Mayan End-Date in A.D. 2012." *Mountain Astrologer* (December 1994).

————. *Izapa Cosmos.* Louisville, Colo.: Four Ahau Press, 1996.

————. *Journey to the Mayan Underworld.* Boulder, Colo.: Four Ahau Press, 1989.

————. *Maya Cosmogenesis 2012: The True Meaning of the Maya Calendar End-Date.* Santa Fe, N.M.: Bear & Co., 1998.

————. *Mayan Sacred Science.* Boulder, Colo.: Four Ahau Press, 1994, 2000.

————. *Mirror in the Sky.* Boulder, Colo.: Four Ahau Press, 1991.

————. *7 Wind: A Quiché Maya Calendar for 1993.* Boulder, Colo.: Four Ahau

Press, 1993.

———. *Tzolkin: Visionary Perspectives and Calendar Studies.* Garberville, Calif.: Borderland Sciences Research Foundation, 1994.

Johnson, Kenneth Rayner. *The Fulcanelli Phenomenon.* London: Neville-Spearman, 1980.

Kelley, David H. *Deciphering the Maya Script.* Austin: University of Texas Press, 1976.

Knoll, Max. "Transformations of Science in Our Age." In *Man and Time: Papers from the Eranos Yearbooks.* Edited by Joseph Campbell. Princeton, N.J.: Princeton University Press, 1951.

Krishna, Gopi. *Kundalini: The Evolutionary Energy in Man.* Boston: Shambhala Publications, 1985.

Kuhn, Thomas S. *The Structure of Scientific Revolutions.* Chicago: University of Chicago Press, 1962.

Kurlansky, Mark. *The Basque History of the World.* New York: Penguin Books, 1999.

Landscheidt, Theodor. *Cosmic Cybernetics: The Foundations of a Modern Astrology.* Translated by Linda Kratzch. Aalen, Germany: Ebertin Verlag, 1973.

Langdon, Stephen. *Tammuz and Ishtar.* Oxford: Oxford University Press, 1914.

LaViolette, Paul. *Beyond the Big Bang: Ancient Myth and the Science of Continuous Creation.* Rochester, Vt.: Park Street Press, 1995.

———. *Earth under Fire: Humanity's Survival of the Apocalypse.* Schenectady, N.Y.: Starlane Publications, 1997.

Lings, Martin. "René Guénon." *Sophia: The Journal of Traditional Studies* 1, no. 1 (1995).

Lipsey, Roger. *Coomaraswamy 3: His Life and Work.* Princeton, N.J.: Princeton University Press, 1977.

Lowe, Gareth W., Thomas A. Lee Jr., and Eduardo Martinez Espinoza. *Izapa: An Introduction to the Ruins and Monuments.* Papers of the New World Archaeological Foundation, no. 31. Provo, Utah: Brigham Young University, 1982.

MacKenzie, D. N. "Zoroastrian Astrology in the *Bundahishn.*" *Bulletin of the School of Oriental and African Studies* 27 (1964).

Macrobius. *Commentary on the Dream of Scipio.* Translated by William H. Stahl. New York: Columbia University Press, 1952.

Markman, Sydney David. *Colonial Architecture of Antigua, Guatemala.* Philadelphia: American Philosophical Society, 1966.

McKenna, Dennis, and Terence McKenna. *The Invisible Landscape.* New York: Seabury Press, 1975.

Meeus, Jean. *Mathematical Astronomy Morsels*. Richmond: Willmann-Bell, 1997.

Michell, John. *At the Centre of the World: Polar Symbolism Discovered in Celtic, Norse, and Other Ritualized Landscapes*. London: Thames & Hudson, 1994.

Michell, John, and Christine Rhone. *Twelve-Tribe Nations and the Science of Enchanting the Landscape*. Grand Rapids, Mich.: Phanes Press, 1991.

Milbrath, Susan. *Star Gods of the Maya: Astronomy in Art, Folklore, and Calendars*. Austin: University of Texas Press, 2000.

Muktananda. *Play of Consciousness*. South Fallsburg, N.Y.: SYDA Foundation, 1978.

Nasr, Seyyed Hossein. *An Introduction to Islamic Cosmological Doctrines*. Cambridge: Harvard University Press, Belknap Press, 1964.

———. *The Need for a Sacred Science*. Albany: State University of New York Press, 1993.

Norelli-Bachelet, Patrizia. *The Gnostic Circle: A Synthesis in the Harmonies of the Cosmos*. New York: Samuel Weiser, 1975.

———. *The New Way: A Study in the Rise and Establishment of a Gnostic Society*. 2 vols. Kodaikanal, India: Aeon Books, 1981.

Norman, V. Garth. "Astronomical Orientations of Izapa Sculpture." Masters thesis, Brigham Young University, 1980.

———. *Izapa Sculpture, Part 1: Album*. Papers of the New World Archaeological Foundation, no. 30. Provo, Utah: Brigham Young University, 1973.

———. *Izapa Sculpture, Part 2: Text*. Papers of the New World Archaeological Foundation, no. 30. Provo, Utah: Brigham Young University, 1976.

Oldmeadow, Kenneth. *Traditionalism: Religion in the Light of the Perennial Philosophy*. Colombo, Sri Lanka: Sri Lanka Institute of Traditional Studies, 2000.

Ovason, David. *The Secret Architecture of Our Nation's Capital*. New York: HarperCollins, 2000.

Pallis, Marco. "A Fateful Meeting of Minds: A. K. Coomaraswamy and René Guénon." *Studies in Comparative Religion* 12, nos. 3 and 4 (1978).

Perry, Whitall N. "Coomaraswamy: The Man, Myth, and History." *Studies in Comparative Religion* 11, no. 1 (1977).

Picknett, Lynn, and Clive Prince. *The Stargate Conspiracy: The Truth about Extraterrestrial Life and the Mysteries of Ancient Egypt*. New York: Berkley Books, 1999.

Plato. *The Republic of Plato*. Translated by Francis MacDonald Cornford. Oxford: Oxford University Press, 1941.

———. *Timaeus*. Translated by Francis MacDonald Cornford. New York: Liberal Arts Press, 1959.

Porphyry. *De antro nympharum* (Cave of the Nymphs). Passages in Roger Beck,

"The Seat of Mithras at the Equinoxes: Porphyry, *De Antro Nympharum* 24." *Journal of Mithraic Studies* 1, no. 1 (1976).

Portal Market. At www.portalmarket.com.

Posnansky, Arthur. *Tihuanacu: The Cradle of American Man.* New York: Augustin, 1945.

Pozzato, Maria Pia. *L'idea deforme.* Milan, Italy: Bompiani, 1989.

Quinn, William W. Jr., *The Only Tradition.* Albany: State University of New York Press, 1997.

Reich, Wilhelm. *Cosmic Superimposition: Ether, God, and Devil.* New York: Farrar, Straus & Giroux, 1973.

Reiser, Oliver L. "Cosmecology: A Theory of Evolution." *Journal of Heredity* 28 (1937).

———. *Cosmic Humanism: A Theory of the Eight-Dimensional Cosmos Based on Integrative Principles from Science, Religion, and Art.* Cambridge, Mass.: Schenkman Publishing Company, 1966.

———. *Cosmic Humanism and World Unity.* New York: Gordon & Breach, 1975.

———. *The Intent of Creation.* Lakemont, Ga.: CSA Press, 1978.

———. *The Promise of Scientific Humanism.* New York: Oskar Piest, 1940.

———. *This Holyest Erthe: The Glastonbury Zodiac and King Arthur's Camelot.* London: Perennial Books, 1974.

Richer, Jean. *Delphes, Délos et Cumes.* Paris: Julliard, 1970.

———. *Sacred Geography of the Ancient Greeks: Astrological Symbolism in Art, Architecture, and Landscape.* Translated by Christine Rhone. Albany: State University of New York Press, 1994.

Roob, Alexander. *The Hermetic Museum: Alchemy and Mysticism.* London: Taschen, 1996.

Sahagún, Bernardino de. *Florentine Codex, General History of the Things of New Spain* bk. 7. Translated by Arthur J. O. Anderson and Charles E. Dibble. Santa Fe, N.M.: School of American Research, Archaeological Institute of America, 1953.

Santillana, Giorgio de. *The Crime of Galileo.* Chicago: University of Chicago Press, 1955.

———. *Reflections on Men and Ideas.* Cambridge: Massachusetts Institute of Technology Press, 1968.

Santillana, Giorgio de, and Hertha von Dechend. *Hamlet's Mill: An Essay on Myth and the Frame of Time.* Boston: Gambit, 1969.

Schele, Linda, and Peter Mathews. *The Code of Kings: The Language of Seven Maya Temples and Tombs.* New York: Simon & Schuster, 1998.

Schoch, Robert M., and Robert A. McNally. *Voices of the Rocks: A Scientist Looks at Catastrophes and Ancient Civilizations.* New York: Harmony Books, 1999.

Scholem, Gershom. *Kabbalah*. New York: Meridian Books, 1974.

Schwaller de Lubicz, Isha. *Her-Bak: The Living Face of Ancient Egypt*. New York: Inner Traditions International, 1978.

Schwaller de Lubicz, R. A. *Sacred Science: The King of Pharaonic Theocracy*. Translated by André VandenBroeck and Goldian VandenBroeck. Rochester, Vt.: Inner Traditions International, 1982.

———. *The Temple of Man*. Translated by Deborah Lawlor and Robert Lawlor. Rochester, Vt.: Inner Traditions International, 1999.

Sellers, Jane B. *The Death of Gods in Ancient Egypt: An Essay on Egyptian Religion and the Frame of Time*. New York: Penguin Books, 1992.

Sesti, Giuseppe M. *The Glorious Constellations: History and Mythology*. Translated by Karin H. Ford. New York: Harry N. Abrams, 1991.

Shearer, Tony. *Beneath the Moon and under the Sun*. Albuquerque, N. M.: Sun Books, 1975.

Smith, Huston. *Forgotten Truth: The Primordial Tradition*. New York: Harper & Row, 1976.

Sophia: The Journal of Traditional Studies. At: www.sophiajournal.com.

Straiton, Valentia. *The Celestial Ship of the North*. New York: Albert & Charles Boni, 1927.

Sullivan, William. *The Secret of the Incas: Myth, Astronomy, and the War Against Time*. New York: Crown Publishers, 1996.

Tedlock, Dennis. *Breath on the Mirror: Mythic Voices and Visions of the Living Maya*. San Francisco: HarperSanFrancisco, 1994.

———. *Popol Vuh: The Definitive Edition of the Mayan Book of the Dawn of Life and the Glories of Gods and Kings*. New York: Simon and Schuster, 1985. Revised and expanded 1996.

Timms, Moira. "Raising the Djed," 1992. At: www.Alignment2012.com/djed.html.

Tompkins, Peter. *The Eunuch and the Virgin*. New York: Bramhall House, 1962.

———. *The Magic of Obelisks*. New York: Harper & Row, 1981.

———. *Secrets of the Great Pyramid*. New York: Harper & Row, 1971.

Ulansey, David. *The Origins of the Mithraic Mysteries: Cosmology and Salvation in the Ancient World*. New York: Oxford University Press, 1989.

———. "Mithras and the Hypercosmic Sun." *Studies in Mithraism*. Rome, Erma di Brettschneider, 1994.

Urton, Gary. *At the Crossroads of the Earth and the Sky*. Austin: University of Texas Press, 1981.

VandenBroeck, André. *Al-Kemi: A Memoir—Hermetic, Occult, Political, and Private Aspects of R. A. Schwaller de Lubicz*. Rochester, Vt.: Inner Traditions International, 1987.

Varāhamihira. *Bṛhatsamhitā*. Translated by M. Ramakrishna Bhatt. Columbia, Mo: South Asia Books, 1995.

Vergara, Miguel Angel. *Chichen Itza: Astronomical Light and Shadow Phenomena of the Great Pyramid*. Nolo, Yucatan, Mexico: Centro de Investigacion Maya Haltun-Ha and K'u-Kuul-Kaan Academy, at: www.1spirit.com/kukuulkaan.

Vermaseran, Maarten. *Corpus Inscriptionum et monumentorum religionis mithriacae*. 2 vols. The Hague: Martinus Nijhoff, 1956, 1960.

Volguine, Alexandre. *L'Ésotérisme de l'astrologie*. Paris: Dangles, 1953.

Wasson, R. Gordon. *Soma: Divine Mushroom of Immortality*. New York: Harcourt, Brace, Jovanovich, 1968.

———. *The Wondrous Mushroom: Mycolatry in Mesoamerica*. New York: McGraw-Hill, 1980.

Waters, Frank. *Mexico Mystique: The Coming Sixth World of Consciousness*. Chicago: Sage Books, 1975.

———. *Mountain Dialogues*. Athens, Ohio: Sage/Swallow Books, 1981.

Watkins, Alfred. *The Old Straight Track: Its Mounds, Beacons, Moats, Sites, and Mark Stones*. London: Abacus, 1970.

Watts, Alan. *The Supreme Identity: An Essay on Oriental Metaphysic and the Christian Religion*. New York: Pantheon Books, 1950.

Weidner, Jay, and Vincent Bridges. *A Monument to the End of Time: Alchemy, Fulcanelli, and the Great Cross*. Mount Gilead, N.C.: Aethyrea Books, 1999.

West, John Anthony. *Serpent in the Sky: The High Wisdom of Ancient Egypt*. New York: Harper & Row, 1979

Wethey, Harold E. *Colonial Architecture and Sculpture in Peru*. Cambridge: Harvard University Press, 1949.

Wilcock, David. *Convergence III*. At: www.Ascension2000.com.

Wood, Florence, and Kenneth Wood. *Homer's Secret Iliad: The Epic of the Night Skies Decoded*. London: John Murray, 1999.

Yogananda, Paramahansa. *The Autobiography of a Yogi*. 1946. Los Angeles: Self-Realization Fellowship, 1993.

Yukteswar, Swami Sri. *The Holy Science*. 1949. Los Angeles: Self-Realization Fellowship, 1990.

Zimmer, Heinrich. *Myths and Symbols in Indian Art and Civilization*. Edited by Joseph Campbell. Princeton, N.J.: Princeton University Press, 1946.

Index

Books of Related Interest

MAYA COSMOGENESIS 2012
The True Meaning of the Maya Calendar End-Date
by John Major Jenkins

TIME AND THE TECHNOSPHERE
The Law of Time in Human Affairs
by José Argüelles

THE MAYAN FACTOR
Path Beyond Technology
by José Argüelles

EARTH ASCENDING
An Illustrated Treatise on Law Governing Whole Systems
by José Argüelles

SECRETS OF MAYAN SCIENCE/RELIGION
by Hunbatz Men

THE HIDDEN MAYA
A New Understanding of Maya Glyphs
by Martin Brennan

THE TUTANKHAMUN PROPHECIES
The Sacred Secret of the Maya, Egyptians, and Freemasons
by Maurice Cotterell

FROM THE ASHES OF ANGELS
The Forbidden Legacy of a Fallen Race
by Andrew Collins

Inner Traditions • Bear & Company
P.O. Box 388
Rochester, VT 05767
1-800-246-8648
www.InnerTraditions.com
Or contact your local bookseller